THE MORNING STAR

THE MORNING STAR

Wycliffe and the Dawn of The Reformation

by

G. H. W. PARKER

M.A., M.Litt. (Cantab.)

Lecturer in History in the University of Canterbury
Christchurch, New Zealand

Wipf and Stock Publishers
199 W 8th Ave, Suite 3
Eugene, OR 97401

The Morning Star
Wycliffe and the Dawn of the Reformation
By Parker, G. H. W.

ISBN: 1-59752-563-4
Publication date: 2/6/2006
Previously published by Wm. B. Eerdmans Publishing Co., 1965

Paternoster
9 Holdom Avenue
Bletchley
Milton Keyes, MK1 1QR
Great Britain

CONTENTS

PREFACE

There have been scores of studies on Wycliffe, Lollardy and the developments that led to the Reformation. Understandably enough, Church historians have long been concerned to probe the fourteenth and fifteenth centuries in western Christendom for the origins of that later crisis, and Englishmen in particular have been proud of Wycliffe as in some sense its herald. Yet interpretation of this pre-Reformation period has varied with the years, and if any plea is necessary for a fresh survey it can be justified on the ground that changes in our understanding have been unusually violent since 1900. Fifty years ago it was still possible to portray clearly those English and Continental affairs that brought Luther's break with the Papacy in a general setting of developments in Christendom agreed on by all historians. But with the immense growth of specialist knowledge about late mediaeval and Reformation periods, that landscape of political, social, economic and other features has been swept away and a very untidy world put in its place. What form to give to the progress of Christian affairs in this new terrain is a matter of conflicting claims and disputes. Increasingly it is argued that, as much as any simple rupture between the pre-Reformation world and that of Luther, there was continuity in a whole range of ideas and activities. The deplorable nature of papal government and life in the earlier centuries was recognized on all sides and provoked far-reaching plans for reconstruction among papalists hardly less than with Wycliffe, Hus or the conciliar reformers; and many of the doctrines elaborated led into strange paths in the sixteenth century.

No simple pattern suffices for explaining all that was most influential in the growth of the Christian Church through these centuries. But in all kinds of situations and ways it is possible to see that God's Spirit was at work, calling individuals to renewed spiritual life in the knowledge of Christ and the study of the Scriptures. My attempt has been to present some picture of these developments in the light of conclusions and insights in recent scholarship, though there can be no finality on many matters where discussion remains lively about origins, influences, ideas and the like. I have included a selected number of footnotes, chiefly to show where there have been revaluations of older conclusions; the Bibliography is intended to give more general direction for those interested in further study.

My thanks are due to Professor F. F. Bruce for his guidance as General Editor, and to Mr. Howard Mudditt for patience and encouragement in awaiting the manuscript; to the staff of Canterbury University Library in securing books for me throughout the length and breadth of New Zealand; and to my wife for her help in countless ways.

G. H. W. PARKER.

Department of History,
The University of Canterbury,
Christchurch, New Zealand.
October, 1964.

CHAPTER I

CHRISTENDOM IN THE MID-FOURTEENTH CENTURY

THE TWO CENTURIES THAT STRETCHED FROM WYCLIFFE'S BIRTH TO the age of Luther were characterized in Christendom by recurrent and unresolved crises in ecclesiastical and doctrinal affairs at the same time as they witnessed political and social upheaval. Through these years the cry for reform in the Christian Church was constant, urgent and sincere. Such concern is always to be found in those responsive to the promptings of God's Spirit where the Church cannot yet be perfect, but it was felt with particular depth in reaction to the glaring needs and abuses of the fourteenth and fifteenth centuries. What to later eyes appears remarkable is not that Luther eventually challenged the existing system and ideas in 1517, and was driven to break from Rome, but that reformation had not been brought about on more than one occasion in the generations before, whereby the deep divisions of the sixteenth century could possibly have been avoided. Luther's defiance was not unheralded, and in the efforts to cope with the religious and ecclesiastical failings in Christendom from the fourteenth century onward, many ways of reform were pursued. Whether by collective or individual action, these attempts ranged from schemes to reconstruct the Roman Church's authority and organization to total rejection by the laity of all clerical claims and order, or the newer appeal to Humanistic principles which did not always accord with Christian presuppositions and aims. From all these movements, Luther and others of his generation drew much of their inspiration directly or indirectly, in order to formulate protests and draft plans of reform. The debt was profound, even though for the most part earlier criticisms were made about corrupt practices and life in the Church, rather than directed more fundamentally to that reappraisal of Christian doctrine which appeared with Luther's grasp of the idea of justification by faith. In this context of mounting dissatisfaction, Wycliffe's denunciations had their place, and only therein may his significance and rich legacy for later years be properly assessed.

More widely the Christian world of 1350 that cradled the Wycliffite movement can be described as a society at the cross-roads. Older accepted patterns of ideas and hopes were breaking down and men, disillusioned or perhaps with fresh vision, were turning to seek for new principles, still within Christian terms, for coping with unsettling developments. Christendom or Christian society visibly organized under the Pope, the clergy and the secular rulers could still be understood as reaching out to embrace peoples distant and even pagan; and the missionary work of the friars through the preceding century that left only Lithuania unconverted in Europe and extended beyond to Africa and the farthest limits of Asia gave substance to the most ambitious hopes for converting the world.[1] Christendom comprised the Greek Orthodox Church of Constantinople and other countries as well as the Latin Church under the Pope, even though the two communions had been split since 1054 and papal attempts at reunion were always in terms unacceptable to the East. Relations between the two churches were strained enough with doctrinal differences, but even more severely through political and military contacts where Byzantium had been harmed as much as helped by the Crusades of the West. Byzantine rulers long held off growing pressure from the Turks to the East, but by 1350 their Empire was closely beleaguered in Ottoman attack from Asia Minor. All Christians shared in the opposition to Islam, and leaders in the West were not unmindful of the plight of their separated brethren, but efforts to bring aid were intermittent and vitiated by suspicions and lack of knowledge. Indeed, despite the far-flung activities of Christian missionaries, Turkish Islamic power menaced the Eastern Mediterranean by the middle of the fourteenth century, and the widespread adoption of Islam by the Mongols throughout Asia soon after effectively limited the confines of Christendom to those of Europe.[2] Such a process of geographical contraction continued through to the sixteenth century as the Turks steadily advanced, and it was only offset by the early explorations and conquests of the Iberian powers in the New World.

Within the Latin West itself, religious and ecclesiastical developments by 1350 posed grave problems of division and dispute. The older theocratic unity which the Popes had sought to realize and impose by their external government and organization had been severely undermined and in some respects abandoned. The papal development of power and administration over the Christian world, in political and judicial as well as religious terms, reached its climax in the fourteenth century, but at the same time the Popes found their claims challenged with increasing success as they came into conflict with secular kings and princes. Under the impact of various ideals and aims, the older unity of Christendom was disintegrating where

[1] Cf. D. Hay, *Europe, The Emergence of an Idea* (Edinburgh, 1957), pp. 56 f.
[2] Ibid., pp. 59, 83–4.

men became anxious to pursue their material interests in trade and wealth and to secure political independence in the sovereign control of their own lands. In traditional conflict, the Popes for centuries had argued and fought with the Holy Roman Emperors over rival theories for leadership of Christendom, and this battle was decided in papal favour before 1300. The wearisome and somewhat unreal arguments that followed between the Emperor Louis of Bavaria and the Popes concerning the independence of imperial authority were finally settled in 1356 by the Golden Bull of Charles IV. This regulated the future control and constitution of the Empire – virtually only Germany – without any need for papal sanction. In their struggles for supreme government over the Christian world the Popes were able to defeat the Emperors, but by the start of the fourteenth century they were coming to face more dangerous foes as national rulers sought to consolidate their sovereign powers over territories and subjects. Boniface VIII in 1303 had his boundless claims to rule the French king flouted by violence and Philip IV's appeal to Gallican sentiment among the clergy of France, and six years later Clement V moved to Avignon as his residence.

For nearly seventy years the Popes stayed in Avignon, which was nominally a fief of the King of Naples but yet an enclave within the papal possession of Comtat-Venaissin adjoining France, and it was purchased for the Holy See in 1348.[1] Sound considerations of security and order led the Popes to prefer Avignon to Rome for most of the fourteenth century and in theory they remained completely independent. In fact they were not all nominees of the French king nor did they lack in concern for the religious welfare of Christendom at large, but symbolically and in their actions the Avignonese Popes showed that the Papacy was under serious attack from the new national monarchies. Although abandonment of Italy made no difference to their well-known claims of universal Christian rule as Bishops of Rome, the successors of Clement V at Avignon were unable wholly to avoid partisan actions in the conflicts of the Hundred Years' War between France and England after 1337. More generally their efforts to set up a new capital at Avignon involved financial expenditure at the very time when they were able to complete and exploit their vast machinery of government for such a need. As a result, Avignon became supremely a great bureaucratic organization, efficient at raising funds from Christendom not only for long-established projects like crusades but also for the papal palace, for patronage in literature and

[1] The authoritative, if somewhat too sympathetic, account of the Avignonese Papacy is by G. Mollat, *The Popes at Avignon*, 1305–1378, translated from the ninth French edition (London, 1963).

the arts, and for the wars which the Popes found it necessary to wage in protecting their Italian possessions.

This centralized power over western Christendom was exercised pre-eminently through taxation and the control of ecclesiastical appointments, supported by the Curia's judicial and penitential discipline in the use of excommunication, interdict and indulgences for regulating matters of sin. The possible scope for indulgences was greatly enlarged in 1343 by the bull *Unigenitus* concerning Christ's Treasury of Merits, which the Popes claimed to be able to use in dealing with the remission of punishments incurred by Christians. More immediately reprehensible were the fiscal devices exploited by the Papacy in dealing with offices and justice. Great ecclesiastics in western Christendom had to make all kinds of payments to the Pope for their appointment and consecration to offices and to pay fees to expedite any business at all at the Curia. They were required more extensively to hand over part of the first year's revenues enjoyed in a new office, and though such annates, when introduced in 1306, were demanded only in special cases – where an incumbent resigned or died whilst at the papal court – they were progressively extended to include nearly all instances of fresh appointments by 1370. The French clergy alone were exempted from these burdens, and similarly were not taxed as heavily as other churches in the relentless papal clamour for money in crusades, Italian wars and the expenses of Avignon.

Apart from annates, procurations and the rights of spoil were matters which stood out in the general charges for any dealings with the papal court after the reign of John XXII. Procurations originally were the bounty or hospitality enjoyed by a bishop as he visited his benefices, but they were made into fixed money taxes in 1336 and later were allowed as sums to be shared between the Popes and the bishops with no requirement for episcopal visitations. The rights of spoil were claimed by long-established custom, and allowed patrons to take the property of bishops at their death, and bishops or abbots in turn to seize whatever was left by incumbents under their control. Such rights the Popes in the fourteenth century gradually arrogated to themselves at the same time as they extended their claims to appoint to all benefices, with the result that a valuable income in money and kind flowed into Avignon. It is reckoned that the papal library in this way acquired twelve hundred books in the years from 1343 to 1350, whilst in 1362 Urban V claimed that he should have the inheritance of any ecclesiastic, secular or regular, whose death occurred in his pontificate, except in England and France where special reservations were made.

The effects of this fiscality were wholly bad, not least where clergy were impoverished, benefices were left vacant and the ordinary Christian laity saw their ecclesiastical leaders excommunicated for failing to meet the financial demands of the papal commissioners. Some excuse could be made for the Popes who were not all wealthy, and found themselves the prisoners of circumstances partly beyond their control. Foundations for a papal treasure were laid by John XXII, and his successor Benedict XII left over a million gold florins in the coffers at Avignon, but despite their great income in taxes and other profits the later Popes ran into increasing difficulties and debt, with expenses at the court and liabilities in wars in Italy. But beyond exploiting their unique financial machinery the Popes attempted to consolidate central authority over Christendom by controlling ecclesiastical appointments in reservations. The origins of reservation were found in the thirteenth century, but John XXII systematically exploited the device, and under the last Avignonese Pope, Gregory XI, it was taken to logical extremes. By reservation, the Pope asserted his control to nominate or appoint to benefices, irrespective of any other local rights of election or collation. These claims to papal reservation were at first only made in particular circumstances but they were steadily amplified to include every case where appointments appeared unusual, even the normal translation of a bishop from one see to another. To reservation were added the papal assertions to "provide" to benefices over the heads of the official patrons, and to grant "expectancies", promising offices in advance to individuals before the existing incumbents had moved or died. Under Gregory XI, sweeping claims were stated for papal powers of nomination to all archbishoprics, bishoprics and abbacies whenever they fell vacant, and it was clear that at Avignon the Popes tried to exercise centralized control over Christendom to a degree which they had never achieved before.

Papal preoccupation with government and finance was not allowed at every point nor without protest. Quite apart from the fierce and at times exaggerated denunciations of Avignon by people as diverse as Petrarch and Bridget of Sweden,[1] the great claims of the Popes, damaging though they could be, were often far from realization. Little could be done in Germany when Louis of Bavaria was actively opposing the Popes, but even with his successor, the "priest-emperor" Charles IV, control of episcopal elections remained quite firmly in German hands. All that the Popes could do in defence of their claims was to declare individual elections void, and then to nominate the person who had earlier been chosen by the chapter with the local prince's agreement. Papal power in France was necessarily tempered at times in favour of national wishes, whilst in England the government

[1] Cf. Mollat, op. cit., p. 279.

took deliberate steps by legislation in the 1350's to curb interfering practices from Avignon. But beyond this the storm of criticism against the Popes in their leadership and corruption was loud and grew louder every year. It was easy to understand complaints about papal attempts to control ecclesiastical appointments or impose crushing burdens in taxation in Christendom, but to these protests were added more radical suggestions concerning the nature of the Church, the functions of the Pope and clergy, and the foundations for salvation and Christian living. Many of the ideas explored were voiced in the political struggles of those who challenged papal theocratic doctrine. Philip IV's supporters against Boniface VIII exploited theories similar to those used by the Colonna cardinals in their own conflict with that same Pope. These themes were taken up again by Marsiglio of Padua, John of Jandun and William of Occam to refute the attacks of John XXII and his successors on Louis of Bavaria. In university circles more widely, extreme ideas of all kinds were entertained and speculation ran deeply into surprising conclusions. The age was one of sharp religious argument, not only over the Pope's position and the privileges of the clergy but also between groups within the ecclesiastical order, where the seculars were often bitterly jealous of the intrusion and favoured rôle of the friars, and the latter, particularly the Franciscans and the Dominicans, disputed their rival claims to orthodoxy, scholastic pre-eminence and Christian zeal.

Apart, however, from any concern with the faults of ecclesiastical authorities and institutions, the mid-fourteenth century was also an age of religion in popular terms. Anti-papal and anti-clerical sentiments were characteristics not of a situation in which Christian ideals had lost their hold so much as of one where religious life was flourishing among the peoples of western Christendom. Traditional doctrines and practices were still largely accepted and the Christian faith remained the unquestioned framework of most people's thoughts and reactions. This did not necessarily imply that popular piety paid more than lip-service to the demands of Christ; but it was true that elements of non-Christian thought derived from Islam or the study of classical Latin and Greek works were not so widely influential in the period as is sometimes suggested, nor were they accepted outside the Christian structure of ideas. Certain groups and doctrines were known and isolated or condemned for what they were. The Jews in Christendom had long been separated and distinguished from others locally by official restrictions on life, occupation and dress, and they were the object of periodic persecutions that all too frequently turned into mob riots and massacres. But more widely, heresy had been recognized and defined from earlier centuries, and its manifestations were made the subject of judicial enquiry and condemnation by the Inquisition under the control of the Popes. Groups like the Waldensians, the Albigensians or the Spiritual Franciscans, with their widely-differing doctrines and aims, were all successively condemned as heretical, and it was clear in the fourteenth century that the line between orthodoxy and heresy could be drawn and enforced where the Papal Inquisition was permitted to act – and this was not the case in England – or where the local hierarchy and government were concerned for the purity of Christian beliefs.

The machinery for rooting our heresy in fact operated but imperfectly. Some individuals or groups were branded as heretics on trivial or inessential grounds, whilst many continued to prosper in secret, only occasionally making their mark on events with ideas and hopes that ranged from simple concern for Christian living, for Bible reading and communal fellowship, to visions of apocalyptic or Messianic kingdoms on earth and the overthrow of all existing government and order. The perennial activities of the Beghards in the Netherlands and Germany, and of the more questionable and widely organized Brethren of the Free Spirit, showed the strength of movements which in the eyes of the authorities hovered on the line between orthodoxy and heresy. They revealed moreover how widespread was Christian piety which often possibly offended only in its anti-clericalism or independence of the priesthood.[1] The vast majority of the people did not doubt fundamentals of belief, even where their complaints about ecclesiasticism in many forms were deeply felt and sometimes violently expressed. They loved church services, the sermons and homiletic teaching of the friars or devout clergy, they went in great numbers on pilgrimages to shrines such as those of James of Compostella or Becket at Canterbury, and they found popular and continuing entertainment in the religious mystery or miracle plays. Writings of religious devotion or instruction were widespread, and the contemplative pursuits and preaching of people like Catherine of Siena, Bridget of Sweden or Rolle and his successors in England brought deep respect and response from the ordinary people of different countries. Such features all illustrated the fact that religious life had a vitality and place central to the interests of the communities of western Christendom in 1350.

Yet these religious or spiritual attitudes did not mean general calm or stability of outlook in the world, even where Christian doctrines remained unquestioned. In fact it seems that the very concern for orthodoxy so often found was in part prompted by uncertainties

[1] Cf. N. Cohn, *The Pursuit of the Millennium* (London, 1957), pp. 164 f., for discussion of the Beghards and the Brethren of the Free Spirit.

which loomed large on the political and social scenes in Christendom. Alongside the cultural splendour and wealth of Avignon, and the progress in reconstruction in State and Church attained by the Emperor Charles IV in his hereditary land of Bohemia, there were reverses and threats to Christendom on its frontiers, and within the Latin West itself political and social upheavals that crowded the world with anxieties in 1350. From about the year 1000 and until the early part of the fourteenth century, there was a steady expansion in population and wealth in western Europe which helped to foster the hopes for the spread of Christianity at the same time as knowledge of the world beyond Europe grew. But this progress was halted with social disorders, class conflicts in the cities of Germany, France, England and around, the disruption of industries, and famines and epidemics which culminated in the natural and universal calamity of the Black Death in 1348 and 1349. The plague decimated population in every country, and with recurrent outbreaks through the rest of the century it brought misery that was profound in effect and a dark memory for generations. In addition, political circumstances in various lands helped to create or intensify the troubles of the people, and in particular to encourage feelings of uncertainty or apprehension common in the age. The struggles of both Louis of Bavaria and Charles IV as Emperors were against rival German princes as much as with the Popes, and the petty competition between local lords and the towns in Germany led to widespread anarchy and distress. In northern France, the early stages of the Hundred Years' War and the rivalries of the Burgundian dukes with the French kings created social troubles, whilst more widely there were urban class struggles in the Netherlands. Even the temporary ending of war between England and France in 1360 did not improve conditions, since the disbanded militia formed Companies of Free Men that roamed and terrorized parts of France and Germany. Hardship at the time led also to the popular French rising of the Jacquerie, whilst twenty years later, by contrast, improving conditions in England provoked the Peasants' Revolt of 1381. In each case the Black Death contributed to the developments, whether in the initial creation of misery and despair or in the more lasting disruption of feudal bonds and duties, where labour shortages enabled the peasantry to press for better wages and conditions of work. Social and political discontent combined in more than one way and in addition directed criticism against churchmen wherever they were seen as landlords and nobles alongside the secular magnates.

These developments played no little part in upsetting conservative religious attitudes. They encouraged apocalyptic ideas or more mildly the appeal of the popular preacher, who could gain a ready response by castigating current ills and pointing out what was promised in the Bible and could be hoped for in social change. Concern with death and the after-life, concern also with the vision of a better world, possibly in revolutionary or anarchistic terms, were elements marking the outlook of common people in western Christendom in the fourteenth century. In the early stages of their work, the friars uniquely captured attention and support with their teaching and evangelism, but by 1350 they were condemned by many for their luxury and privileges, and their place was being taken by preachers and leaders of all kinds, lay as well as clerical. The pressure of circumstances could lead men and women to seek withdrawal from the world in contemplation and a solitary life of prayer – and mystical thinkers and leaders were notable in the age – but developments could equally encourage less worthy pursuits among the people. Whilst witchcraft and the study of magic flourished in Germany, many more general fears and aspirations were brought to a head by the calamities of 1348 which witnessed a remarkable and widespread revival of the older movement of the Flagellants.[1] In these proceedings, groups of people took part in processions and elaborate ceremonies to scourge themselves and re-enact the physical sufferings of Christ. They went from town to town, proclaiming repentance and asceticism, and prophesying the end of the world within a number of years. Whole regions of southern Germany were possessed or terrified by the Flagellants whose excesses turned initial papal and episcopal approval of their practices into outright condemnation. Rigorous efforts were made to stamp out the organization but it retained its appeal, and Flagellants were still to be found in the following century, with the support even of a man like the Dominican Vincent Ferrer.

Religious life revealed strong and at times obscure currents in western Christendom in an age when calamities seemed to be overwhelming and to presage the end of the world. Such conditions made it inevitable that matters of religion and belief should become closely entangled with political or social issues, particularly where the acknowledged structure for argument was still Christendom or the Universal Church as the Body of Christ. What complex hopes and ideas existed, however, were most sharply revealed in the manifold criticisms of the Popes at Avignon. They were all too easily blamed for the disasters that engulfed the countries of Christendom as a whole. By their corruption, it was alleged, they brought down God's judgment upon the world at large. Yet the Popes were not unaware of many of the faults of the system at Avignon, and it would be unjust to suggest that they did not want to do anything for remedying them or did not

[1] See Cohn, op. cit., pp. 129 f. for an account of the Flagellants.

wish to return to Rome. In the event, it seems, Gregory XI made up his own mind to abandon Avignon in 1377 rather than respond to the pleas of Catherine of Siena to end the sinful "Babylonish Captivity". But it is no less certain that his death at Rome in the following year precipitated the general crisis of complaint about the Papacy in Christendom. The cardinals proceeded to elect first one Pope and then another, thereby creating the scandal of schism in the headship of the Roman Church. It was a fateful decision and profound in its effects upon Christendom through the following century. But it had scarcely less importance for John Wycliffe, whose career came to a public climax in England in 1378 and to a considerable extent was directed into its last and most revolutionary phase by the opening developments of the Great Schism.

CHAPTER II

WYCLIFFE AND HIS AGE

IN A GENERATION WHEN WESTERN CHRISTENDOM WAS CONVULSED by crisis in its religious leadership and its kingdoms were divided in political rivalries, John Wycliffe stood out with his torrid denunciations of abuses in the Christian Church. More works have been written about him than any other medieval Englishman, and yet to explain what he sought to do or achieved paradoxically remains difficult. The greater part of his life was spent in a university career and academic disputation, and very little is known of the details of this period before he emerged into public affairs. For the last dozen years or so before his death, he became entangled in English ecclesiastical and secular politics, and in this career eventually gave his attention more exclusively to demands for the reform of doctrines and abuses. These last were the achievements for which he was later honoured by Foxe in his martyrology, and by all those who followed Foxe, but to appreciate Wycliffe's reforms in more proper perspective it is essential to set them against the features of his earlier career and ideas.

He was born probably about 1330,[1] of a family which held property near Richmond and including the village of Wycliffe-upon-Tees in Yorkshire. There remains no record of his early life and reactions to developments in the English world, but it would seem that he could not have failed to respond to issues which aroused criticism and interest in contemporaries around him. Apart from the vast bureaucratic expansion of papal power at Avignon, there were developments closer at hand in the English Church making bishops into royal civil servants and ministers of State, whilst the clergy's landed wealth – popularly reckoned as being one-third of the nation's total – and their exemptions in justice and taxation helped to kindle anti-clerical feeling. Accounting possibly for one-fiftieth of the population, the clergy were to be seen on every side in society, and the monasteries and abbeys were known as great economic enterprises, engaged above all in sheep-farming and jealous of their possessive rights as landlords. At the same time, popular piety flourished, where people flocked to

[1] The dating accepted by K. B. McFarlane, *John Wycliffe and the Beginnings of English Nonconformity* (London, 1952), p. 14, and other modern scholars in preference to that of 1324 given by H. B. Workman in his authoritative study, *John Wyclif*, two volumes (Oxford, 1926).

churches on Sundays and Holy Days for Masses and the sermons of the friars and pardoners, whatever resentment was aroused by the hawking of relics and indulgencies for raising money. There were the special dramas of nativity and miracle plays and other festivals associated with the episodes of Christ's Life and Passion, the services of vernacular carols at Christmas, Easter and Harvest, and through all the year the instruction of children and adults by the village priests in Christian and other lessons.[1] Not least of all in Yorkshire in Wycliffe's childhood, there was particular concern with the writing and study of English preaching manuals at the Minster and around,[2] and a spirituality among the people reflected in the career and influence of a man like Richard Rolle.

The young Wycliffe would undoubtedly have shared in many of the religious practices of his home and its neighbourhood, just as later he came openly to approve or reject them, but with greater certainty he is known to have come into contact with the political and public influences of the age where his family village and manor in 1342 fell under the lordship of John of Gaunt, the Duke of Lancaster and second son of Edward III. Noble and royal patronage counted for much in a society in which the king still depended upon feudal obedience and baronial co-operation, and Parliament as yet had little place for initiative on the parts of its burgesses and knights. But such favour was even more important in the special circumstances of Edward III's reign, for royal weakness increasingly gave scope for intrigue and ambition among the king's sons and allied noble families. With his feudal lands and loyalties in the northern part of England, Lancaster was well placed to attempt to realize his own schemes for controlling the government, and it seems that early on Wycliffe was introduced to his patronage and given that support which was to be all-important in his public career.

More immediately, however, Wycliffe was launched upon a university training that was recognized as one of the major avenues to advancement and leadership in both ecclesiastical and civil life in fourteenth-century England. He probably first went to Oxford at the age of fifteen in 1345 to commence the long course for a full academic career in theology, and these years of study were interrupted with the general dislocation of university life in the repeated epidemics of the Black Death between 1349 and 1353. Thereafter he continued his work, figuring in public records as a junior fellow at Merton College in 1356 and then as Master of Balliol at some date before 1360. At

[1] Cf. B. L. Manning, *The People's Faith in the Time of Wyclif* (Cambridge, 1919), for a fine picture of fourteenth-century religious life in England.

[2] Cf. G. R. Owst, *Preaching in Medieval England* (Cambridge, 1926), pp. 226 f.

the time, the colleges in Oxford were few in number and their membership was confined to the secular clergy, totalling about eighty in all and for the most part graduates.[1] But apart from the colleges, and often in opposition to them, were the houses, priories and halls of the monks and friars, which had been built up during the thirteenth century and had gained a widespread influence in university studies through their teaching and willingness to look after penniless students who came to the city. The friars indeed provided some of the greatest scholars and preachers in Oxford and England as a whole – men such as Archbishop Peckham, Duns Scotus or William of Occam – but their influence in the university was resented and by 1350 was on the wane. At that time Archbishop Fitzralph of Armagh attacked their behaviour, singling out for especial condemnation amongst other practices the friars' trick of giving freshmen hospitality and then making them take vows of mendicancy.[2] Wycliffe came to voice similar complaints, but for most of his academic career was willing to acknowledge that he learned much from the friars, masters and students alike. Outside the colleges and houses of the orders, however, most undergraduate clerks in residence – in all, about fifteen hundred – lived simply in halls supervised or rented by individual graduates of the university, and Wycliffe probably spent some of his years in such lodgings.

He remained as Master of Balliol until May, 1361, when he was instituted to the rich college living of Fillingham in Lincolnshire, so that he would have a sufficient income for continuing his studies at Oxford. This was accepted practice at the time for financing such academic pursuits where individual colleges held the appointment to livings. Wycliffe shared fully in the system for his own advancement, even though later he came to criticize absenteeism or pluralism in ecclesiastical holdings. He may have served the parish at Fillingham in the years before obtaining a license for non-residence in 1363,[3] but in the same period he also sought and obtained an office as a prebend at Aust on the Bristol Channel. This appointment he clearly held in absence, as did the other prebends of Aust, who were supposed to pay vicars to serve there in their stead. This they did not always do, and according to an episcopal visitation of 1366 Wycliffe was one of the defaulters.[4] He continued to pursue his studies at Oxford, his life being almost entirely that of a scholar training in theology and teaching his subject as he became qualified. His degree of Bachelor of

[1] McFarlane, op. cit., pp. 16–18.
[2] J. Foxe, *Acts and Monuments*, edited by S. R. Cattley (London, 1837), Vol. II, p. 760.
[3] M. Deanesly, *The Significance of the Lollard Bible* (London, 1951), p. 10.
[4] McFarlane, op. cit., p. 26.

Divinity he took in 1369 and his doctorate three years later. For a brief period after 1365 he became Warden of the new Canterbury Hall and was involved in disputes with the regulars about its establishment, but in his further years at the university he resided for the most part at Queen's. His academic work throughout was financed by stipends from livings, and by preferment he was appointed in turn Rector of Ludgershall in 1368, relinquishing Fillingham, and Rector of Lutterworth in exchange for Ludgershall after April, 1374. He retained his living at Lutterworth until his death in 1384, but it was only in the last three years of his life that he remained and worked continuous in the parish.

Until 1371 Wycliffe's career was that of the academic in university study and teaching. He took longer than most on the arduous theological course, partly because of his concern with administration, but such studies had a meaning and purpose recognized in the age, for those completing them were finely fitted for leadership in public life, no less than students who gave their attention to canon or civil law. As they had appeared and developed from the eleventh century onward, the universities were pre-eminently the training ground for government and administration as much as for scholarly study, and the basic courses common to all degrees provided the necessary discipline for minds engaged in the problems of the day. The typical programmes of the *quadrivium* and the *trivium*, with their repeated emphasis on argument, dispute and discussion, were well-designed to sharpen thought and expression, and the scholar, once having graduated as a bachelor, took a growing share in teaching and examining to fulfil requirements for his final degree. As a method of argument, scholasticism had become over-developed by the fourteenth century. The fine balance presented in the time of Abelard and perfected by Aquinas had been upset as schoolmen all too frequently came to lose themselves in the gymnastics of debate and pushed their principles to absurd extremes. Wycliffe was thoroughly imbued with such a tradition, he was the "last of the schoolmen" in his training, outlook and exposition, and he shared alike in the virtues and faults of the system. For this reason – even where many of his arguments eventually led to radical and reforming demands – Wycliffe can only fairly be approached and understood in the first instance as the Oxford philosopher debating acute points with his opponents.

In true academic fashion Wycliffe once confessed to Oxford as his greatest love, and against the background of the scholarly world it is possible to suggest what many of his arguments implied and why he stood in such a strangely prominent position during the last dozen years of his life. By 1371, he was renowned as the leading philosopher and theologian of the age at Oxford, that is to say, he was second to none in his scholarship in western Europe in which Oxford, for a period, had come to surpass Paris in its reputation and attainments. Wycliffe's contemporaries, even his opponents, did not doubt his brilliance. Insofar as scholasticism was in decline and its methods were under criticism, his achievement must more generally be questioned since he shared so completely in the discipline of the schools, but qualifications on this score do not necessarily mean that his ideas were the less profound in their conclusions. For two reasons, indeed, he was able to go far in his statement and pursuit of principles. In the first place, his arguments were cast for a long time in accepted scholastic form and the issues in which he was involved were understood as academic problems. They were allowed and excused within the bounds of university license and prerogative. In great measure, Wycliffe's writings were the formulations of academic argument, betraying the scholar's delight in intricacies and unending debate. Moreover, as a university teacher, Oxford's most shining product in the age, he continued to enjoy freedom to expound and defend ideas which outside the city would speedily have been suppressed.

Secondly, Wycliffe was a moderate Realist. Of the two great schools of philosophy which had come to dominate and divide the universities in the later Middle Ages, the Realists affirmed a fundamental belief in the final existence of universals, of concepts or virtues like Truth or Humanity or the Church. The Nominalists by contrast insisted that only particulars had reality or meaning, that individual men and women were real rather than humanity, individual Christians rather than the Church, and that true actions carried out were of value rather than an abstract labelled Truth. Some midway positions had been adopted between these extremes, and great syntheses of thought created by thinkers like Aquinas or Bonaventura in the thirteenth century, but in later years the tide of speculation swung increasingly in favour of Nominalism with the teaching of Duns Scotus and William of Occam. These criticized and challenged all concepts, so that God and the supernatural were elevated to the unknown and unknowable, beyond comprehension or examination, and Man was left only with the world which he could see and touch and classify. Nominalism was disruptive of all philosophical systems that sought to comprehend the universe in one single framework embracing God and Man, Supernature and Nature, and it was "scientific" in its outlook and concern with the material world. Although Nominalism could lead to more complex speculation about the mystery and holiness of God and Man's dealings with Him by faith, as Nicholas of Cusa showed in the fifteenth century,[1] at Occam's

[1] See pp. 151 f. below.

death in 1349 it appeared rather as the leading system of thought in Europe to threaten Christian principles and sweep God out of human reckoning. At Oxford alone there was reaction against this movement, and Wycliffe in the forefront reasserted the validity of universals as concepts alongside particular notions. This meant that philosophically he was conservative, even reactionary, in attempting to lead dispute back along old paths and into what were regarded as dead ends of thought. The consequences were far-reaching where he and his Oxford followers were left isolated in Europe and the Nominalist scholars of Paris became all-important in championing Conciliarism and condemning Wycliffite ideas. But the Realist standpoint was also deeply significant for crystallizing protest and in extending arguments already stated about the evils in the Church. Working from his principles, Wycliffe was able to explore and restate fundamental concepts in Christianity – such as the nature of the Church or God's Word – and in this way penetrate more profoundly in theological argument than a Nominalist like William of Occam, despite his extreme rejection of papal and ecclesiastical organizations.

The substance of Wycliffe's arguments was presented in academic and political controversies before his more radical entry into theological debate and rejection of traditional doctrines. Within the walls of Oxford itself, he entered into dispute over the questions of wealth and property, dominion and grace, which were debated bitterly and in confusing terms both between monks and friars and between seculars and regulars as a whole. Wycliffe was a secular clerk, but initially he joined in the argument on the side of the friars, where the Franciscans questioned the ownership of property and land by the older endowed monks and canons in the university. Two Oxford monks, Uthred of Boldon and William Binham, attacked "mendicancy" or the dependence upon alms in the friars' activities, and in 1366 or 1367, Wycliffe issued tracts to rebut these criticisms. He gave his support to views which derived from the Spiritual Franciscans, William of Occam and Marsiglio of Padua in the general denunciation of landed wealth held by abbots and monasteries, and with the appeal to apostolic poverty for renouncing worldly possessions. But though the Spirituals earlier had expressly attacked the Popes and had suffered excommunication for their views, Wycliffe's condemnations of monastic wealth did not at first involve him in any criticisms of Avignon.[1] At the same time, he drew his more specific arguments from another closer source, Archbishop Fitzralph of Armagh, who had been Chancellor of Oxford University and at the centre of academic

[1] For this account, cf. D. Knowles, *The Religious Orders in England*, Vol. II (Cambridge, 1955), pp. 65 f.

disputes before his death in 1360. Fitzralph expounded and left to Wycliffe a doctrine of lordship or dominion which allowed only those enjoying God's grace to have true lordship or possess property. The thesis involved the nature of the Church where Egidius Romanus had advanced most extreme papal arguments at the start of the fourteenth century, with claims that such lordship could only be found in the Pope's government of the Church. Outside Christian communion, Egidius stated, the heathen, heretics and excommunicants enjoyed no lawful power. Fitzralph gave this argument a particular twist so that he could attack wealthy monks and suggest that in their actions and attitudes they lacked the grace essential for lordship. It was this point which Wycliffe further exploited.[1]

Alike in his academic tracts, in his university lectures, and in his longer works, *On Divine Dominion* and *On Civil Dominion*, published after 1371, Wycliffe argued that lordship was held only from God and in consequence was conditioned according to moral principles. Lordship could be possessed, along with God's other gifts, only by the righteous man, the man in a state of grace. Such a person could be truly called "lord of the whole universe", and was to possess all things in common with other righteous men, just as Christ had shared everything with his disciples, or as had been the case in the early Church. By contrast, the unrighteous man without grace, the man in mortal sin, had no claim to genuine lordship or possession. Therefore, Wycliffe deduced, only Christians who carried out their proper duties were endowed with such lordship, and if they abused their offices they automatically lost all legitimate authority. This doctrine was capable of startling and even revolutionary application, but Wycliffe generally was careful to allow that in sinful human society there remained a place for civil power and private property, whilst in other contexts he could argue positively for the control and initiative of royal government in Christian affairs.[2] But all ecclesiastical matters were to be judged according to the New Testament principle concerning property, and on these grounds Wycliffe argued against the "possessioners", the abbots and monks, the priories and other foundations, holding land and wealth in abundance. The proper function of all regular clergy precluded the accumulation, ownership or even administration of material possessions, and in consequence every abbot or monastery was *ipso facto* attempting to exercise a lordship not properly enjoyed. Only by the surrender of all their wealth or claims to administer property could individual monks and monastic institutions,

[1] For Egidius and Fitzralph, cf. A. Gwynn, *The English Austin Friars in the Time of Wyclif* (Oxford, 1940), pp. 35 f.

[2] See pp. 52 f. below for Wycliffe's arguments about secular authority and reform.

somewhat paradoxically, recover their right standing with God and the lordship which was the attribute of every true Christian.

Wycliffe's first use of this theory of lordship was within university circles and for academic dispute between ecclesiastics, but plainly it was capable of far wider application and relevance in a society characterised by clerical privilege and wealth. In his later, more comprehensive attack on abuses, Wycliffe elaborated some of the implications of this doctrine, but at the start of the 1370's it was his scholarly reputation in the Oxford argument that thrust him into the world of English politics and for a few years made him develop and mould his criticisms for immediate governmental ends rather than anything else. The situation at large in England during that decade was uniquely and favourably balanced for the ideas that Wycliffe could develop in anti-clerical and anti-papal terms. Following the renewal of war with France in 1369, the country was brought to the brink of domestic crisis, where it was quickly shown that earlier English victories before 1360 were transitory and that Edward III's government needed to act with vigour and purpose in the new campaigns. Unfortunately, the most pressing if inevitable demand was for money to pay for the war, and attempts to levy taxes brought feeling against the clergy and Papacy to a head in the country. Under the king, Bishop Wykeham of Winchester as Lord Chancellor controlled the government, and with his ecclesiastical colleagues he incurred mounting criticism as royal demands for clerical grants met with refusals or unsatisfactory compromises in Convocation. A tide of anti-clerical feeling swept through England in 1370 such as had never been known before, where lay resentment against the financial exemptions of the clergy was particularly acute,[1] and this popular reaction played into Lancaster's hands in his hopes for becoming all-powerful in England. His father was declining in dotage, and his brother and heir to the throne, the Black Prince, returned at the start of 1371 from fighting in France, ill and unlikely to retain for long a firm grasp on the direction of government. Until 1371 indeed, Wykeham was able to divert heavy demands upon the clergy and to retain his own position, but in February of that year he was overthrown at the meeting of Parliament, and a secular, noble council under Lancaster assumed power. In these circumstances, Wycliffe was brought into public affairs to champion royal causes, possibly under the patronage of the Black Prince in the first stage, but more continuously with Lancaster's protection.

Wycliffe himself was present at the Parliament of 1371, in which lay demands were voiced for the submission of the clergy and their

[1] Knowles, op. cit., p. 67.

exclusion from governmental office, but it does not appear that he spoke even though he clearly inspired the arguments of the friars who attacked the "possessioners". The view was advanced that in the economic troubles of the day the government, pleading necessity, could take over all ecclesiastical lands or property, for such goods had originally been gifts from laymen, and lawfully they – or their heirs – could resume what had been bestowed. This was a point well taken, as Wycliffe himself revealed in reporting that one nobleman added, "If we are involved in war, then we should seize the clergy's temporal possessions which belong to us and the kingdom as a whole". This revolutionary idea was completely rejected by the bishops and abbots and at the time was not pressed further. The convocations of the two provinces responded to the threat and agreed to contribute substantially to the needs of the king. But Wycliffe did not stop at that point – he followed out his arguments in a number of pamphlets to crystallize the theory of lordship and apply it more widely in criticism of ecclesiastical endowments. No clerical possessions, he argued, could be held in perpetuity, and beyond the bare needs of the clergy they could be seized by the government in national emergency or if they were misused. It was indeed a government's Christian duty to act in this way to further God's kingdom on earth. Wycliffe's suggestions were most welcome to Lancaster and the royal council, if only to be used as threats, but meanwhile the Pope's position was drawn under fire in developments involving England with Avignon.

In the fourteenth century, feeling against papal authority in England was most directly and keenly experienced by the clergy, not the laity: it was the clergy that had to pay the taxes demanded by Avignon. Like other national hierarchies, however, the English Church was taxed by the secular power as much as by the Pope, and both authorities made increasingly pressing demands as the years passed – the Pope had the costs at Avignon, Edward III his expenses in the French war. But royal control grew so powerful that the king allowed papal taxation of the English clergy only insofar as he took a high percentage of the proceeds. The curious result of this development was that during the first stages of the Hundred Years' War to 1360, the Avignonese Popes took no taxes from the English Church, since to have done so would financially have benefited Edward III most of all in his conflict with France. When therefore Gregory XI found himself in desperate straits and tried to impose a tax on the English clergy in 1372, the latter shrilly protested and, ironically enough, found the royal government rising to their defence. The Pope lowered his demands, but Edward III's council curtly forbade all papal levies and took the opportunity to raise general complaints over provisions and papal jurisdiction.

The system extended throughout Latin Christendom in centralized curial control of offices and justice was known in England as elsewhere, but practice never completely matched theory. In particular, there existed a working compromise between king and Pope for applying the machinery of provisions with respect to bishoprics, even though popularly there were reiterated protests at what were believed to be general abuses of control from Avignon. The Popes undoubtedly made regular use of their powers to appoint to archdeaconries, deaneries or canonries in cathedrals so that as many as a third of these offices could be held by non-resident foreigners, including French cardinals,[1] and public resentment at this situation led to the passing of the first statute of Provisors (1351) and the first and second statutes of Praemunire (1353, 1365). But this legislation had little effect since Edward III never intended it to upset his understanding with the Pope which ensured effective royal control over higher ecclesiastical appointments.[2] During the fourteenth century, papal provisions to the English episcopate were almost entirely of men native to the country, and these were chosen by the king rather than the Pope. Edward III was vitally concerned to have on the bench those most able in government and administration. As a result, there were few among the bishops who were not publicly distinguished and capable, even though they could rarely give the religious or spiritual leadership so desired in the Church of the day.[3] The method of provision allowed the king to secure his nominees as bishops, whilst the Pope retained the formal right of approval and appointment, and papal complaints showed that royal control was usually decisive. Clement VI in 1345 commented about the nomination of Thomas Hatfield to the see of Durham with the words, "If the King of England were to petition for his ass to be made a bishop, we could not say him Nay"; and later in 1360, royal wishes prevailed in the appointment of Robert Stretton as Bishop of Coventry, although the nominee was so illiterate that he was consecrated "without examination" after failing three times to satisfy the authorities, and with his profession of obedience read for him.

Royal action against the Popes was intermittent and calculated as a rule to further national ends. This was the case in 1373, when the government endeavoured to exploit the financial crisis in raising other complaints against papal claims of control. An embassy was sent to Gregory XI at Avignon, with a list of demands to curb the Curia's judicial interference with royal power, citations to the Papal

[1] Cf. G. M. Trevelyan, *England in the Age of Wycliffe*, fourth edition (London, 1909), pp. 117–9.

[2] M. McKisack, *The Fourteenth Century* (Oxford, 1959), pp. 280 f.

[3] McKisack, op. cit., presents a reasonable case for the value of this system. Cf. also W. A. Pantin, *The English Church in the Fourteenth Century* (Cambridge, 1955), Chapter IV.

Court, taxation of the English clergy during the French war, and the practice of reservations and provisions. Gregory temporized, agreeing to suspend his activities until a fuller discussion had been held, and this was arranged at Bruges in the summer of 1374. Wycliffe appeared at this point as one of the commissioners sent to the conference to negotiate a settlement with the papal envoys, but despite his high ranking as a theologian, he played no distinguished part in events. When the commission went to Bruges again in the following year, Wycliffe was omitted from its membership. The English government's efforts to browbeat the Pope came to nothing, probably because of the disastrous fortunes of war that lost England nearly the whole of Aquitaine by 1374, and the needs of the Duke of Lancaster to make peace with the Pope as well as France to preserve his own power in the disintegrating situation at home. By a compromise with Gregory in 1375, remedies were provided for past appointments and appeals, but the Pope conceded no point of principle to limit his future action. At the same time, he was allowed to levy the subsidy which he had earlier demanded from the clergy, and despite the wide discontent that this caused in England, Lancaster was able to deflect criticism against his government on to the whole system of the appointment of aliens and absentee clerics.

In these developments Wycliffe had his part, for after 1374 he not only continued to support the duke's political schemes but also turned his thoughts more specifically to the subject of practical reform in England. He was disappointed in ecclesiastical preferment where he was promised but not given a prebend at Lincoln, and then was passed over for the Bishopric of Worcester in 1375. These setbacks, it seems, gave him an added sense of grievance against authority, but he continued to hope for possible papal action in introducing reform until after the start of the Great Schism. In the meantime, political involvement as a pamphleteer for the English government led him steadily on to the crisis of his career in 1378. The see-saw of events in 1376 forced Lancaster temporarily to yield to attacks on his authority in the Good Parliament and to accept recommendations for radical changes, but these he repudiated later in the same year after the Black Prince's death. Wykeham, restored briefly to public notice, was banished from court and his temporalities were confiscated. Such actions Wycliffe endorsed by condemning the bishop as a "Caesarean" cleric, a servant of Caesar in his pursuit of worldly ambitions and affairs.

This defence of Lancaster's cause hardly redounded to the credit of Wycliffe and in the event it proved unwise for him. The disgraced bishop had influential and energetic support in William Courtenay, the young and popular Bishop of London, who not only made it possible for Wykeham to attend Convocation at the start of 1377 but also summoned Wycliffe to St. Paul's to answer charges about his teaching. A dramatic, if somewhat inconclusive, scene followed, involving ecclesiastical dignitaries, the secular leaders of the country and the London mob. Lancaster saw that Courtenay was seeking to attack him through Wycliffe, and left no doubt about supporting his servant. He supplied four theological doctors – one from each of the mendicant orders – to defend Wycliffe, and went in person with Henry Percy, the Marshal, to overawe the bishop and clergy in the assembly. The manners of the noblemen were resented and when Lancaster threatened Courtenay, popular feeling ran so high that the Duke and the Marshal had to flee precipitately, with Wycliffe in attendance. Proceedings against the Oxford don were certainly suspended, but for a day or so there was dangerous rioting in London at Lancaster's expense. It was not difficult to see that Wycliffe was becoming embarrassing as a political servant for the government, and changing circumstances in England and outside confirmed this fact. Edward III's death in 1377 immediately brought a check to the powers of Lancaster, for his nephew succeeded to the throne as Richard II without any trouble. Governmental attitudes, nevertheless, did not change overnight, and Wycliffe was still consulted for his opinions; on two matters at least he was asked to justify public views. The first concerned the possibility of withholding payment of taxes to the Pope in the interests of national defence, and the question was put to Wycliffe where there was continuing public alarm at the steady loss of money to the Curia. Wycliffe's answer was unequivocal and a logical deduction from his general thesis about lordship: on grounds of natural reason, Christian principles and conscience alike, he argued, it was right to deny payments to the Pope. Not only did Gregory XI possess no claims over endowments made for the Church in England, but he had also generally forfeited any rights to possessions by his corrupt behaviour. Furthermore, Wycliffe urged, the government should take direct action and redistribute ecclesiastical endowments and tithes in England; but at this point, the council abruptly ordered him to be silent, probably because it required only a useful argument or threat to bring pressure on the Pope, and not a radical and practical programme demolishing papal power.

In the circumstances, Wycliffe's ideas seemed to go too far, for political considerations demanded accommodation and compromise. Nevertheless, his views were sought once again in the following year in defence of official action, this time with regard to sanctuary. The privilege of sanctuary, like other privileges attached to English ecclesiastical life, was one of mixed value and uncertain limits in its development through the later Middle Ages. Essentially it was meant to provide an immediate refuge for a man who had committed a crime and was in flight from justice, so that by reaching the safety of a church or consecrated ground he could avoid summary execution, and have the opportunity to abjure the realm within forty days. In an age of rough justice, where the innocent could too easily suffer before any proper investigation into a crime, such a principle was commendable, but it could be abused by deliberate law-breakers and it never commanded complete respect. Becket's murder in 1170 was celebrated as an instance in which sanctuary was flouted, but on occasion through the following centuries as well, the idea could be conveniently ignored as much as misused in other ways. The circumstances on which Wycliffe was asked to give his opinion in 1378 showed how confused attitudes to the practice had become. In the Spanish expedition of 1367, two English knights, Shakell and Haule, had made a nobleman their personal prisoner, and they later ransomed him in exchange for his son. They hoped eventually to be paid well for the boy's release, but in 1377 the English government negotiated to secure this without any necessary ransom and demanded that the knights should hand over their hostage. This they refused to do, and in consequence they were committed to the Tower; but they escaped in August, 1378, and sought refuge in Westminster Abbey. The royal officers who pursued them flouted any privilege of sanctuary, arrested Shakell and killed Haule, who tried to resist capture at the celebration of Mass. Such action created uproar, and led to defiance and deadlock between civil and ecclesiastical authorities in the country: Archbishop Sudbury of Canterbury excommunicated the royal servants and their masters, with the exception of the king, his mother, and the Duke of Lancaster, and Courtenay and the other bishops supported his measures. On its side, the government deplored the murder, but adamantly upheld civil prerogative to arrest those committing crimes against the king. Wycliffe produced a pamphlet in Parliament to defend the royal case: he did not attempt to justify Haule's murder, but attacked the obvious abuses arising from sanctuary, and concerned himself above all to argue that the clergy should be stripped of all material, worldly privileges to restore them to their proper spiritual life and work.[1] Such sweeping proposals were ignored, and the political crisis was resolved in the following year by legislation that left the problem of sanctuary virtually untouched.[2] Wycliffe went on his own way to

[1] The pamphlet was inserted as Chapters VI–XVI into his longer treatise *Concerning the Church*.

[2] See Chapter XI, p. 173, below for the troubles with sanctuary in the fifteenth century.

probe more extreme ideas, in a situation where he was no longer acceptable as a government writer. It was not merely that his theories were politically awkward: his position generally had been radically changed by papal condemnation of his ideas and the start of the Great Schism.

Wycliffe's older monastic enemies did not forget him in the 1370's, and Uthred's mantle was taken up by Adam Easton who in 1376 drew the attention of the Pope to a number of the Oxford scholar's writings and teachings. As a result, Gregory XI submitted these works to a commission of cardinals, and in May, 1377, issued a series of bulls to authorities in England. One of these was directed to Oxford University, lamenting that error had been allowed to grow within its walls and ordering that Wycliffe should be arrested and handed over to Sudbury and Courtenay. Separate instructions were sent to these ecclesiastics for them to enquire into Wycliffe's teachings on the basis of eighteen propositions, which had been taken from his writings and condemned at Avignon. The Pope complained that some of the Englishman's ideas smacked of heresies condemned in the Spiritual Franciscans, but significantly the points of error listed concerned ecclesiastical authority and organization rather than basic credal beliefs. To attack the Church's order was grave enough in view of papal claims, but Gregory XI seemed willing to allow that Wycliffe could clear himself of subscribing to dangerous ideas. The Pope, however, ordered that, if he were found guilty, then he should be punished and his teaching eradicated. If it proved difficult to arrest him, Gregory ordered that Wycliffe should appear at Rome in three months.

But what the Pope stipulated was never carried out. There was considerable delay in any attempt to implement the bulls, and although Wycliffe was eventually summoned before Sudbury and Courtenay at Lambeth, he was not even arrested. The English ecclesiastical lords were not disposed to comply exactly with papal demands, especially where it seemed to them that Gregory XI was trying to exercise his authority in a case of heresy. Oxford was vigorous in support of its most eminent teacher, and Richard II's government was anti-papal, willing indeed to dally with some of Wycliffe's ideas, despite Gregory's attempts to suggest that his teaching on lordship had revolutionary implications.[1] He retracted none of his opinions before his examiners, who merely ordered him to stop arguing the points at issue in public or in the university "on account of the scandal which they excited among the laity" against the clergy. Gregory XI died before he could take more positive measures, and there was no pontiff after him who

[1] Cf. Workman, op. cit., Vol. I, p. 298.

was able to resume the subject and possibly enforce condemnation on Wycliffe for his ideas. The double papal election of 1378 left two Popes – Urban VI and Clement VII – claiming and having to bid for universal allegiance in Christendom. In their rival ambitions to retain or acquire the English obedience, neither could afford to press investigations against Wycliffe, and for his part he continued to enjoy the protection of powerful noble and governmental figures in England.

At the same time, it is not difficult to see that he had no further political utility or possible rôle for national reform in Church and State. Not only was Lancaster losing his dominating influence as Richard II became a focus for rallying opposition to him, but with two Popes competing in schism it was easier to secure reasonable objectives in English affairs by compromise rather than with dire threats or ultimatums. It has been suggested[1] that for a brief period around the end of the year 1377 there was the possibility of genuine criticism and reform in the structure of the whole English Church, and the greatest threat to the established order under the Pope before the summoning of the Reformation Parliament by Henry VIII in 1529. Had Lancaster been prepared to continue supporting that anti-clericalism voiced in popular terms, he could have carried through some kind of reform and Wycliffe would have been at the centre of developments with his ideas. But the moment passed, and with it Wycliffe's particular opportunity. Thereafter he was isolated, not least in continuing to defend those points singled out by Gregory XI, and although the peculiar circumstances of the Great Schism afforded him protection from any Pope, his episcopal and monastic enemies in England scanned every opportunity for going further in securing an official condemnation. The year 1378 was a turning point for Wycliffe in his public career, but it also marked a watershed in his attitudes and thought. Until 1378, as university teacher and political writer, he developed his arguments to suit particular requirements of the day, but in turning from a life in royal service and for ecclesiastical preferment he moved more systematically into doctrinal and theological discussion. Although his fundamental principles remained unchanged, in this development he stepped firmly from the orthodoxy of the day into heresy. What he might have contributed in ideas and a practical programme in any reformation before 1378 would certainly have been drastic, but it would probably have been too heavily exploited in the interests of Lancaster and his friends. Moreover, in all likelihood, any such scheme would have lacked that deeper theological content and

[1] G. A. Holmes, *The Later Middle Ages* (London, 1962), pp. 172–3.

vision which appeared in the programmes subsequently hammered out by Wycliffe after his retirement from the duke's service. It was with those ideas in the last years of his life that he emerged supremely as a reformer.

CHAPTER III

WYCLIFFE THE REFORMER

FROM 1378 UNTIL HIS DEATH IN 1384, WYCLIFFE WAS INCREASINGLY withdrawn from public affairs in England, yet in this same period he crystallized his ideas more methodically and starkly than ever before in constant writing, and became the key figure in the widening movement known as Lollardy. His career in these years is simply told, for he continued to teach at Oxford until 1381 when he was banished from the university, and thereafter his final days were spent in the living at Lutterworth. Many of the details of his life through that period are lost, beyond the clear fact that he wrote unremittingly in reaction to circumstances, with feverishness and haste after suffering a stroke in 1382 and on to his second and fatal attack two years later. In such an outpouring, his ideas advanced far, so that his support fluctuated and altered in character, whilst he himself finally set out a programme of positive and radical reform that revealed him as more than the mere political propagandist or university don.

In many respects, Wycliffe only repeated the burden of complaint common to the age, whether against the Pope or the clergy, and such points equally found expression in the writings of his great contemporaries, Langland and Chaucer, or in the sermons and actions of exceptional bishops like Thoresby or Brinton. But whereas these critics condemned what was wrong in practice, Wycliffe went deeper in his arguments to develop fundamental principles in attacking clerical abuses and dependence of the laity on the priests, and to urge reformation in all Christian living and objectives. In 1378 he had still not reached his final conclusions, certainly not where he could think hopefully about the friars and the Papacy. His friends included men like Thomas Winterton, later Provincial Prior of the Augustinian Friars, or the Franciscan William Wodeford, who willingly debated with Wycliffe, whilst a younger student could speak of him at that time as "the venerable doctor, master John", words which were crossed out a year or so later and replaced with his condemnation as "an execrable seducer".[1] Meanwhile, Wycliffe had high expectations of Urban VI, the new Pope at Rome, for although not completely happy at the start of the Schism, he saw in it the chance of reform

[1] Gwynn, op. cit., pp. 238–9.

if Urban were to abandon all the organization and corruption of Avignon.[1] But all too quickly he was disillusioned and with increasing bitterness came to condemn the new as well as the old Pope, whilst after 1381 he turned against the friars for abandoning him. His reputation remained high at Oxford until his teaching and conclusions were challenged late in 1380. The episode that followed when he was ordered to stop his lectures and preaching saw the Duke of Lancaster attempting in vain to persuade Wycliffe not to give further offence in the university with his writings and views.

What were these views? They concerned three subjects in particular – the Church, the Eucharist, and the place of Scripture for Christian doctrine and life – and already in 1378 Wycliffe's publications revealed the trends of his thought on these matters. His arguments about lordship sketched out conclusions that could be exploited to attack all ecclesiastical abuses, but beyond this the principle fitted well enough with his more comprehensive understanding of the nature of the Church, which he discussed in a full-length tract in 1378. The fundamental premiss for his argument was that the Church was the predestined body of the elect – an idea which he had on occasion applied before, and for which he had been attacked, implicitly at least, in some of Gregory XI's articles. Predestination had been argued out most fully, if not clearly, by Augustine in the early Christian Church, and although the doctrine thereafter had not been abandoned in official teaching, it was not prominently proclaimed during the medieval centuries. Part of the reason for this neglect was to be found in the importance that men attached to the organized Church in its authority and to the sacraments for salvation. Renewed and vigorous exposition of predestination only came in the fourteenth century, when the Oxford scholar, Thomas Bradwardine, engaged in fierce controversy with the Occamists.[2] Bradwardine attained public pre-eminence as Archbishop of Canterbury for a few weeks in 1349 before succumbing in the Black Death, but more lasting and important was his influence upon Wycliffe over the subject of predestination. Wycliffe took his specific concepts and arguments from the older scholar, but characteristically pursued them much further. More logically and extremely than his predecessors, more extremely too than Calvin after him, Wycliffe argued in Biblical terms that God had predestined some for salvation, whilst others – condemned to damnation – He merely "foreknew". The true Church was composed of the "congregation of the predestined" as the Body of Christ, where

[1] Gwynn, op. cit,, p. 254.

[2] G. Leff, *Bradwardine and the Pelagians* (Cambridge, 1957), is a full study of this dispute and its importance for Wycliffe.

> neither place nor human election makes a person a member of the Church but divine predestination in respect of whoever with perseverance follows Christ in love, and in abandoning all his worldly goods suffers to defend His law.[1]

Only God could know who belonged to this "true" or "general" Church, which Wycliffe set over against the Church as commonly understood in its authority and organization. To be "in" what was often described as the Church Militant did not necessarily mean that a person was "of" the Church as the company of the predestined.

Wycliffe repeatedly directed the force of this argument against any possible human certainty as to who was saved, in order to impugn papal claims, sweep aside ecclesiastical authority and reject the commonly accepted distinction between clergy and laity. In particular he attacked the assertion made in Boniface VIII's bull *Unam Sanctam* that the Pope was the head of the Church and that all Christians had to be subject to him for their salvation. The only Head of the Church, Wycliffe retorted, was Christ. Neither the Pope nor anybody else could claim such a position for authority and government, even in the organized Church Militant, since nobody knew if an individual were predestined to salvation. The Pope, Wycliffe allowed,

> . . . if he is predestined and exercises his pastoral office, is the head of as much of the Church Militant as he governs, so that if he thus rules pre-eminently the whole of the Church Militant according to Christ's law, then he is the particular head of it under the Supreme Head, Jesus Christ.[2]

But no Christian had the power to make or even proclaim the Pope head or a member of the true Church. Moreover, Wycliffe dryly asked, what sort of claim to any headship could the Pope make if Christ in His wisdom judged it better for the Church Militant that He as Head should leave the earth after His Resurrection?

God's grace was available for every Christian without the need to believe in the claims of any ecclesiastical leader, whose commands each time had to be tested by Scripture. Developing themes which he had already touched on in discussing lordship, Wycliffe castigated the Church of his day, repudiating not only ecclesiastical authority but all privileges or concern for civil affairs, and corrupt and superstitious practices such as pilgrimages, the cult of saints, or the selling of indulgences with its accompanying belief in a Treasury of Merits for pardons. His appeal to predestination to cut away all pretence to authority or institutionalism in the Church was matched by a vigorous

[1] *De Ecclesia*, edited by J. Loserth (London, 1886), p. 76.
[2] Ibid., p. 19.

positive statement of the need for renewed spiritual life based on Christ's precepts in the Bible. Insofar as anything could, such life would demonstrate the fact of divine election. More comprehensively, Wycliffe put forward the primitive organization of the apostolic Church as the ideal for membership and behaviour. It was wholly wrong, he claimed, to speak of the Church as merely the Pope and priests, however corrupt their life, and to exclude laymen following God's Law. Manner of life made Christians what they were, and the priests' ordination counted for nothing if they themselves were unrighteous – an important point which Wycliffe more fully afterwards developed to deny that an unworthy priest could administer the sacraments. Though predestination was decisive in the end for constituting the true Church, Wycliffe insisted that charity and obedience to the Law of God in Christ were essential in the Church Militant. The king was God's regent and had the Christian authority to reform the Church's hierarchy and cut away its corrupting privileges.

There was nothing new in attacking papal doctrines of power and government over an organized Universal Church, even when Wycliffe sought to claim that the clergy's functions were supposed to be spiritual and should therefore have nothing to do with secular power and wealth. The Anonymous of York in the eleventh century had advanced arguments for the supreme Christian authority of kings and princes; Marsiglio of Padua and William of Occam at a later date had deeply exploited the concept of the Church as a purely spiritual, non-organizational body of all the faithful. Nevertheless, Wycliffe did go further than other critics in his unusual stress upon predestination, and this in the end made him more radical and damaging than, say, Occam or those who advocated a General Council to bring about reform. He did not face the full consequences of the doctrine, which logically could lead to the denial not only of all authority and hierarchy in the Church but also of any necessary sacramental life or righteous conduct. Such spiritual anarchy Wycliffe desired no more than the social or political disruption which could follow from his doctrine of lordship. He was emphatic in demanding a return to Gospel principles and the pattern of the unorganized primitive Church for Christian living, and it was upon these foundations that his practical schemes were further built. But he never attempted to reconcile or explain satisfactorily the working of predestination with the validity and need of righteous living in the Church. It can be allowed that in the last analysis no rational human explanation of this paradox is possible, and that Scripture offers none. Even so, Wycliffe's polemical concern where he wrote on the subject, and his sweeping use of the idea of the Church as the predestined, chosen Body of Christ to destroy his opponents' schemes, prevented him from showing adequately that this truth had to be harmonized with the equally vital principle of practical righteousness.

Wycliffe's ecclesiology, it can be claimed, was defective, but his particular stress on predestination was necessary and deeply valuable in the age. He brought back into prominence features in the doctrine of the Church and the whole working of salvation which for too long had been overlaid by other considerations of authority, sacerdotalism and organization. Simply and logically from the fundamentals which he posed there followed the conclusion that the individual Christian – layman no less than cleric, if such a distinction were made – could commune face to face with God. No mediating priesthood remained necessary, for implicitly there was a priesthood of all believers in the Church in which none could lay claim to binding authority. The lordship which could only be possessed by God's grace in righteousness meant that each Christian as a vassal, in feudal imagery, held directly of God Himself as liege lord. Thereby the individual was left privileged and responsible in direct relationship to God through Christ, and all argument for priestly intercession or government in the Church was swept aside. In upholding the reality of particulars against universals, the Nominalist William of Occam could claim that a single man might be true to God and all the rest of the world – including the Pope – be wrong; but Wycliffe was not one whit less radical in developing his Realist ideas to defend the responsibility and worth of the individual Christian.

These principles also underlay Wycliffe's arguments about the second great subject – the Eucharist – which claimed his attention. Philosophically and in doctrinal terms, his work on the Church was challenging enough to orthodoxy,[1] and this was quickly followed by other attacks on the Pope and arguments for royal action to deal with abuses. But in 1379 and 1380, Wycliffe clearly went into heresy by attacking accepted dogma on the Eucharist in his Oxford lectures and in his tracts *On Apostasy* and *On the Eucharist*. The ideas which he then expounded he returned to again and again in the last years of his life, and pre-eminently they made it possible for the authorities to condemn him and his followers as heretical. What brought Wycliffe's criticisms to the surface were both the practices and the theories of the Eucharist and Mass in his age. The particular service was central in religious life, worship and ceremonial, where attendance at least once a year

1 Gwynn, op. cit., p. 251, rightly notes that Wycliffe had become heretical in his doctrine of the Church from the Roman point of view, and yet only his Eucharistic ideas brought general concern in England.

and in connection with confession to the priest was obligatory on every Christian, and where too injunctions were issued frequently for more regular communion by the faithful. The ordinary people held the Mass in veneration, with all the accompanying symbolism that directed attention to Christ's Passion and Death. Recognition of the need to explain what the service was about was to be found in the production of a Lay Folks' Mass Book, first in French and then in English verse, for the benefit of the ordinary layman.[1] At the same time, the appearance and multiplication of chantries, where patrons gave endowments for the saying of Masses for their souls in Purgatory, demonstrated in another way what attention was given officially and popularly to the service.

Wycliffe was categorically opposed to the idolatry encouraged by practices in the Mass, and above all to the fact that the priest was given an immensely important place in "making" Christ's Body, but as a Realist too he was long uneasy with the doctrine of transubstantiation and the numerous efforts to make rational sense of it. Transubstantiation had been declared a dogma of faith at the Fourth Lateran Council in 1215, and it stated plainly that in the priestly consecration of the elements, the bread and wine were transubstantiated into the Body and Blood of Christ, that is, that Christ's Body and Blood were truly and objectively created, and there remained only the appearance of bread and wine. From such a doctrine sprang the worship of the Host in the Mass, but it was difficult to explain scholastically, and thinkers like Aquinas, Duns Scotus and Occam came to present widely contrasting definitions. All used the familiar philosophical distinctions between a substance and its accidents, between the essence of a thing and its many qualities of form, taste and colour, and in such categories they endeavoured to explain how Christ could bodily be present in the Eucharist whilst the bread and wine appeared to remain. Aquinas accepted that the accidents of the bread continued in existence when its substance was transubstantiated, but Occam as a Nominalist rejected the idea of accidents remaining apart from their substance, and in consequence taught that in transubstantiation the bread and wine were annihilated, leaving only an illusion of their existence thereafter. Wycliffe was especially unhappy with this view which wrenched appearance and reality apart, but he continued to accept an official explanation of transubstantiation until other disputes led him into Biblical questioning and a direct break from the doctrine in 1379. He then completely rejected it, in philosophical terms and as un-Scriptural in encouraging idolatry and a wrong view of the priest.

[1] Cf. Manning, op. cit., Chapter I, for an account of the place of the Mass in ordinary devotion.

On historical grounds, he easily showed that transubstantiation was of recent origin in its formulation by Innocent III and defence by later Popes. In contrast he appealed back to the Bible and the early Christian Fathers, as well as to the statement which Berengarius of Tours had to accept in 1059 to demonstrate his orthodoxy on the subject of the Eucharist. In this official declaration, Wycliffe argued, Berengarius clearly understood "that the same bread and wine which were placed before the Mass upon the altar remain after the consecration both as sacrament and as the Lord's Body".[1] As late as the eleventh century after Christ's Resurrection, therefore, no dogma of transubstantiation was known; Satan had been bound for the first thousand years, and only thereafter had begun to work actively in spreading error, with the Pope as Antichrist.[2]

In theological terms, Wycliffe maintained that the elements of bread and wine remained what they were before consecration, although after that act they also became in some sense the Lord's Body and Blood. It was clear what he rejected, but his efforts more positively to state the nature of the Eucharist were confused, partly because he continued to argue in accepted scholastic terms. The bread, he explained, remained bread after consecration, and there was no basis for arguing that it became *identical* with Christ's Body: it was the sacrament or sign of Christ, who was present in the bread as the soul in the human body. It was indeed Christ's Body, but not in substance or essence, only virtually, spiritually and sacramentally – three modes of being which Wycliffe attempted to define, each time clearly rejecting any thought of a material presence or substitution of Christ for the substance of the bread.[3] His nearest approach to a simple statement on the matter was the explanation that "Under the form of bread and wine is sacramentally the Body of Christ",[4] but despite the lack of finality in his discussion, it seems that essentially Wycliffe was concerned with a "receptionist" view of the Eucharist. The determining factor to validate Christ's presence and reception in the Eucharist was the faith of the individual participant. His doctrine of remanence, that the bread and wine *remained* substantially as well as in their accidents, alongside the sacramental Body of Christ, was too subtle for his own followers[5] and left problems of meaning for later reformers, but his general view has been summed up as "sacramental, in the only proper sense of the word, namely, as a material substance symbolizing a spiritual content".[6] What he plainly and utterly rejected

[1] *De Eucharistia*, edited by J. Loserth (London, 1892), pp. 30, 31.
[2] Ibid., pp. 286–7. [3] Ibid., pp. 11, 12. [4] Ibid., p. 49.
[5] See below, pp. 51, 176, for Lollard views of the Eucharist.
[6] Spinka, M. (editor), *Advocates of Reform from Wyclif to Erasmus* (London, 1953), p. 30.

in such argument was any thought of sacerdotalism and the idolatry nurtured upon belief in transubstantiation. In this respect, his argument was conservative as well as logical, where he claimed to be reverting to the older, purer teaching in the Church of the first millennium of the Christian era.

From 1379 onward, Wycliffe came under specific attack at Oxford for his views on the Eucharist, and in 1380 defended a set of a dozen conclusions in his teaching at a council summoned by Berton, the Chancellor of the University. In this debate, the friars abandoned Wycliffe to join the monks in opposition to him and his secular supporters. Early in the following year, his doctrine of remanence was condemned at Oxford, and when he appealed to the king, the Duke of Lancaster came in person to the city to dissuade him from further dispute. Wycliffe's reply was to publish his *Confession* in May, 1381, which defended and amplified his known conclusions and represented perhaps the last attempt to keep the dispute within academic bounds. The work, however, only served to deepen the divisions in Oxford and to stimulate the ecclesiastical authorities in having Wycliffe and his teaching condemned. Within the university, there were feuds between the regulars and seculars, whilst Robert Rygge, the new Chancellor elected in 1381, was sympathetic to Wycliffe as the great Oxford scholar, though shortly before he had helped to condemn his teaching on remanence in Berton's council. From these developments there came the Blackfriars Synod of May, 1382, in which Wycliffe's doctrines and following were more formally proscribed, but by that time Wycliffe himself had moved on from verbal criticism to schemes for implementing practical reform. His appeal did not remain confined to university circles: it was channelled by his own personal scholarly disciples to a wider audience through the country. In this was to be found the substance of Wycliffe's more enduring legacy, where it was shown that the arguments and conclusions primarily of a schoolman – even if presented in violent form on occasion – were also relevant for ordinary people and could be translated into terms which they were able to understand and employ.

These developments sprang directly from Wycliffe's concern in the third of his basic principles – the supreme place and authority to be given to Scripture. In all his arguments he came to stress with growing emphasis that God's Word, the Bible, was the final and only justification for any conclusion. This conviction was given practical expression in two major enterprises which together helped to define the Lollard movement: one was the translation of the Bible into English and use of vernacular writings for teaching, the other was the organizing of "poor preachers" to evangelize the country at large. In neither undertaking did Wycliffe lack forerunners, nor were his contributions very direct or complete before his death, but both bore the imprint of the ideas and hopes of his last years of work.

In all his scholarly writings, notably where theological issues were under discussion, Wycliffe quoted extensively from Scripture as well as from canon law and the Fathers, but it seems that only gradually and in the course of his university disputes did he come to regard the Bible as supremely authoritative for belief and life. Though he came to exalt Scripture in uncompromising terms, it was only late in his life that he did so, whilst even later was the plan crystallized for producing a vernacular Bible.[1] In his arguments on lordship, on the Church and on the Eucharist, it is possible to see Wycliffe's increasing reliance on Scripture alone as the all-sufficient authority for right conclusions, and it is not surprising therefore that in 1378, when he published his work on the Church, he also issued a lengthy discussion entitled *On the Truth of Holy Scripture*. As in other arguments, he repeated the appeals of earlier opponents of the Pope to the Scriptures as the authority for showing and judging corruption, but once again he went further, not only in distinguishing sharply between the Bible and all other writings but also in asserting the right of every Christian to read and know it for himself. His principal argument was simple: Holy Scripture was the highest authority for every believer, the standard of faith and the foundation for reform in religious, political and social life. It was grounded in its divine inspiration in every part as God's Law,[2] and witnessed to Christ and the whole scheme of salvation in Him.[3] In itself it was perfectly sufficient for salvation, without the addition of customs or traditions such as canon law, prayers to the saints, fastings, pilgrimages or the Mass.[4] Elsewhere, Wycliffe could speak with more sympathy of the use of such customs, but their place was insignificant when measured against the claims of Scripture for regulating Christian affairs. Knowledge of the Bible alone was essential, he argued, and failure to know it was failure to know Christ;[5] as it stood, it could be understood by anyone who read in faith and sought the teaching of God's Holy Spirit. If anything appeared false in Scripture, the fault lay in the reader's understanding, not in the text, where difficult passages were to be interpreted by those more easily grasped.[6] Wycliffe was insistent on the fact that

[1] Workman, op. cit., Vol. II, p. 156.

[2] *De Veritate Sacrae Scripturae*, edited by R. Buddensieg (London, 1905–7), Vol. I, pp. 392, 394–5, 401.

[3] Ibid., Vol. I, pp. 125 f.; Vol. II, p. 242.

[4] Ibid., Vol. I, p. 181; Vol. II, pp. 116, 144, 270.

[5] Ibid., Vol. III, p. 242.

[6] Ibid., Vol. I, pp. 192–6.

every passage had one sense – the literal – and that though a spiritual meaning could be discerned behind this, there was no place in Biblical study for the tortuous, involved interpretations or glosses common to the age. In practice, it can be observed, Wycliffe himself did not always strictly follow his own rules.

Where he assigned such weight to the Bible as the sole arbiter for Christian doctrine and behaviour, it was logical that he should also urge and eventually undertake its translation into ordinary language for common use. The project as ultimately realized broke new ground, but it did not lack some precedents, nor did Wycliffe originally plan much more than what had already been done by contemporaries. Generally speaking, the English clergy in the fourteenth century used the Bible as far as they could in the Latin Vulgate, with the glosses and commentaries of medieval scholars, but all too often their knowledge of Latin extended only as far as the Ten Commandments and the Lord's Prayer. It was in consequence by no means unknown for preachers to quote Biblical texts in the vernacular and for bishops to attempt to meet popular needs with instruction books in English. Amongst such were the Lay Folks' Mass Book in various versions from an original French edition of an earlier century, and the Lay Folks' Catechism issued in Latin and English by Archbishop Thoresby in 1357. These contained passages of Scripture for learning or liturgical use by the laity. But there also existed from earlier centuries translations of parts of the Bible into various languages – the Psalms or Gospels into Old English and French – and the whole of the Scriptures in the Norman dialect of French.[1] Typically, however, these products were for reading and meditation by the literate upper classes rather than designed for the common people, and Wycliffe pointedly complained that "As lords of England have the Bible in French, so it would not be against reason that they should have the same words in English".[2] The first attempt to go beyond this limit in fourteenth-century England also showed how far away was the thought of any general vernacular Bible. The hermit and mystic Richard Rolle wrote a psalter in English prose which became widely popular and was later enjoyed as much by the Lollards as anyone else, but it was produced for use by a recluse and intended to aid her in devotions; the glosses and comments of scholars which were included could be valued more highly than the Biblical text itself.[3]

Wycliffe's early idea seemed to have been to provide translations of parts of Scripture for use by the clergy, so that they should have

[1] Cf. M. Deanesly, *The Lollard Bible* (Cambridge, 1920), Chapter V.
[2] F. D. Matthew (editor), *The English Works of Wyclif* (London, 1880), p. 429.
[3] Deanesly, op. cit., pp. 144 f.

manuals of texts or a collection of proofs to demonstrate the truth of the Bible as "God's Law" against the canonists in their support of the Pope. Scripture in this light was a law book, and Wycliffe continued to regard it so as he moved on into the uncompromising demand for its translation in entirety and stripped of all extraneous comment, so that the ordinary layman could see what was true for himself. Under Wycliffe's urging, his followers at Oxford were already planning the scheme by 1380 and the systematic work of translation was started in the last years of his life. His own personal share in the versions eventually produced is judged to have been slight, and it is possible that he contributed directly no part of any translation, but he inspired the enterprise and supervised the writing of others from his rectory at Lutterworth, and his own vernacular sermons richly indicate his familiarity with and quotation of Scripture in English. The first attempt at a translation was made chiefly by Nicholas Hereford, who was a doctor of divinity and an Oxford canon, and whose contribution appears to have been interrupted by his summons to appear at the Blackfriars Synod of 1382. At that point, he had reached Baruch, chapter three, verse twenty, in the Apocrypha, and the translation was completed by other followers of Wycliffe before his death. This version was a great undertaking, but it was a crabbed and literal rendering of the Vulgate and in places almost incomprehensible. It was not intended to be the popular, easily readable book that Wycliffe elsewhere advocated, but rather the new law-book, accurate to the letter, to be used by the clergy and knights of the national, anti-papal party, that still had Lancaster as its leader.[1] General feeling in Parliament and through the country certainly was critical of the Papacy, but by 1382 or 1383, the moment had passed for Lancaster to be able to use such a translation, even if it were acceptable from Wycliffe and his followers. Hereford's version, therefore, never served the purpose for which it was probably intended, but in any case Wycliffe encouraged the start of a major revision in his lifetime, and this was undertaken by John Purvey, another of the Oxford disciples and Wycliffe's secretary at Lutterworth.

Purvey's translation was not completed until about 1395, and was much freer, more idiomatic in its English renderings than the earlier version which it almost completely superseded in use. It was this second Wycliffite translation which came generally to be known as the Lollard Bible, and its popularity is attested by the fact that over a hundred manuscripts of it still survive, despite legislation enacted

[1] Deanesly, *Significance*, pp. 6–13, admirably sets out the purpose and character of this version.

and enforced through the fifteenth century against possessing or reading the Bible in English. The achievement marked a significant advance where for the first time Englishmen could have the whole Bible for reading in the vernacular, and without the encumbrance of involved glosses, but Purvey's work was remarkable and valuable in other ways as well. He wrote introductions and epilogues to many of the books of the Bible, and a general prologue setting out the nature of his task in obtaining a basic text for translation and what he judged were the fundamental principles for doing such a work. He had, he explained, assembled and collated older Latin Bibles, with other writings, to secure the most accurate text possible of Jerome's Vulgate; and had then consulted additional commentators and glosses to reach the exact meanings of obscure passages and words. He paid particular tribute to the Franciscan scholar Nicholas of Lyra, who earlier in the century had specialized in Hebrew studies and used his knowledge in expounding the Old Testament.[1] Setting out next his general principles for translation, Purvey explained that "the best translating . . . out of Latin into English [is] to translate after the sentence [meaning], and not only after the words, so that the sentence be as open, or opener, in English, as in Latin, and go not far from the letter".[2] Finally, in more detail, he illustrated differences of use in the two languages where his purpose was to reach a plain, idiomatic English rendering.

This task was quite formidable in an age when English was only just beginning to replace French in official writing, and where no adequate theological terminology was generally accepted in the native tongue. Quite apart from the multiplicity of Vulgate texts as well, making it difficult at times to determine the true Latin original, there were in Middle English three main dialects and numerous other minor variations. Purvey (like Chaucer in *The Canterbury Tales*) used Midland English which was the dialect of London and came to dominate the whole country, but nevertheless it remained debatable often enough as to what words or constructions were to be used in translation. Occasionally, it seems that Purvey was at a loss to find any English equivalent and merely copied down the Latin word in slightly altered form, just as he could transcribe into his version glosses or comments from Lyra's earlier studies,[3] but the translation was fundamental and deeply influential for the subsequent history of the English Bible. Developments in Lollardy brought the idea of vernacular Scriptures under official censure in the fifteenth century, but Purvey's

[1] Wycliffe too acknowledged Lyra's work as a Biblical commentator and scholar, excepting him from his more general condemnation of contemporary theologians (*De Veritate*, Vol. I, p. 275).

[2] Deanesly, *Lollard Bible*, p. 258. Chapter X deals generally with Purvey's prologue.

[3] Cf. F. F. Bruce, *The English Bible* (London, 1961), pp. 18, 19.

Bible paved the way to the work of Tyndale and his successors and further refinements in translation upon Hebrew and Greek originals. Some idea of the enduring authority of the version, and of its quality, can be gained in this quotation of the first fourteen verses of John's Gospel:

> In the bigynnyng was the word, and the word was at God, and God was the word. This was in the bigynnyng at God. Alle thingis weren maad bi hym, and withouten hym was maad no thing, that thing that was maad. In hym was lijf, and the lijf was the light of men; and the light schyneth in derknessis, and derknessis comprehendiden not it. A man was sent fro God, to whom the name was Joon. This man cam in to witnessyng, that he schulde bere witnessing of the light, that alle men schulden bileve bi hym. He was not the light, but that he schulde bere witnessing of the light. There was a very light, which lightneth ech man that cometh in to this world. He was in the world, and the world was maad bi hym, and the world knew hym not. He cam in to his owne thingis, and hise resseyveden hym not. But hou many ever resseyveden hym, he gaf to hem power to be maad the sones of God, to hem that bileveden in his name; the whiche not of bloodis, nether of the wille of fleische, nether of the wille of man, but ben borun of God. And the word was maad man, and dwellyde among us, and we han seyn the glorie of hym, as the glorie of the oon bigetun sone of the fadir, ful of grace and of treuthe.

In the meantime, there emerged the second great practical scheme from Wycliffe's teaching on the supremacy of Scripture, namely, the organization and work of the "poor preachers". This meant that laymen as well as clerics were to be trained and to minister amongst the people, and again it was a venture by no means clearly planned out by Wycliffe before his death. It nevertheless followed on logically from his arguments, and was functioning vigorously, if haphazardly, in certain centres in the early 1380's. From 1378 onward, the support that Wycliffe commanded was increasingly limited to a few scholars at Oxford – men like Nicholas Hereford, John Aston, Philip Repton, Robert Alington, John Ashwardby – and it was through their enthusiasm that the ideas of the master were spread more widely through the world outside the university. Thus it was that by 1382 more popular groups sprang up at Leicester, possibly through Repton's activity and with the support of laymen like William Smith and William Swinderby, who carried the gospel around neighbouring Midland towns – Melton Mowbray and Loughborough – and south into Hampshire. Strictly speaking, the authorities from the start should have censured such unlicensed preaching, but they took little notice for a time, chiefly because popular evangelism and criticism of ecclesiastical abuse were so prevalent in the age. Wycliffe placed the very highest premium upon preaching as the ministry of God's Word to the whole people. It was, he claimed, "a holier act than the consecration of the sacrament, when only one person received God's Word as the Body of Christ".[1] Again and again he argued that the priest's chief duty, after the example of righteous living, was to offer the Gospel to ordinary people by preaching, and it was to remedy defects in such a ministry that he encouraged the movements spreading through the Midlands. But his criticisms were not unique, and the startling spread of the work of the "poor preachers" was as much in the tradition of older developments as anything entirely new.

Among the parish clergy of the later Middle Ages, preaching in theory had a recognized and important place, but actual standards of ministry and teaching by local priests were generally very unsatisfactory. The abuses in the ecclesiastical system, with pluralities, non-residence and the growth of appropriations, helped to disrupt and demoralize the regular parochial system, and many of those who had the cures of souls were not university graduates or properly literate. In 1281, Archbishop Peckham had issued a series of constitutions for Canterbury Province requiring preaching in the vernacular at least four times a year to explain "the fourteen articles of faith, the Lord's Prayer, the Ten Commandments of the Decalogue, the two precepts of the Gospel, the seven works of mercy, the seven mortal sins, the seven principal virtues and the seven sacramental graces". These regulations were re-issued by Thoresby for York in 1357 and expanded with an English rhyming version that became known as the Lay Folks' Catechism. The priest was ordered to instruct his congregation each Sunday on such matters. Wycliffe undeniably approved of these rules, since a version of them was later made with long interpolations for Lollard ideas, and this was widely used in the spread of the movement.[2] But Thoresby's orders seem to have been ignored rather than obeyed, and the Poor Parson of Chaucer's tale "that Christ's Gospel truly would preach" was the exception to that general class of clergy condemned as scathingly by Bishop Brinton as by Wycliffe. If anything, the mantle of preaching was donned by those who sought a more secluded religious life – men like Rolle and Walter Hilton – and by the friars and pardoners in their activities.

[1] *De Veritate*, Vol. II, p. 156; *Polemical Works*, edited by R. Buddensieg (London, 1883), Vol. I, p. 261.

[2] All versions are printed in *The Lay Folks' Catechism*, edited by T. F. Simmons and H. E. Nolloth. Both Thoresby and Wycliffe were associated with Yorkshire, but there seems to have been no definite connection between them, and Thoresby would not have approved of the Lollard additions to his regulations. How much was added by Wycliffe himself, how much by his followers, remains conjecture, but it seems probable that the Lollard version did not begin to circulate until well after Thoresby's death in 1373. Cf. Workman, op. cit., Vol. II, p. 157 and note.

From early in the thirteenth century the friars had been prominent in England as in other countries of Christendom, and their peculiar achievement in working among the people had been to make preaching an art. The secular beneficed clergy alone were legally entitled to preach, but the Popes readily gave exemptions for the friars who were welcomed wherever they went as great preachers. In their work, they tended to stress the sermon at the expense of the Mass, and were loud in denouncing ecclesiastical authorities, wealth and corruption. Not unnaturally, the local bishops and clergy quickly came to resent the friars where they upset parish work even if popular in drawing large numbers to hear their sermons and anecdotes; and by 1350, they were regarded with suspicion generally in much of what they did. Their ideals of poverty and spirituality were applauded, but the individual friar usually failed to live up to earlier examples and was renowned rather for preaching solely to gain money from his hearers. Wycliffe's criticisms in his last days against "begging" friars were not more trenchant than those implied in Chaucer's portrait of a mendicant with his wealth and skill in hearing confessions or preaching for alms. The friars after 1350 continued to contribute positively towards popularizing religion, and Wycliffe acknowledged their ability and work, but their failings were a powerful spur to the Lollard attempt to bring in remedies.

More surprisingly, the pardoners also helped to prepare the ground for Wycliffe's preachers. As officials licensed generally by the Pope and more individually by the local bishop to sell indulgences around the country, pardoners were notorious for their practices, not least of all in using relics among the superstitious people of the day. With papal sanction behind them, they could override even the protests of bishops in commandeering pulpits for their preaching and selling. Not unexpectedly, their intrusion was bitterly disliked by both local clergy and friars, and their activities became suspect among the ordinary people as they found themselves exploited. On all sides pardoners were condemned or considered beneath contempt, even if, as Chaucer noted, they could gain a ready response with their attractive wares. Yet they made the appearance of Lollard preachers natural as much as welcome. In the papal license, a pardoner was not required to be a cleric, and some English bishops protested that the whole ministerial office was suffering abuse as laymen appeared as pardoners and preached from pulpits.[1] In the end, both papal and episcopal regulations cut down these irregularities, but in Wycliffe's age laymen frequently preached the value of indulgences and sold their relics from pulpits denied to sub-deacons. Such a situation not only added to official

[1] Owst, op. cit., p. 104.

resentment against pardoners but also made it easy for the people to accept Lollard lay preachers and missionaries alongside the clergy.

In these ways, therefore, the Wycliffite development of a lay ministry in evangelism built upon specific ideas by no means unfamiliar to contemporaries. Yet the scheme was new as witnessing the first deliberate attempt to do anything practical about the needs in religion throughout the country.[1] Wycliffe did not intend to set up any new order or a rival ministry to the parish priesthood but simply to fill the gap in preaching the Gospel, notably with a different stress in what was said. He roundly condemned the kinds of sermons well known in his age – the scholastic expositions of the theologians and the mendicants' strings of popular stories – and by contrast urged that the "bare text" of Scripture should be taken and expounded, for the most part in practical terms. In such preaching, the purpose would be that

> . . . the law of God be well known, taught, maintained, magnified . . . , the great open sin that reigneth in divers places be destroyed, and also heresy and hypocrisy of Antichrist and his followers . . . , and true peace, prosperity and burning charity be increased in Christendom, and namely in the realm of England.[2]

Wycliffe has been called the greatest English preacher of his day, and his surviving sermons in Latin and the vernacular reveal how simply and carefully he sought to take the Scriptures and expound their meaning, notably in relation to Christ and His salvation and for the practical needs of the congregation. Such sermons lacked much of the lively appeal of the stories with which the friars entertained their hearers, but they had the impact of direct, relevant spiritual teaching from the Bible, and for this teaching people were hungry. The Word of God was the rule of life for Wycliffe, and this conviction he imparted to his followers who evangelized during the last years of his life and thereafter.

Such were the crucial practical measures – translation of the Bible into English and a popular evangelistic movement – that sprang from Wycliffe's concern with Scripture and took his ideas everywhere. The final shape in each scheme was the work of his disciples, but already before his death they were known as Lollards and their activities had provoked important reactions. The movement clearly struck a deep, responsive chord among the ordinary people but at the same time it attracted heavy official censure because of its disruptive implications, and for this reason was dubbed Lollardy. The term "Lollard", deriving from a word meaning "to mumble", was applied

[1] Owst, op. cit., p. 131.

[2] *English Works*, p. 276.

to the Flemish Beghards and Beguines for learning and reciting Scripture and saying prayers, though possibly it also reflected the fact that such people preached and argued too much for some ears; but more generally it came to be synonymous with "heretic" and in this sense was used in England and applied to the Wycliffites.[1] The Oxford disciples were first called Lollards, and then more widely the clerical and lay recruits to Wycliffe's ideas, whilst the movement itself rapidly became known as Lollardy where its adherents clung to three or four basic views concerning the Eucharist, the Pope, a vernacular Bible and the independence of the laity from all priests. The Wycliffite theories were given simpler, more comprehensible form in these tenets, but Lollardy itself was no completely new phenomenon in the 1380's. As a popular anti-clerical movement, sceptical of all authority or hierarchy in the Church, and affirming individual autonomy in spiritual life, it was undoubtedly of far older lineage. Despite the concern of English people in the fourteenth century for traditional practices in their religious life, there also existed an underlying, stubborn current of popular piety outside organized ecclesiastical control. At times, this current had affinities with earlier and contemporary anti-clerical tides on the Continent – such as Waldensianism and the Beghard movement – but it was given precise direction and a particular purpose in Wycliffe's teaching and hopes. This programme, it can be claimed, was argued out lengthily and in scholastic confusion by Wycliffe, but even though trimmed into simpler form by popularizers, it would scarcely have spread so quickly and widely had the ideas not fallen into receptive ears. As it appeared in and after Wycliffe's lifetime, Lollardy was moulded and labelled by particular reference to his ideas, but its roots more generally were fastened deeply and obscurely in an earlier England.

Clear indication of the ease with which the formulations of the university philosopher and theologian could become, or were believed to become, the simple slogans of the common man, was given in the Peasants' Revolt of 1381. England knew uncertain social and economic conditions in the decades after 1350, with war, plague and famine causing popular discontent as well as government anxiety. Labour shortages following the Black Death meant that traditional peasant burdens had to be relaxed, and the statute of Labourers in 1351 caused resentment precisely because the government thereby sought to limit wages and to bind workers generally to their occupa-

[1] The word was also thought to derive from "loller", a loafer, and was made to pun with the Latin *lolia*, the tares in the Bible. Cf. Deanesly, *Lollard Bible*, p. 70; Workman, op. cit., Vol. I, p. 327. The Host in Chaucer's *Canterbury Tales* seemed to fear heresy and a long sermon from the Poor Parson as a "lollere".

tions. Grievances repeatedly voiced after 1351 were from a peasantry which had tasted better conditions, and wanted no return to older, oppressive ways. These feelings were aggravated by fresh taxation for war after 1379, and the poll-tax levied in 1380 and 1381 led directly to wide-spread insurrection. Peasants rose against their lords and Wat Tyler marched on London, occupying it with the aid of the citizens who had their own complaints against the authorities. The demands basically were economic, whether against taxes or oppressive landlords who included the abbots and monasteries, and the provisions presented and granted temporarily by Richard II in London were practical and limited. But there was also much talk of the overthrow of the government and Archbishop Sudbury was seized and murdered in the capital. A number of minor clergy joined the rebellious groups, and these included John Ball, notorious for years in his denunciations of social and political injustices, and as the preacher who stirred the forces gathering to march into London with his sermon on the tag, "When Adam delved and Eve span, Who was then the gentleman?" In his and others' teaching, there were hopes of establishing an egalitarian society and of ushering in the Millennium,[1] and it was later alleged that Ball confessed to having studied under Wycliffe for two years and to having tried to apply his ideas. There was no such connection between Wycliffe and Ball, but it seems probable that the ideas of the Oxford reformer had some part in the revolutionary programme.

Wycliffe's arguments on lordship or predestination and his unequivocal appeal to Scripture had serious implications for social and political issues. Within university walls, it was possible to speculate academically in extreme terms, and Wycliffe was careful in his published arguments almost entirely to stress conservative conclusions, avoiding suggestions that the English government or secular authority more generally could or should be overthrown. Indeed, he placed great weight upon what he considered civil power should do in carrying through reform. The ramifications of the idea that lordship could only be anchored in God's grace he confined rigidly to the ecclesiastical realm, whilst arguing that the king and nobles – the "captains" of the Christian polity – should act to remedy religious affairs.[2] It was in this connection that Wycliffe spoke provocatively of the need for God "to obey the devil". Furthermore, in denouncing social injustice and the failures of the lords to deal in Christian ways with their servants and tenants, Wycliffe strongly urged that wrongs

[1] Cohn, op. cit., pp. 210–7.

[2] Cf. H. Kaminsky, "Wyclifism as Ideology of Revolution", in *Church History* XXXII (1963), pp. 57–74.

should be patiently borne rather than used as the pretext for rebellion.[1] Bishop Brinton and the Dominican John Bromyard each said as much, and they certainly did not want revolution.[2] Finally, there was a radical difference of outlook between Wycliffe and those in the Peasants' Revolt – many in 1381 looked forward to the Millennium, but this for Wycliffe had already come and gone, and his appeal was to secular authority to fight against Satan in his renewed activity after the thousand years' bondage. No shred of evidence exists of any formal connection between Wycliffe or his known followers and the leaders of the revolt. Yet his principles were inflammatory, susceptible to interpretations other than those he gave, and he was unwise enough to defend the murder of Sudbury. He allowed that a subject could resist a ruler if obedience would mean sin against God, and although he refused to probe what this implied, such an argument gave scope ultimately for justifying rebellion, as in later Calvinism. But no less obviously, Wycliffe's principles of lordship, predestination, even millennialism, could be argued to challenge authority and proclaim anarchy, with the Scriptures to appeal to for such conclusions. There were these ideas in Lollardy, and they remained, however muddled or muted they became. In 1381, they coincided with popular sentiment so that John Ball and Wycliffe's enemies alike used the opportunity, if for different ends.[3]

Wycliffe's *Confession* appeared shortly before the uprising, and its tone left Lancaster embarrassed in his efforts to continue shielding the author; but more significantly the sequence of events that included the murder of governmental leaders before the suppression of Wat Tyler's revolt was exploited to discredit the whole Lollard movement with the authorities. The Lollards themselves were branded as subversive, rebels against both civil and ecclesiastical order. In this manner, circumstances led to more determined official action against Wycliffe and his teaching in the last year or so of his life, and the leader of the attack was Courtenay as the new Archbishop of Canterbury. With regard to Wycliffe himself, action was restrained, so that at the Blackfriars Synod of May, 1382, his name was not even mentioned. That assembly convened by Courtenay was packed with monks and friars at the expense of the seculars, and the Archbishop asked for its judgment upon twenty-four conclusions selected from Wycliffe's writings.

[1] *English Works*, pp. 226–43.

[2] Cf. M. A. Devlin, editor, *The Sermons of Thomas Brinton* (London, 1954), Vol. I, p. xxv; G. R. Owst, *Literature and Pulpit in Medieval England*, second edition (Oxford, 1961), p. 583.

[3] Cf. M. E. Aston, "Lollardy and Sedition", in *Past and Present* 17 (1960), pp. 1–44, for the general discussion of the political implications of Lollard ideas in the 1380's and after.

Ten of the total were condemned as heretical, four of them relating to the Mass, whilst the rest were judged only as erroneous.[1] It was not necessarily true that the conclusions selected gave a fair picture of Wycliffe's views for condemnation, but they served as a basis for attacking the Lollards, and continued to be influential later in the Hussite process.[2] Wycliffe himself was not summoned to appear at the synod, nor was he expressly attacked, but his followers were. Courtenay, acting with care and effect, compelled Aston and others to attend at Blackfriars to explain their views. As a result, Aston was condemned, though he escaped, for rejecting transubstantiation and defining his belief in the Real Presence in Wycliffe's terms. Hereford and Repton were similarly excommunicated and went into hiding for failing to satisfy the synod about their views, although they were willing to allow that the conclusions were heretical and erroneous. An earthquake brought proceedings abruptly to an end, and was taken on both sides – and for different reasons – as a sign of God's judgment.

Wycliffe thereafter was allowed to remain virtually unhindered in retirement at Lutterworth, possibly since Courtenay judged that his stroke would leave him harmless. The archbishop acted more deliberately against Lollardy as he found it infesting Oxford, where he banned Hereford and others from teaching and broke the hold of the Lollard masters with an official condemnation of Wycliffe's ideas. But at Lutterworth the leader himself was not silent. Wycliffe never seemed to have felt sufficient pressure upon him to conform publicly, nor even to cease from writing, and in the last two years of his life, he poured out an astonishing number of tracts. In these works, he reiterated his main conclusions on the abuses of the age, castigating with particular sharpness the Pope as Antichrist and the friars as the four sects upholding "Caim's (Cain's) castles"[3] for Satan. One of the tracts – the *Trialogue* – was a systematic and comprehensive statement of Wycliffe's arguments, and uniquely important for the Reformation in the sixteenth century as it was printed in 1525. But in 1384, the *Trialogue* and the other pamphlets of that time were the writings of a man whose teaching had in part been condemned, and scope for their reading and influence was severely limited to those who clung loyally to the master and were prepared to risk punishment for possessing or copying his works.

Wycliffe died officially orthodox in his faith, and it was only in the next century that he was posthumously condemned as a heretic.

[1] The conclusions are translated in Workman, op. cit., Vol. II, pp. 416–7.

[2] See Chapter V, pp. 76 f., 80 f. below.

[3] "Caim" was made up by Wycliffe from the initial letters of the four mendicant orders – C (Carmelites), A (Augustinians), I (Jacobites or Dominicans), and M (Minorites or Franciscans).

In 1384 it seemed that his theological ideas and the work of his followers had been discredited by Courtenay's vigorous action, whilst his reputation could be judged as that of a brilliant schoolman, even if erratic and irresponsible in leading Oxford astray. The confused passage of the last dozen years of his life through politics and into retirement could be explained as the aberrations of an ageing scholar, who strayed too far beyond the bounds of academic license. Had Wycliffe died at the age of forty, his reputation would have been that of the theologian and philosopher, radical in outlook and brilliant in playing with ideas, but not so markedly different in argument or conclusions from other contemporary critics. More generally, too, he was a figure of his age, hardly wearing the garb of a complete reformer as suggested by John Foxe and by those who have improved upon Foxe.[1] Wycliffe's personality remains elusive and in some ways unattractive. Part of the reason for this is that he is known too exclusively through his writings, which were nearly all angry denunciations and refutations, whether in academic argument, for the political cause of the hour, or more objectively for Christian truth. He wrote almost nothing of devotional nature apart from some sermons, or nothing has survived such as gives vivid insight today into the personalities of his contemporaries like Rolle or Dame Julian of Norwich. Despite his attachment to the Bible and its "bare text" as God's rule for men, he hardly wrote any commentaries as did Luther and Calvin later, or most medieval theologians before him. His achievement was largely intellectual, that of a schoolman after the model of Aquinas, but with a difference – Wycliffe's interest lay not so much in creating a synthesis or *Summa* of knowledge as in applying his mind and scholarship to revealing and condemning abuses, and to formulating the remedies to apply.[2] In this pursuit, he shared for most of his career in corrupt practices that he condemned, since the absentee and plural holding of livings made his university life possible, whilst events showed him ambitious and disappointed in his hopes for particular ecclesiastical preferment.

But this catalogue of qualifications, failings and difficulties in Wycliffe's personality and life does not explain all that he was, nor why, at his death in 1384, he was of profoundly greater consequence

[1] Foxe, op. cit., Vol. II, pp. 792–800; Vol. III, pp. 1–50, gives Wycliffe's career, but with scarcely any detail of his personal life: the text is largely made up of official documents. Foxe's picture of Wycliffe as a reformer was therefore much less exaggerated with fanciful detail than that painted by many who copied and enlarged upon his sketch after the sixteenth century.

[2] Many of Wycliffe's theological works were issued as parts of a greater *Summa*, but this was never completed, and it is clear that he dealt in random fashion with what subjects most immediately concerned him in his other interests (e.g. the Church).

than Courtenay hoped. With all his faults, he showed himself increasingly consistent in his principles as official support was withdrawn, and he refused to compromise on issues which so clearly he came to formulate. Moreover, from those principles he drew conclusions and practical schemes that corresponded amazingly well to popular hopes and he inspired the affection and loyalty of a band of followers to carry his plans on. More than twenty years later, William Thorpe, who claimed to have been one of Wycliffe's early adherents, paid high tribute to his master's personality and life. In examination before Archbishop Arundel in 1407, Thorpe asserted that Wycliffe "was holden of full many men the greatest clerk that they knew then living; and therewith he was named a passing ruely man and an innocent in his living: and herefore great many commoned [communed] oft with him, and they loved so much his learning that they writ it, and busily enforced them to rule themselves thereafter".[1] In the last analysis he was not just a scholarly Oxford don with a biting pen and heterodox ideas: he was a revolutionary in religious criticism, who set out in uncompromising terms the basic principles for reform and left a legacy for spiritual independency which was richly treasured in later centuries.[2] He was indeed the precursor or "Morning Star"[3] of a later Reformation, but his heirs were not Luther, Calvin or the leaders of official reform in England so much as those who championed freedom of individual belief and nonconformity in the sixteenth century and later. The last years of Wycliffe's life revealed that he was more than an ordinary figure of his age; and the continuing transmission of his ideas and plans through the centuries that followed made plain to what extent the authorities were mistaken in supposing that the danger as they saw it was ended in 1384.

[1] Foxe, op. cit., Vol. III, p. 297.

[2] J. Stacey, *Wyclif and Reform* (London, 1964), has recently analysed in detail Wycliffe's contribution to the later Reformation; in general he confirms the conclusion that Wycliffe was too much the scholar for his own success (cf. ibid., p. 160), but that his legacy in ideas and the Lollard movement far outran his life.

[3] Wycliffe seems first to have been called "the Morning Star of the Reformation" by Daniel Neal, *History of the Puritans*, Vol. I (London, 1732), p. 3, possibly in allusion to Christ's name in Rev. 22:16. But Neal appears to have echoed Foxe who spoke of Wycliffe as "the morning star" in a wider and somewhat different context. Foxe saw the Millennium as lasting from A.D. 324 – his date for Constantine's final triumph in making the Roman Empire Christian – until 1324, and in describing the "ignorance and darkness of God's truth" that followed, he stated that Wycliffe "stepped forth like a valiant champion, unto whom that may justly be applied which is . . . spoken of one Simon, the son of Onias: 'Even as the morning star being in the midst of a cloud, and as the moon being full in her course, and as the bright beams of the sun; so doth he shine and glister in the temple and church of God'" (Foxe, op. cit., Vol. II, p. 792). The quotation from the Vulgate text of Ecclesiasticus 50:6, 7, was used to show how Wycliffe – like Simon the High Priest in repairing the Temple – stood out as the greatest of a band of witnesses in the surrounding gloom that followed Satan's reviving work after 1324 (cf. W. Haller, *Foxe's Book of Martyrs and the Elect Nation* [London, 1963], pp. 162 f.).

Elsewhere Foxe spoke of that time as the period when "there seemed . . . to be no one so little a spark of pure doctrine left" and claimed that through Wycliffe "the Lord would first waken and raise up again the world" (Foxe, ibid., p. 796). Moreover, he was familiar with the view that linked Wycliffe, Hus and Luther together in succession – a view expressed by John Aylmer in 1559 (Haller, op. cit., pp. 87 f., 165) and illustrated pictorially in a 1572 Bohemian psalter, with Wycliffe striking the spark, Hus kindling the coals and Luther brandishing the lighted torch of Truth (Workman, op. cit., Vol. I, p. 8). But Foxe was not primarily concerned with any limited idea of the Reformation of which Wycliffe was a forerunner, nor did he use the title "morning star" to describe him in this sense. His interest was in the cosmic, continuing struggle between Christ and Satan which had a succession of champions for God through the centuries, notably in British history, and was leading (so Foxe hoped) to the establishment of Christ's Kingdom under Elizabeth as a second Constantine (cf. Haller, *passim*). In this history, Wycliffe could be called "the morning star" in the words of Ecclesiasticus, but without implying that he heralded later developments, certainly not in any unique sense, for Foxe used the text later in reference to another person. In speaking of William White, the Lollard martyred in 1428, he praised him as one "to be reputed amongst the number of them of whom the wise man speaketh, 'He was as the morning star in the midst of a cloud' " (Foxe, op. cit., Vol. III, p. 591). Only with Neal's description was the title "the morning star" confined exclusively to Wycliffe and given the clear sense of a herald or precursor.

CHAPTER IV

THE PROGRESS OF LOLLARDY TO 1431

IN THE FOURTEENTH CENTURY ENGLAND WAS NO LESS PART OF LATIN Christendom than France or Italy, and the canon law of the Roman Church was the ordinary law of the English clergy. Moreover, Wycliffe's ideas owed much to earlier movements beyond his country and had their own repercussions throughout the Christian world. But despite these wider affiliations and influences, it was in relative isolation that Lollardy developed in England during the fifty years after Wycliffe's death, when at times great hopes were found in events. His teaching and immediate disciples stood condemned in 1384, but the period that followed to 1431 witnessed not only a continuing Lollard activity but also change in its character, with high confidence on more than one occasion that official reforms would be carried through, before final defeat by the government. Lollardy throughout implied adherence to those basic principles that swept away any essential distinction between lay and cleric in the Church, questioned authority and priestly functions and left the ordinary person free to study, expound and preach God's Word and live his own Christian life. Implicit, and sometimes explicit, in such arguments were the underlying themes of lordship and predestination, not least where programmes were presented for disendowing monasteries or the clergy as a whole, but Lollardy often included additional and even contradictory ideas. Chronologically, the movement passed through two overlapping phases, the first where its remaining association with Oxford was brought to an end by 1415, and the second in which it retained political attachments and aspirations until 1431. In successive stages, both the intellectual leadership at Oxford and the noble or gentry support in society at large were almost completely lost to Lollardy.

Courtenay's strict measures at Oxford in 1382 broke the core of university support for Wycliffite teaching, where individuals were banished from the city and few remained to defend the arguments in the schools. Many from the orders laboured after Wycliffe's death to rebut what he had taught at the university – men like Easton, Roger Dymoke and Thomas Netter – but not all was lost, and a steady stream of Lollard tracts in the vernacular poured out, some of them popular translations of Wycliffe's Latin works, others new pamphlets in the master's style.[1] In addition, there appeared about 1395 the second, more idiomatic rendering of the Bible by Purvey. Wycliffite teaching and study clearly persisted at Oxford, if in secret, and in 1395, the government was suspicious enough to arrest some of the fellows of Merton College, and to order the university to root out such teaching. Meanwhile, as a more general movement in its support and ideas, Lollardy persistently attracted attention from the ecclesiastical and civil authorities, mainly because of official fears about possible revolution after 1381 and with the occasional preaching about temporalities and the payment of tithes. As early as May, 1382, Parliament authorized sheriffs and other local officials to arrest troublesome preachers noted by the bishops, and two months later, letters patent were granted to apply in the Province of Canterbury for imprisoning those teaching heretical conclusions; these instructions were extended to York as well in 1384.[2] Repeated references thereafter to individuals in the countryside, dressed simply "in the guise of great holiness" and stirring up dissension by their preaching, were eloquent testimony to the wide-ranging and lively growth of Lollard activities.

The development nevertheless remains difficult to chart, for Lollard teachers, converts and groups were forced to work with circumspection, and, not unlike the early Christians in the Roman Empire, they were only heard of when they came to the notice of the authorities. Wild stories circulated as to the numbers and location of Lollards, where primitive communications and anxieties about social unrest helped to magnify rumours, but it seems that the cause must have spread widely, if erractically, and it gathered converts from all ranks in society. As Archbishops of Canterbury, both Courtenay and Thomas Arundel were consistent and determined in their efforts to stamp out the heresy, more so than many individual bishops, and the political circumstances of the day meant that the kings fully support orthodox policy. On attaining his majority, Richard II was always anxious to demonstrate a traditional religious attitude. His successor Henry could do no less, for he owed his crown largely to Arundel whom he restored to the primacy in 1399 after extrusion under Richard II for plotting against the king. Lollards were exposed to continuing efforts by the authorities to hunt them out and make them abjure, and they no longer possessed the kind of powerful patronage which Wycliffe had known in the Duke of Lancaster.

[1] Many of the English writings earlier attributed to Wycliffe in the collections of Arnold and Matthew are now accepted as having been the work of men like Hereford and Purvey. Cf. Workman, op. cit., Vol. I, pp. 329–32.

[2] Cf. Aston, op. cit., pp. 4, 5; H. Gee and W. J. Hardy, editors, *Documents Illustrative of English Church History* (London, 1896), No. XXXVIII, pp. 110–2.

The leaders who were scattered from Oxford and held to their Lollard principles took the teaching to various regions. Before the close of 1382, Repton submitted to the archbishop and abjured Lollardy; he later became Bishop of Lincoln and a cardinal. Aston also submitted, but only for the moment, and subsequently he evangelized along the Welsh border and as far south as Gloucester before his death in 1388. Meanwhile, Hereford fled to Rome in order to appeal to Urban VI, but was promptly imprisoned by the Pope. He eventually escaped to return to England in 1385, and was active in Worcester and later again in Nottingham. After Wycliffe's death, Purvey travelled in the south-west, teaching among the cloth-workers of Bristol and continuing his translation of the Bible. Hereford was re-arrested and recanted his Lollard ideas as early as 1391, whilst Purvey was eventually caught in 1401 and forced similarly to abjure, after his long ministry in teaching and writing. He was given a living, but was unhappy and disappeared in 1403, leaving a reputation of being "neither hot nor cold", in Thorpe's rather hard words. Purvey's services were immeasurable in the Lollard cause, for he was perhaps the most scholarly of Wycliffe's followers, and left as his great achievement the vernacular Bible without which Lollardy would scarcely have survived. But other followers, lay as well as clerical, were equally vigorous in evangelism and on occasion more defiant against officials. The work at Leicester flourished even after Swinderby had left, and it was only when Courtenay visited the town in 1389 that Lollard activity was subdued by the excommunication of eight people. A little later, Northampton became a hotbed of similar ideas, with the support of its mayor and some local clergy, before investigations by the authorities disrupted the Lollard groups in the town.

Swinderby in the meantime showed himself to be of more consequence than other early leaders, and has been judged as "one of the greatest, perhaps the very greatest, of Lollard evangelists".[1] He most typically demonstrated the lay, anti-clerical attitude which was so widespread, and also how Wycliffe's scholastic doctrines could be transmuted into popular terms. Moving through the towns and villages of the south Welsh border, he preached and celebrated Mass as an unlicensed layman, even after a warrant was issued for his arrest in 1388. He was denounced as a relapsed heretic by the Bishop of Hereford in 1390, and under safe conduct appeared at Bodenham a year later to answer charges against him. Swinderby's defence was bold and uncompromising, and brought his conviction for heresy, though he explicitly denied ever rejecting transubstantiation. After

[1] McFarlane, op. cit., p. 135, where the fullest appreciation of Swinderby's career is presented.

the enquiry, he retired into hiding, and appeared no less defiant and able to argue on a further occasion at Hereford, when the bishop confirmed judgment that he was heretical and schismatic. He was excommunicated, and in answer sent to Parliament an appeal which probably never reached its destination, and certainly had no effect. Finally, Swinderby vanished with a companion into the Welsh hills, and avoided further arrest by any officers.[1] His career was fitful but illuminating and deeply significant, since he made converts wherever he went, and amongst these probably was the young gentleman John Oldcastle.

Other Lollards there were who became known in falling foul of ecclesiastical enquiry in the Midlands and Wesh border country, chiefly along the highways of trade and among artisans or townsfolk, but there were also disturbances in London. The capital had a reputation for civic independence and pride, and though on rare occasions such feelings could be combined with popular support for the clergy, as in 1376 and 1377, anti-clerical attitudes more naturally predominated. These could easily be mingled with and mistaken for Lollard ideas. In view of the keen watch first of Courtenay and then Arundel, it seems improbable that Lollardy spread noticeably in London before the close of the century, but yet disturbances which occurred in 1387 were rumoured to be the work of Lollards, and there was persistent, if misplaced, belief among the Wycliffite followers that the Commons in Parliament were wholly of their persuasion. Support for Wycliffe's ideas was scattered extensively through the more influential class of knights in the countryside, and the call to disendow the clergy and redistribute their possessions among the lay lords plainly made some look sympathetically upon Lollardy.[2] Individuals like Sir Thomas Latimer of Braybrooke in Northamptonshire, Sir John Montague, Sir Lewis Clifford and Sir John Cheyne gave protection to Lollard teachers and hid their writings at different times. Though these were not all Lollards in their ideas, and no solid group in this gentry class championed the movement, there was some organization and coherence in activity. When twelve Lollard conclusions were presented to Parliament in 1395, it is possible that some more specific proposal on disendowment had already been aired to alarm the government. No notice appears to have been taken in Parliament of these conclusions, which condemned general corruption and a whole series of particular practices – clerical celibacy, pilgrimages, confessions to priests – and ideas, including transubstantiation.[3] But a Dominican

[1] Foxe, op. cit., Vol. III, p. 131, suggested that Swinderby was later burnt as a heretic under Henry IV, but McFarlane gives no support to the idea.

[2] Aston, op. cit., pp. 16 f.

[3] Printed in Gee and Hardy, op. cit., pp. 126–132.

wrote expressly to refute them, the archbishops were alarmed, and Boniface IX, on hearing their details, wrote to King Richard to point out the dangers to civil security in Lollard intrigues. As a result, some suspects were imprisoned as Lollards, including members of Merton at Oxford, but more ominous and effective action only came later – in the passing of the statute *De Heretico Comburendo* in 1401 and with the introduction of machinery for dealing with heresy in England.

In its treatment of heresy, the English Church theoretically conformed to the general practices of western Christendom in the fourteenth century, but in practice the country knew virtually nothing of the harsher punishments of the Papal Inquisition, or of a regular ecclesiastical authority for coping with the problem. Partly because of royal claims and in part through the desires of English bishops to guard their independence, the Church in England remained outside the exercise of full papal jurisdiction. Not only were papal financial and judicial claims therefore resisted, but also the activities of the Dominicans – the official Inquisitors – in hunting out heresy as in France and Italy. Notable heretics had indeed been rare in England, despite its strong vein of anti-clericalism. William of Occam was excommunicated for his views, but he stood out as the supporter of the Franciscans and of the Empire, rather than as the founder of any heretical movement in his own country. As a result, when Wycliffe's theological ideas and writings were condemned, and his followers examined and required to recant, the English bishops resorted to normal methods for dealing with the problem, without applying extreme penalties. Suspects were apprehended and examined; if found heretical, they were required to abjure and do penance. If they refused to do this, they were excommunicated and possibly imprisoned in ecclesiastical or civil keeping. One who recanted and was later caught again teaching or otherwise involved in Lollard practices was seen as a relapsed heretic, and therefore open to the severest punishment of burning according to ecclesiastical law. This was demanded in Swinderby's case in 1382, but significantly nothing then happened, nor were there any such instances of punishment in the 1390's. But as Lollardy persisted, and the government became increasingly anxious over possible incitements to rebellion, the archbishops sought to introduce more stringent measures for action. Following the affair of the Lollard conclusions in 1395, Arundel had Wycliffe's teachings condemned anew in a provincial synod two years later, but in Parliament nothing was done until after Henry of Lancaster had seized the throne in 1399.

For several reasons, the new king was not unwilling to take severe measures against Lollardy. Apart from his debt to Arundel, he was more than a little apprehensive about his own position and the influence that preaching might have in stirring up opposition. Henry and Parliament therefore were willing to bring in regulations about this in 1400, before the statute of the following year dealt more comprehensively with heresy.[1] The act recited what dangers generally were being presented to the realm in the spread of Lollardy, and laid down a series of measures to bring remedy. All unlicensed preaching was forbidden, except by "curates in their own churches, and persons hitherto privileged, and others of the canon law granted"; whilst

> . . . none [is to] preach, hold, teach, or instruct anything, openly or privily, or make or write any book contrary to the Catholic faith or determination of the Holy Church, nor that any of such sect and wicked doctrines and opinions shall make any conventicles, or in any wise hold or exercise schools.[2]

The word "conventicle" had a dangerous, subversive connotation, and appeared to be deliberately employed herein. Further provisions ordered that those possessing condemned books were to surrender them, whilst those canonically convicted were to be kept in prison or handed over to the secular court. Anyone refusing to abjure, or convicted as a relapsed heretic, was to be burned at the stake under the secular authority's power. In these terms, the main principles and punishments of medieval law against heresy were finally brought into operation in England, directly for dealing with Lollardy. But it was not the Papal Inquisition which was introduced, nor were the English bishops left wholly alone to put the provisions into effect. The civil government was as much concerned as the ecclesiastical: parliamentary statute defined the problem and the means for dealing with it, and the later additions and alterations to the law made heresy fully the subject of secular enquiry and punishment. It was regarded as a civil and treasonable crime as much as an offence against the Church and orthodoxy, and Lollardy was long seen and treated in this light in the fifteenth century.[3]

Arundel's hopes in 1401 were to use his fresh powers to eradicate the movement, and indeed the first Lollard to be executed according to the tenor of the new law was burned before it came into effect. William Sawtre, a chaplain, fell in 1399 into the hands of the notorious Bishop Despenser of Norwich and recanted his views. He was therefore a relapsed heretic when accused again of Lollard teaching before Archbishop Arundel early in 1401, and after condemnation and

[1] Aston, op. cit., p. 33.
[2] Gee and Hardy, op. cit., No. XLII, p. 137.
[3] Aston, op. cit., p. 34.

degradation, he was burned at Smithfield on royal orders. There seems little doubt that such a harsh punishment was carried out in Sawtre's case as an example for other Lollards. The archbishop continued thereafter to deal systematically with Lollardy, hounding out individuals at Oxford and in the country at large, and earning the reputation of being the "hammer of the Lollards", but not all his episcopal colleagues liked the policy, nor was he completely ruthless in all his actions.[1] Apart from Sawtre, whose execution seemed intended as a warning to others, apart too from those punished after the attempted rebellion in 1414, only one man was recorded as a Lollard martyr during Arundel's primacy. This was John Badby, a tailor of Evesham, who was condemned as an obstinate heretic and eventually burned in 1410. Pleas for him to repent were made by the archbishop and Prince Henry, the king's son, but throughout his trials Badby remained firm in upholding the truths of Scripture and his faith in Christ, and in denying transubstantiation. His conviction and courage in dying in the fire moved his enemies to admiration, if not mercy, and as in Sawtre's case, Arundel again was possibly too much influenced by political considerations of security. By contrast, when he examined William Thorpe in 1407, he seems to have allowed himself to be worsted in argument. Thorpe, who was a priest, claimed to have followed Wycliffe in the early days and to have taught for twenty years or more. He left an account of his examination which sheds significant light on Lollard teaching and on the scholarship and ability which it could command in individuals at the time. Thorpe's narrative made Arundel appear fair in argument and he himself clear and skilled in affirming his beliefs. He insisted on the authority and rule of Scripture, claimed that the supreme office of every priest was to preach, and denied that there was any Biblical warrant from Christ for paying tithes. He argued similarly against oaths and confessions to priests, and ended by questioning Arundel himself. Possibly because he was not a relapsed heretic, Thorpe was not dealt with severely by Arundel at the time, though the archbishop seems later to have imprisoned him.

Meanwhile, Arundel went further in 1407 by adding a series of constitutions to the earlier statute of 1401. These articles were passed in Convocation at Oxford and were designed specifically to suppress Wycliffite influences in the university and to check Lollard practices more widely through the country. Where Wycliffe's philosophical works remained as texts of study in the university, Lollard teaching had continued under some guise of legality, and Bohemian students who came to Oxford for their courses were in this way able to gain

[1] McFarlane, op. cit., pp. 152 f. sympathetically assesses Arundel's character and work.

their knowledge of the heresiarch's ideas.[1] Almost nothing is known of the individuals who disseminated such teaching at Oxford, but St. Edmund's Hall remained a Wycliffite centre and its principal, William Taylor, was willing to preach some of the Lollard ideas openly at St. Paul's Cross in 1406. More serious trouble, however, was provoked by a younger man, Peter Payne, who had been studying at Oxford since the start of the century and was imbued with Wycliffe's ideas. It seems likely that it was Payne who in 1406 sent an encomium on Wycliffe to Prague University, with the seal of his own foundation attached, thus making it appear that Oxford officially applauded the scholar. Such a document was received in all good faith in Bohemia and used by John Hus among others to defend Wycliffe's reputation, but in England the prank alarmed Arundel and led him to convene Convocation at Oxford in 1407.

The new constitutions passed in that assembly forbade any preaching without prior examination and formal authorization to preach by a bishop. They limited the subjects for sermons generally to the matters specified in Peckham's constitutions of 1281, but stipulated that addresses to clergy were to be confined to ecclesiastical affairs, and for the laity they were to deal only with lay issues. Any discussion in them about the sacraments or articles of faith was to be wholly in accord with the Church's definitions: otherwise, excommunication would follow. In similar terms schoolmasters were warned about teaching on subjects of faith. At Oxford and Cambridge, Wycliffe's works were to be allowed for study only after examination and approval by a specified university committee, whilst those in charge of halls were to hold monthly enquiries into the views of their residents and expel those who offended. Finally, on the ground that it was "dangerous to translate Holy Scripture out of one language into another", the articles forbade any new translations into English and laid down that older versions were only to be used with explicit official permission. Such regulations struck heavily at university freedom to study any of Wycliffe's ideas, but generally they had profound importance in curbing preaching and the use of vernacular Scriptures in the following years in England. They were indeed too restrictive to work, and though reaffirmed and promulgated at a provincial synod in 1409, their provisions were relaxed only a year later to the extent of allowing the mendicants to have special licenses for preaching through the country. Later in the century, Thomas Gascoigne as Chancellor of Oxford University was scathing in denunciation of the bad effects of Arundel's restrictions on preaching. But when they were made, however, they did provide a recognizable series of rules

[1] See Chapter V, p. 76 below for these Bohemian developments.

by which to attempt to contain Lollardy and suppress its most dangerous activities at Oxford. The archbishop further visited the university in 1411 to enforce official examination of Wycliffe's writings, and despite protests, the academic authorities submitted to his powers as Visitor, and the last traces of Lollardy were removed. Arundel ordered all in authority to take an oath to refuse admission thereafter to Lollards or suspected Lollards, and this plainly embarrassed Payne, who had become Principal of St. Edmund's Hall and continued to encourage Wycliffe's ideas. Whether or not he took the oath is not known, but it was possibly to avoid arrest that before the end of 1413 Payne fled to Bohemia, where he began a new and prominent career in the Hussite cause.

It is not difficult to understand that strong measures for authority and order had to be taken in England at the start of the fifteenth century, but even so the legislation of 1401 and the years after was hard completely to justify. Attempts to apply these laws were half-hearted where the English bishops were not devoid of all feeling and wished to have the extreme punishment of death as a threat rather than inflict it. The Lollards have been blamed for forcing the government to bring in heresy laws which had not existed before in the civil code. They have been accused of hindering rather than helping the movement for reform in England, for they alienated that official support without which changes could not be introduced, and were not introduced until after 1529 by Henry VIII.[1] Such a judgment, it can be suggested, does less than justice to the faith and hopes of the Lollards, or to the difficult circumstances in which their movement developed. They cannot be condemned merely for presenting arguments in such terms that the authorities could regard them as subversive revolutionaries. Their convictions of the truths of salvation led them into what was considered as heresy, and these convictions could not easily or permanently be abandoned, even if individual Lollards temporarily abjured their ideas under pressure. They were often rash or stubborn in clinging to one or two principles, and it can be allowed that other critics were as outspoken about abuses without bringing the harmful complications found in Lollardy. But for all the clamour about corruption in the English Church, little was achieved before 1400, and what was done did not suggest that the way to reform would be speedier and more complete thereafter than was finally the case.[2] It would have been hard to calculate the best path to choose for ushering in reformation in 1400, but as it was the Lollards were not concerned with organized and comprehen-

[1] This is the main argument of McFarlane, op. cit., pp. 186–8.

[2] Deanesly, *Significance*, p. 16, remarks that there were great obstacles facing Wycliffe "for which there appeared no remedy but radical reform".

sive schemes: they were zealous for the truths which became real in their lives, they read and studied and treasured the Bible which opened to them the path of salvation in Christ. Clearly they made reform in some ways discreditable, but they were unfortunate in finding that their criticisms and hopes, cast primarily in religious terms, flourished at precisely the same time as social and political ideas of revolution. "Sedition and dissent", it has been remarked, "had come of age together",[1] and the official fears of 1381 about Lollardy only deepened as the years passed.

In the early fifteenth century, Lollardy for many retained dangerous political and social implications, even where these were not central or necessary to the religious demands of reform. Consideration in Parliament in 1410 of a scheme for disendowing the monasteries to fill the royal treasury and meet other needs only followed many similar proposals made through the years from 1395. Such ideas roused official suspicions, but Sir John Oldcastle's attempted rebellion early in 1414 dramatized most vividly the continuing political involvements of Lollardy. It is not necessary to suppose that Oldcastle's plot was any logical product of Lollard teaching when it was obviously the desperate action of a nobleman, but there were aspects of Lollard argument favouring hopes of social and political change. Born about 1378, Oldcastle himself came of a good Herefordshire family, and he not only served well in county and country for Henry IV and in the household of Prince Henry, but by marriage in 1408 also obtained a baronial title as Lord Cobham with lands throughout England. He was a convert to Lollardy from earlier years and came to stand out as a leader of the movement. In 1410, he fell under Arundel's suspicions, and the archbishop tried in vain to warn him about his views. Oldcastle, however, retained royal favour, served with distinction in France, and had high hopes for the future when Prince Henry succeeded to the throne in 1413. At that point, evidence about his beliefs was published in Convocation and Oldcastle found himself unable satisfactorily to explain to the new king his possession of compromising Lollard books. He was arrested and brought to trial before Arundel, but remained adamant in upholding Lollard ideas when questioned. The Pope, he declared, had no authority for deciding matters such as transubstantiation, and was the head of Antichrist where the monks and friars were the tail. He insisted that the Eucharist was "Christ's Body in form of bread" and that the bread remained after consecration; whilst pilgrimages, confession to priests and the worship of images he denied. When taxed with St. Paul's words about rejoicing in the cross of Christ, and asked if he would worship the cross that Christ died on, he replied, "Our salvation came not in by that material

[1] Aston, op. cit., p. 36.

cross, but alone by Him who died thereupon . . . . And, well I wot, that holy St. Paul rejoiced in none other cross, but in Christ's Passion and Death only".[1]

Oldcastle was excommunicated and imprisoned in the Tower with forty days' grace, in the hope it seems that he might recant and be restored to royal favour. But with the help of friends he escaped and went into hiding in the city, where he planned a wild plot to overthrow the government and seize the king and royal family in January, 1414. Under any circumstance, such an enterprise could have held out little hope of complete success, but as it was the plans of the rising were betrayed and the rebellion was dispersed before it could properly materialize. The government feared that Lollards in their multitudes were threatening insurrection through the country – and the rebels boasted of mustering an army of twenty thousand – but in reality only a few hundred men responded to Oldcastle's summons. Even so, the enterprise revealed important features about Lollardy and Oldcastle's support in 1414. Through the winter of 1413–14, he was well protected by Lollards and other sympathizers in London, and he was able to call up groups from many parts of the country – Essex, the Chilterns, the Midland towns and Bristol. Only a proportion of those who set out to march to London were Lollards, for some were attracted by military adventure, others by the pay promised or the wild hope of reward in office and power. Those Lollards involved were recruited largely by the local ministry of individual preachers, clerical and lay, and most of them were weavers, fullers or tailors from the textile industry, with its cottage organization and loyalties that stretched beyond local village bounds. Such men were hardy, but they were not trained or militarily equipped, and were no match for royal levies. Only experienced soldiers like Oldcastle and his close retinue stood out in the enterprise. He was able to depend upon some rudimentary structure for summoning out groups, pitifully small though they proved to be, but Lollardy had no close organization or leadership, and a number of Lollards took no part in the rising and avoided subsequent arrest. As it was, the government was able to despatch commissions to towns and counties before the fatal day to seize Lollards and others in numerous localities, and to surprise, capture and scatter the contingents converging on London, where most of the ringleaders were arrested.

Those captured were tried in civil courts and condemned to death for treason, whilst a proportion were also convicted as Lollards by ecclesiastical judges. Some forty were quickly executed, after which investigations were set on foot more widely to rout out Lollards and

[1] Foxe, op. cit., Vol. III, p. 335.

other rebels in various centres. In March, 1414, the king proclaimed clemency for all ordinary people possibly involved in the rising, and Parliament, meeting at the heart of heresy in Leicester, ordered local municipal and other officials to exterminate all shreds of Lollardy. In the clash with the royal forces in London, Oldcastle himself escaped, and as a proscribed heretic and rebel avoided capture for several years. In anxiety to embark upon his French expedition, Henry V willingly extended an offer of pardon to Oldcastle in 1414 and again in 1415, if he were prepared to come out of hiding, but he never responded. He was eventually captured in 1417, brought to London and executed. By that date, the government knew what had been the scope of the abortive rising and how great was the continuing influence of Lollardy, and with an authority sharpened by legislation, it disrupted and drove the movement underground. Oldcastle was genuine in his attachment to Lollard principles and desire for religious reform, about which he corresponded with Hus and other Bohemian leaders, but the whole episode of his career was confusing as well as harmful to the issues involved in Lollardy. It magnified the potential political threat in the Wycliffite doctrines, associated them too closely with active treason, and thereby allowed opponents to strike more deeply and lastingly at Lollard structure and support.

Oxford was purged of Wycliffe's teaching before the events of 1414, and the connection with Lollardy was slight and all but severed thereafter. At the same time, the more politically influential support of gentry and knights was swept away in the government's efforts to hunt down the associates of Oldcastle. Wycliffe's works were officially condemned at the papal council in Rome in 1413, and he himself was posthumously declared a heretic two years later at Constance. Eventually in 1428, his bones were exhumed and burned, and scattered in the river Swift at Lutterworth. Yet Lollardy survived as a political ferment after 1414, and continued to worry the authorities in these as well as more general terms for another twenty years. In 1421, several notable Lollards had to provide securities for their behaviour, and two years later, William Taylor was finally condemned and burned for arguments, amongst others, that could be construed as treasonable about priestly government and civil power. Robert Hook, Rector of Braybrook, which had long been a centre for Lollard activity, was required to explain his views in 1425, and in 1428, another priest, Ralph Mungyn, had similarly to answer before Convocation, where he was already known for possessing Scriptures in English illegally. In the meantime, Lollard activities thrived notably in East Anglia and the West of England, as well as London, and records showed individuals and groups buying, reading and studying the

Bible in English, teaching Lollard principles, and seeking to apply Christian ideals in their lives. Many amongst these were humble in class and wealth, working people with little contact with the clergy, even where Lollard priests still counted. One carpenter's wife, Margery Backster, was accused at Norwich in 1428 of trying to persuade other women to visit her and her husband at night for the reading of "the law of Christ", and in the following year, another deposition in the same town stated that Nicholas Belward "hath a New Testament which he bought at London for four marks and forty pence, and taught the said William Wright and Margery his wife and wrought with them the space of one year and studied diligently upon the said New Testament".[1] The Bishop of Norwich was particularly active in hunting out Lollards after 1429, and similarly in London there was persecution, with the burning of priests – William White in 1428, Richard Hunden two years later and Thomas Bagley in 1431. But Lollard issues reached their climax in another incident of the same year in which Bagley was martyred.

Under the leadership of a weaver, William Perkins, a fresh rising was planned on the model of the earlier attempt of 1414. Perkins clearly sought to profit from older mistakes in his organization by arranging, for example, that the army to be assembled was to meet well outside London before marching on the capital. His programme was directly based on the petition of 1410 and proclaimed the disendowment of the clergy and, more distantly, the disestablishment as well of the lay lords, whilst the Lollards were to assume power. But the rising never took place, Perkins himself was betrayed as he was journeying about to distribute pamphlets, and he and a few companions were arrested and executed. Significantly there were no members of the landed gentry known to have lost their lives in this conspiracy, though it is possible that some were implicated and the government arrested one or two on suspicion. The revolutionary purpose to be found in parts of Oldcastle's programme and even more blatantly unfolded by Perkins largely disappeared from Lollardy with this episode of 1431, and the subsequent history and composition of the movement took forms different from those so prominent in the early years of the century. Lollardy was marked down as heresy in official terms because of certain Wycliffite doctrines, but it was eyed with added suspicion by the authorities for its dangerous political and social implications during the fifty years following Wycliffe's death. But from 1431 onward, as a movement of criticism and dissent, its enduring influence became more completely religious than it had been through the earlier decades.

[1] Foxe, op. cit., Vol. III, pp. 594 f.

In the meantime, Lollardy took root in Scotland where it spread rapidly and encountered sharper efforts at repression by the government. The political and religious situation in the country gave scope for disseminating such ideas, for bad feeling between the Scottish kings and Parliament and the Popes exacerbated criticism of clerical abuses and papal controls. Attendance of Scottish students at Oxford in the latter part of the fourteenth century made it easy for Wycliffe's ideas to travel to Scotland, and by 1407 when Thorpe admitted to having preached for twenty years in the north of England, there was ample evidence of Lollard work over the border. In the war between England and Scotland, James I was captured and held by the English government, and the Duke of Albany ruled as Regent. He became known as a "hater of Lollards and heretics", and allowed the introduction of an inquisitorial court into Scotland after 1405. Its vigorous work indicated plainly that individual Lollards and groups were numerous in the country. In 1407, James Reseby, an English priest who fled north of the border, was condemned and burned at Perth, and another Lollard, Quintin Folkhard, was similarly executed three years later. The University of St. Andrews was officially required in 1416 to defend the Church against Lollard attacks, whilst at the Council of Constance itself, John Gerson, the Chancellor of Paris University, complained of the spread of Lollardy in England and Scotland. Another Lollard was burned in 1422, and two years later the Scottish Parliament passed laws to deal with the movement more widely. Finally, there was the case of Paul Craw, the Bohemian emissary who came to Scotland with Hussite teaching for those who still followed the ways of Wycliffe. Craw was arrested, condemned and executed by the Inquisition in 1433. The Lollards, it seems, were not numerous, nor did they present any obvious political threat such as worried the English government, but in Scotland they remained stubborn and loyal, if obscure. Inquisitorial efforts throughout the fifteenth century failed to stamp out all the groups of those who placed their faith in God's Word, used it in the vernacular for study, denied sacerdotal power and transubstantiation, and sought in their own lives to show the true spirit of Christ's Law. No less than those in England, the Scottish Lollards remained to contribute vitally to developments in the sixteenth century,[1] but Wycliffe's ideas provoked response more widely than in the British Isles alone. By 1431 they had become entangled deeply in the affairs of all Christendom through Hussitism and the Conciliar Movement – and both of these developments were crucially important as further attempts to bring about reform and reconstruction in the Church.

[1] See Chapter XI below for these sixteenth-century activities.

CHAPTER V

HUS AND BOHEMIA

THE FULL WEIGHT OF OFFICIAL REPRESSION IN ENGLAND AND Scotland fell upon the Lollards in the early part of the fifteenth century, and though they survived to be more important in the age of the Reformation than has sometimes been thought, Lollardy after 1431 certainly had no direct influence on affairs outside the British Isles. In the sixteenth century, Wycliffe's works were hardly known apart from the *Trialogue*, which was reprinted at Basel in 1525. Otherwise Luther's information about the Oxford heresiarch extended only as far as the opinions condemned in 1382, together with those added in Prague and declared heretical at the Council of Constance.[1] But by contrast he was explicit in speaking of the deep impression made on him by Hus's treatise about the Church, and in his enthusiasm Luther more generally aided the publication and knowledge of the Bohemian leader's writings in the 1520's. The teaching, career and achievement of Hus were more obviously meaningful for sixteenth-century developments than Wycliffe's challenge where Luther was accused of the heresy of Hussitism and the Englishman's thought and work were known supremely through the Hussite tradition. Developments in Bohemia in the early years of the fifteenth century brought the Church under criticism in ways similar to those expressed in English Lollardy, and the free trade of scholarly life and ideas between the universities of Europe, between Oxford and Prague as well as Paris, provided an all-important link for explaining how this could be. Quite in what manner the two movements were related has, however, been a subject of changing opinion. Hus was credited with originality in his demands for reform until most of Wycliffe's Latin works were published in the late nineteenth century and after, when the claim was developed that the Bohemian leader had only taken over the Oxford scholar's ideas and that Hussitism was nothing more than Wycliffism in Bohemian dress – and a poor change of

[1] By 1559, Wycliffe could be seen as "begetting" Hus, just as Hus "begat" Luther, but he was only prominently fitted into the pre-Reformation tradition by Foxe in his *Acts and Monuments*, which was first published in 1563 and given more final form in 1570. Cf. p. 56, note 3 above, and Haller, op. cit., passim.

costume at that.[1] In the light of further study,[2] this judgment is now seen to do grave injustice to both men and to the fact of native ideas of reform in Bohemia that antedated knowledge of Wycliffe and issued eventually in a dramatic national rebellion convulsing all Christendom for twenty years.

Evangelized from Byzantium in the ninth century, Bohemia retained its ties with the Eastern Church rather than Rome until after 1300, and it was proud and jealous in defence of religious practices and ideas – such as communion in both kinds for the laity – that were peculiar to the land. With its privileges and prosperity, it stood out from other European States in the fourteenth century. Much was achieved by the Luxemburg kings, above all by Charles IV, who reigned over Bohemia from 1336 to 1378 and was also the Holy Roman Emperor[3] after 1346, with imperial claims to rule central Europe and rank alongside the Pope. In fact, Charles's power in Germany was only a shadow of what imperial authority once had been, and he had little more than titular control over many princes, towns and leagues, but in Bohemia the situation was different. He built up the political and social institutions of the country, drew power into royal hands and inaugurated reforms in the Church. He was greatly concerned to encourage learning and culture and was influenced by the early Italian Renaissance spirit as well as by the work of the University of Paris. In 1344, he had Prague separated from Mainz and elevated into an archbishopric by his tutor and friend, Clement VI, and thereafter he worked closely and strenuously with the first two primates, Ernest of Pardubice (1344–64) and John Ocko of Vlasim (1364–80), to raise standards of clerical life and eradicate corruption in Bohemia. As a man of letters, Charles met and corresponded with Petrarch, the greatest classicist of the age, but more noteworthy was his foundation of the University of Prague in 1348, with German scholars from Paris, and a constitution of four "nations" – Saxon, Bavarian, Polish and Bohemian – to order its life. The chancellor of the university was Archbishop Ernest, who worked with enthusiasm to develop its studies and scholarship. The king's aim generally was to transform Prague into the leading city of Europe, to have its university famed throughout Christendom alongside Paris and Oxford.

[1] J. Loserth championed this view, arguing it at length in *Hus and Wiclif*, first edition (Munich, 1884), second edition (1925), and repeatedly in his editing of texts for the Wyclif Society.

[2] By Czech scholars, whose conclusions have been presented in English in numerous articles and monographs by R. R. Betts, S. H. Thomson and M. Spinka.

[3] Like other rulers of the Holy Roman Empire, Charles was strictly King of the Romans until papally crowned, and this was in 1355. But for simplicity, all were called Emperors after election since they enjoyed effective imperial power, and coronation rarely followed closely afterward, if at all.

Undoubtedly, Bohemia's reputation for learning and culture attained great heights in the century. Teachers and students flocked to the city, particularly after the start of the Great Schism in 1378, when French recognition of the Pope remaining at Avignon made Paris unwelcome for German scholars. At the same time, the division of the academic schools in Prague somewhat fortuitously linked Oxford and the new Bohemian university.

The model for Prague University was Paris, in its forms of study and Nominalist principles for argument, but Bohemian students who went to Paris from early in the fourteenth century were there registered with Irish, Scots and others in the "English" nation. Thereby they came under strong influences for a Realist outlook such as Wycliffe championed. As a result, Bohemians who studied at Paris and then returned as masters to their own country, more often than not possessed an attachment in philosophy and theology to the Realist outlook rather than to Nominalism.[1] With this they coupled an increasing sense of resentment at German domination in the University of Prague, so that national feeling came to figure prominently in the wider movement of reform by 1400. At the same time, some of the university teachers and leaders outside the university were trenchant in criticizing ecclesiastical abuses and questioning the true purposes of religious life. Such complaint was not unlike that voiced in England or other countries, but it had its own distinctive note in Bohemia, where reformers shared a Realist philosophical attitude and mystical concern with Christian principles. In addition, they drew inspiration partly from the older movement of Waldensianism which had spread into Bohemia in the thirteenth century and retained a buoyant life, notably in the southern part of the country. Despite repeated efforts by the Inquisition and the archbishops to root out such beliefs, popular, anti-clerical and Biblically-centred in character, Waldensianism still counted in ordinary religion in the 1370's and after.[2]

An early university critic was the Augustinian friar, Conrad Waldhauser, who died in 1369 after six years of preaching in Prague, and who was later honoured by the Bohemians for his condemnation of luxury and formalism, though he was a German. His contemporary, John Milič of Kremsier, however, stood out far more defiantly in attacking contemporary evils. Sharing some of the mystical attitudes of Bridget of Sweden and Catherine of Siena, Milič was the inspiration of many in his vernacular preaching, writings, and deep attachment

[1] Cf. R. R. Betts, "The Influence of Realist Philosophy on Jan Hus and his Predecessors in Bohemia", in *Slavonic and East European Review*, XXIX (1950–1), pp. 408–9.

[2] Cf. S. H. Thomson, "Pre-Hussite Heresy in Bohemia", in *English Historical Review* XLVIII (1953), pp. 23–42.

to the Bible as the final authority for Christian life.[1] He was accused of heresy and indeed was possibly influenced by the Waldensians in his whole apocalyptic outlook and denunciation of the Papacy. He twice answered papal summons to account for his views, and after suffering imprisonment at Rome in 1367, was later detained at Avignon where he died in 1374. Men like Adalbertus Ranconis, who probably studied at Oxford as well as Paris, where he was rector for a time, and Thomas of Štítný were the friends and followers of Milič, and they furthered the reform movement in publicizing ideas. His greatest disciple, however, was Matthew of Janov, a scholar and theologian who achieved renown at Paris, but nevertheless returned to Prague as a Realist and fervent in decrying the ills of the day. The Universal Church he understood as the ideal spotless Bride of Christ, in its essence unchanging and perfect, and this in the 1380's he was unable to discern in any of the three "particular" churches – the two competing for allegiance in the Latin West and the Greek Church of the East. With his commentaries on the Bible, Janov was the first to give the Bohemian reformers a doctrinal programme, and he moreover connected the movement closely with Prague University. Both Milič and Janov looked fundamentally for reform in individual life and practice, and held a high view of the Eucharist, seeing in frequent communion and devotion to Christ the means for bringing spiritual renewal more generally in the Church, and restoring the unity which had been lost.[2] They had no faith in the clergy or the State, nor for that matter in the schemes of their philosophical opponents, the Nominalists, which currently found expression in the idea that a General Council should have supreme authority in the Church and enforce reforms. The concern in the Bohemian programme was more realistic and practical, and throughout it looked to moral and ethical activities rather than to doctrinal issues for argument, trusting in preaching to bring reform in the hearts of men.

Janov died in 1394, and in the following decade, Bohemian masters and reformers like Stanislas of Znojmo, Stephen of Páleč and Stephen of Kolín became leaders at Prague University. But these same years witnessed two other significant developments – the spread of Wycliffe's writings and ideas into Bohemia, and the appearance of John Hus on the academic scene at Prague. Connections between England and Bohemia had been nurtured academically, as Ranconis's career suggested, but they were considerably strengthened in diplomatic and political terms in 1382 by the marriage of Richard II to

[1] Cf. R. R. Betts, "English and Czech Influences on Hus", in *Transactions of the Royal Historical Society*, 4th series, XXI (1939), pp. 93–5.

[2] Ibid., pp. 96–7.

Anne of Bohemia, the sister of King Wenzel who had succeeded his father, Charles IV, in 1378. Though the marriage was not successful politically and Anne died in 1394, and though it was unlikely that Wycliffe's ideas passed directly to Bohemia through such associations, the alliance encouraged interchange of scholars between Oxford and Prague. Wycliffe claimed to have scattered his ideas world-wide in answer to the Pope, and unique evidence remains of enterprising missionary effort seemingly by an English Lollard in the Adriatic in 1383,[1] but more generally and certainly the spread of Wycliffite thought came through the travels of Bohemian students to England and their studies at Oxford. By 1398, they had taken back to Prague Wycliffe's metaphysical and logical works, that is to say, his philosophical treatises which were not necessarily seen as heretical or forbidden for study and teaching. Such works acted as catalysts in helping to precipitate in clear form the Realism of earlier Bohemian teachers and to provide the leaders of the day with the systematic means for argument against clerical abuses. Meanwhile, in Prague a public platform for airing criticisms and schemes of reform was established in the Bethlehem Chapel, founded in 1391 with the stipulation that two preaching services should be held every Sunday and holiday. Stephen of Kolín preached at the chapel for some years, using his post influentially to proclaim the cause of reform, but in 1402, his pupil John Hus was elected to the office.

At the time, Hus was just over thirty but already renowned academically. After progressing through his studies at Prague in the 1390's, he was ordained priest in 1400 and became dean of the faculty of arts a year later. He was known for his reforming zeal and preaching ability, qualities which marked him out not only for using the pulpit at the Bethlehem Chapel but also for leadership in the wider movement. As a scholar, he was familiar by then with Wycliffe's philosophical tracts, but in 1402, his friend, Jerome of Prague, returned from Oxford with more of the Englishman's writings, in particular the *Dialogue* and the *Trialogue*, both of which presented cogent attacks on corruption. Jerome was enthusiastic in supporting Wycliffite ideas, and narrowly escaped arrest at Oxford for his Realism, but Hus was not then fully cognizant with such thought and did not adopt fresh principles to the exclusion of what he had earlier learned in his own training. Thus it was that in the immediate university crises that followed, he remained distinctly less radical than some of his academic superiors, and only later did he move further in his conclusions.

In May, 1403, the Germans at Prague, under the rector Walter

[1] M. Brandt, "Wyclifism in Dalmatia in 1383", in *Slavonic and East European Review* XXXVI (1957–8), pp. 58–68.

Harasser, who was himself a Bavarian, presented for condemnation a set of forty-five articles supposedly drawn from Wycliffe's writings. These articles comprised the twenty-four conclusions condemned at Blackfriars and twenty-one additional statements worked out by a German teacher at the university. The motion provoked a stormy debate in which some of the Bohemian masters, including Hus, challenged the condemnation and accused the Germans of misrepresenting Wycliffe's teaching. A modified prohibition was temporarily agreed upon, but the English scholar's views were debated in full in the following year. In the dispute, Hus was chosen by the reformers to defend Wycliffe's ideas, probably because he had become well-versed in them, and it was notable that he remained moderate in stressing still the fact of misrepresentation. His overmastering concern was to attack corruption around and to demand spiritual reform: it was not to follow Wycliffe or anybody else slavishly in their teaching. In ensuing developments, however, within and outside the university, he was thrust inexorably into leadership of a cause that embodied many Wycliffite principles. At the university the Germans gained the support of Archbishop Zbynek to renew their attacks in 1408, and as a result several Bohemians were indicted for defending Wycliffe. Znojmo and Páleč, cited to the papal court at Rome, were forced to recant their views on Wycliffe, and at a later date they returned to Prague to become leading opponents of Hus. In the meantime there seemed to the authorities little danger of a further spread of unorthodox ideas in Bohemia, and Zbynek boasted that there was no heretic in the country.

Except in practical issues, Hus did not consider that he was following or borrowing from Wycliffe until after 1408. His career to that date was auspicious, both in official and popular terms. He appeared increasingly as a national advocate of practical reform, but was also confessor to Queen Sophia and court chaplain, and on two occasions – in 1405 and 1407 – was appointed by Zbynek to preach at the Prague synod. Such distinction did not suggest that he was known for heretical views, outspoken though he was about current wrongs, but events of 1408 thrust him into leadership of the reforming party, and in the following year he clashed with the archbishop. The dispute arose from reaction to the involved efforts to end the Great Schism, in which the cardinals held a council at Pisa to depose the two existing Popes and agree on a single new choice. King Wenzel and the Bohemians generally were in sympathy with this procedure, but the Germans and Zbynek maintained their allegiance to one of the existing Popes, Gregory XII at Rome. The division in the university showed strong national feeling against the archbishop and the Germans, and this was voiced by Hus and Jerome, though for a time Hus was ill and Jerome initiated action that led to the royal edict of Kutna Hora at the start of 1409. By this decree, the academic body at Prague was reconstituted to provide the Bohemian "nation" with a predominant voice of three votes, against the other three "nations" who were left with only one each. A few months later, the Germans withdrew to found a new university in Leipzig, whilst Hus was elected rector at Prague. Zbynek was forced to submit to the new Pope at Pisa – Alexander V – but he harboured resentment against Hus, and ironically enough secured from his fresh master a commission to act drastically in dealing with Wycliffite teaching in Bohemia.

Zbynek was given a specific mandate to suspend preaching in the Bethlehem Chapel, but this order Hus refused to obey. When moreover the archbishop sought to have all of Wycliffe's books surrendered, he met with still stronger protests from the university and the king, and with appeals to John XXIII, who succeeded Alexander V in 1410. Nonetheless, Zbynek had many of Wycliffe's writings burned and he excommunicated Hus and his supporters. In the storm of popular and national feeling that followed, he tried at first to maintain his position, and then took care to have the dispute about Hus put before the papal legate, Cardinal Colonna. The latter excommunicated Hus for contumacy in 1411, and this action was to prove of fateful consequence later for the Bohemian leader. Meanwhile, compromise was reached between the other parties, chiefly because John XXIII wanted to placate Wenzel. So that the archbishop's sentence of excommunication should be removed, Hus on his part was willing to deny categorically the heresies alleged against him. He still thought of himself as wholly orthodox in faith, more clearly so than Jerome at that point, and he was certainly moderate and discriminating in his ideas. But it seems that he had progressed in learning of Wycliffe's arguments, for from 1410 onward he was modifying the bases of his criticisms to add theological considerations more completely to those moral or ethical; and circumstances pushed him further into more extreme and dangerous views.

Quite possibly the episode over Wycliffe's writings could have ended with the official reconciliation, for Zbynek died later in the same year and Hus continued to enjoy royal and national support in Bohemia. This could be seen even when he defended Wycliffe in public debate against the English doctor, John Stokes. But in 1412 he clashed violently with the Pope over indulgences. In Italy John XXIII had his own territorial ambitions which involved a war with King Ladislas of Naples, and against him he proclaimed a crusade at the close of 1411. Plenary indulgences were offered to all who should take part in the campaign or contribute towards its cost, and Wenzel Tiem, the Dean of Passau, was authorized to sell these letters in regions that included Bohemia. Strangely like the Dominican Tetzel a century later, Tiem abused his commission in blatantly hawking indulgences around solely for the money to be gained. The device was widely condemned in Europe, and Hus, in open opposition to the sale of indulgences for such a purpose, spoke of the Pope as Antichrist in June, 1412. He argued that no Pope or priest could absolve from the penalty and guilt of sin, but only God Himself; the Pope should not fight like any secular lord, but deal rather with spiritual matters and use the Word of God. It was therefore quite right, Hus claimed, for Christians to disobey the papal summons and have nothing to do with the simoniacal and anti-Christian traffic in indulgences. Some of these ideas came directly from Wycliffe and were stated even more sharply by Jerome, but the consequences were grave. The petty war occasioning the need for indulgences was soon settled, but Hus's outspoken criticisms lost him royal support, made Páleč and Znojmo his bitter enemies and in particular left him in a perilous position where he was still under Cardinal Colonna's ban of excommunication. The Bethlehem Chapel was closed and Hus was denounced to the Pope, who ordered that he should be seized and his adherents excommunicated and tried if they refused to submit. Appealing to Christ as the Supreme Judge "who is neither influenced by gifts nor deceived by false witnesses", Hus left Prague in October, 1412, so that the city should escape interdict.

By that date he was seen as the leader of a popular national movement against the Germans and the Pope, against even Wenzel or his brother Sigismund who had been elected Holy Roman Emperor in 1410; the murder of some of Hus's student supporters in Prague before his flight into hiding only served to confirm the people's enthusiasm for him. Through 1413, friends at the university continued to uphold his views, and Wenzel went so far as to banish some of his opponents in the vain attempt to effect a compromise. Apart from occasional secret visits to Prague, Hus spent most of his time in exile in writing extensively, with the object of giving practical expositions of reform and sermons of instruction where he no longer had his pulpit in the city. These writings showed plainly his position and what he urged others to believe. The Pope he allowed to be Christ's Vicar only insofar as he followed the Law of Christ, and otherwise he was Antichrist. His own hope he placed in God and love of His Word which, Hus argued, all should obey as Christians. From such work in hiding, he later agreed to emerge so that he could attend the General Council at Constance. This was summoned by John XXIII chiefly to end the scandal of three competing Popes, but also to stamp out heresy, which above all meant Wycliffite ideas and the teachings of Hus in Bohemia. Where Wycliffe's works and the forty-five propositions presented at Prague had already been condemned as heretical by John XXIII in the council at Rome in 1413, Hus's position was pre-judged by the Pope, and it became clear that the leaders at Constance thought no differently.

Hus went to Constance in 1414 with the promise of a safe conduct from Emperor Sigismund whereby he imagined that he could freely leave after the Council's hearing. Undoubtedly he believed somewhat optimistically that he was to defend and explain his views at the Council, even to modify them if it was shown that they were contrary to God's law in Scripture. But the conciliarists at no time looked on him as other than a heretic, in terms clearly misleading and unjust, where the only defence offered for their actions was to say that no faith could be broken with those who broke faith with God. At Constance, Hus was imprisoned first of all by John XXIII, who treated him as still under indictment from 1411, and Sigismund's protests failed to secure his release. When the Pope fled from Constance, prior to his own deposition, the leaders at the Council continued to act against Hus on the same questionable basis. A concession was made to Sigismund in that Hus was allowed an extensive public hearing in his trial, where normally canon law required secret sittings, and some of the conciliar leaders, including Zabarella and d'Ailly, appeared genuinely anxious to save him from punishment as a heretic. In his own defence, Hus himself was not always tactful and in exasperation at one point declared that a king in mortal sin was not a true king in God's sight. Thereby he tacitly adopted much in Wycliffe's argument about lordship, and in particular annoyed Sigismund who subsequently gave up any effort to save the Bohemian leader. Nevertheless, the Emperor was morally culpable in abandoning his promise of a safe-conduct, however awkward its keeping would have been for the Council, whilst the judicial hearings of Hus were less than fair. He was, it seems, confronted with the forty-five Wycliffite articles and a series of propositions from his own writings, and asked to recant them. In many places he argued that he had never said or held the opinions attributed to him, and therefore could not recant them, but his refusals only led to condemnation as a heretic, and he was burned at the stake in Constance in July, 1415.

The events that led to Hus's death were clear and the Council unequivocally judged him as a Wycliffite, but the records show that he was condemned for what he was supposed to believe rather than for what he insisted on as his faith. Hus had many enemies at Constance whose opposition sprang from non-theological motives – there were his erstwhile Bohemian colleagues jealous of his popularity, the French Nominalists as philosophical rivals, even Wenzel and Sigismund fearful about royal power in Bohemia – and he was by no means simply a follower of Wycliffe. Insofar as he was condemned for insisting that the Church was the whole body of the predestined in contrast to any organized, authoritative structure – and he did emphasize this view in his preaching and writing – then he was at one with Wycliffe and learned much from his works. Where too he laid fundamental stress on the Scriptures and the right of each man to interpret and use them as the test for any ecclesiastical action, he followed the same arguments as Wycliffe and reached the same all-important conclusion. Like Luther later at Worms in 1521, Hus's final appeal was to the individual Christian in his trust in Christ against all the world, Pope, Emperor, Council or bishops. But beyond these points of similarity, Hus was not so closely or obviously dependent upon Wycliffe, for throughout he looked back to his native reform movement and framed many of his criticisms and demands in practical terms that had meaning in the Bohemian situation. Moreover, in using Wycliffe's works for his own tracts, Hus, it can be argued, was selective and critical, always master of his own arguments. Verbally, as Loserth demonstrated,[1] Hus borrowed many passages from the Englishman in his writings, but it was always with careful rearrangement where generally his tracts were more tightly-knit, pungent and practical than the academic and highly technical theses of Wycliffe. In this way, Hus's work on the Church contained passages from Wycliffe amounting to about one-eighth of the book, but these borrowings were very selective, carefully woven together into Hus's own discussion and drawn from nearly forty different tracts of the Oxford reformer, not just from his *On the Church*.[2] Hus's main arguments about the nature of the Church were similar to those of Wycliffe: he claimed that it was composed of the predestined under Christ, and that the Pope, cardinals and all the clergy possessed ministries only insofar as they lived according to God's Law in Scripture; he denounced simony in any form, and denied any sacerdotal power to remit sin. In addition, he upheld the right of individual judgment against ecclesiastical authority. Yet he certainly did not press all these ideas to the conclusions reached by Wycliffe, and it was noteworthy that at Constance he was indicted on the evidence of a copy of his tract containing Wycliffite interpolations – and this copy he flatly repudiated.

[1] In *Hus und Wiclif.*

[2] Cf. M. Spinka, *John Hus and the Czech Reform* (Chicago, 1941), p. 16, and more generally S. H. Thomson's remarks in his Introduction to John Hus's *De Ecclesia* (Cambridge, 1956), pp. viii f.

Hus had dealings with the English Lollards and corresponded with Oldcastle and Richard Wyche, but in general thought and attitude he stood in a far more moderate position than Wycliffe. At Constance he was ready to reject many of the other reformer's alleged conclusions, and stated that "Whatever truth was propounded by Wycliffe, that I accept, not because it is Wycliffe's, but because it is Christ's truth". Though he took predestination as the keynote for his definition of the Church, he did not pursue it so far as Wycliffe, whilst he was willing to qualify in certain ways the fundamental authority of Scripture. He spoke of the relative inspiration of the Old alongside the New Testament, and could acknowledge as guides for Christian living under Scripture, "God, the apostles, the holy doctors of the Church, and the Catholic Church", even the General Council. Hus was not the intellectual radical or revolutionary that Wycliffe ultimately had been, and he stood well short of anarchy: he neither placed so much reliance upon civil power nor explored theories like lordship anchored in grace which threatened to upset all government and rights of property. Only in the heated exchanges of Constance and under sentence of execution, did Hus speak out more extremely, but even then without the carefully argued theses of Wycliffe, and he never elaborated a sweeping anti-papal or anti-clerical programme. The essential distinction which he sought to draw was between office and person, where worthiness of character and life remained all-important. Hus was willing to allow the rightful exercise of jurisdiction by the Pope, bishops and other ecclesiastics, and that they should have some property, and when at Constance he gave a list of fifteen Popes whom he regarded as having been unworthy of office, he did not deny the validity of their power as far as their function allowed.

Above all, he differed radically from Wycliffe over the subject of transubstantiation, which he was always prepared to accept on the basis that Christ's Body was sacramentally present in the Eucharist. His orthodoxy on transubstantiation he consistently maintained at Constance, although d'Ailly tried to make out that he followed Wycliffe on the point and had him finally condemned for upholding remanence amongst other doctrines. Hus again was emphatic in stating that the worthiness or otherwise of the priest made no difference to the sacrament, where Wycliffe had argued that this was of decisive importance. More generally he refused to adopt the dangerous ideas suggested by Jerome and trod rather in the footprints of earlier Bohemian reformers by seeking change inside the existing structure, above all, in moral regeneration of life. It was illuminating that the demand which he took up as fundamental from his contemporary, Jacobellus of Stribro, was for communion in both kinds, that the laity should have the cup as well as the bread in the Eucharist. Despite his philosophic Realism, Hus did not argue that transubstantiation was doctrinally wrong, nor did he explore the subject as deeply as Wycliffe in its sacerdotal implications.[1]

The judgment passed at Constance on Hus was therefore misleading as well as criminal, for the Bohemian leader remained in many respects fully orthodox and moderate in his proposals, his own hopes high for reconciliation with the conciliar leaders. But from their point of view, both Hus and his teaching had to be destroyed for in the last resort he challenged what they claimed to possess – authority to suppress individual speculation, delimit heresy and punish it with death. In his final appeal to Christ and the Scriptures, he rejected conciliar assertions of supreme authority no less than those of any Pope and condemned both with equal severity. The conciliarists had their own troubles in trying to vindicate claims to supremacy over the Pope and dared not show themselves less zealous than the papalists in upholding orthodoxy. On grounds of doctrine, therefore, where the General Council was declared to have supreme authority in faith, and for expediency, the Fathers at Constance condemned Hus, and drove him to argue as radically as Wycliffe in standing by the right of every Christian to find salvation in Christ alone, in appealing to the Scriptures, and in challenging and rejecting ecclesiastical authority.

Events that followed on Hus's death showed how profoundly were his enemies mistaken in their hopes. Hus undoubtedly was more fortunate than Wycliffe in the national support that he inspired, even where he seemed to lack political discretion in refusing to compromise over indulgences. But in addition, the movement that he left was stronger and more organized in popular hopes than Lollardy had ever been or could be, for in Hussitism there were non-religious political and social factors that had no place in England. As a result, the Hussite movement, so far from vanishing at the death of its leader, entered upon an amazing period of development and defiance against the rest of Christendom which left a number of reforms in Bohemia and a pattern of what might be attempted in the future. The betrayal and execution of Hus enraged the Bohemian people, and their nobles in 1415 spurned the Council's orders to root out heresy. They not only declared that Hus had been a great and good Catholic, but also bound themselves by oath to maintain the gospel and its preachers, and appointed a committee to prepare the defence of the country against attack. At the same time, however, they maintained that they were willing to recognize papal jurisdiction so long as it was not repugnant to God, and to allow the Bohemian hierarchy to negotiate with a

[1] M. Spinka, *John Hus*, presents this general view of Hus's relationship to Wycliffe.

Pope for settlement. But at Constance in 1415, there was no certainty as to who the next Pope would be or when he would be elected, and the leaders of the Council hoped instead to weaken Hussite influence by their treatment of Jerome of Prague, who in many ways was as important as Hus in forging the national movement, and was ranked with Wycliffe and Hus as a champion against Rome by sixteenth-century Protestants.

Jerome was slightly younger than Hus, taking his B.A. at Prague only in 1398, and throughout the years his career was interwoven with that of his friend. But his life was much more variegated, for Jerome travelled ceaselessly across Europe, teaching and disputing his Realist principles in different universities. Wherever he went, he made converts and gained official censure. His stay at Oxford ended abruptly in this way in 1402, after which he studied at Paris, where he aroused Gerson's condemnation before escaping from the city in 1406. Following further travels to Heidelberg and Cologne, he returned to Prague to dominate the university with his oratory and take the initiative, while Hus was unwell, in the developments that led to the refounding of the Bohemian university in 1409. Thereafter he travelled again, first to Hungary, where he preached as a layman before Sigismund and was imprisoned briefly, then to Vienna to answer charges of heresy. After sharing in the Prague disturbances of July, 1412, over indulgences, Jerome went in the following year to Lithuania and White Russia to engage in efforts for re-opening contacts with the Orthodox Ruthenians. He shocked many in the West by his characteristic assertion that the Ruthenians were better Christians than the Dominican friars who were at work in the country, and more generally his activities were fiery and popular in ways that Hus did not cultivate. His views were more extreme, and he was notorious for stirring up riots and for iconoclasm. Yet at the same time Jerome was acknowledged as one of the most able scholars and classicists of his age. He accompanied Hus to Constance, tried to leave for a safer retreat, but was seized and imprisoned in the city for nearly a year. From him the conciliarists secured a public recantation before the end of 1415, but this had no effect in halting events in Bohemia. After keeping Jerome further months in solitary confinement, his enemies examined him more thoroughly, under the influence of Gerson's argument that not even recantation should save a heretic from execution. In the new hearings, Jerome repudiated his earlier confession, eulogized Hus, and out-argued his accusers brilliantly and convincingly. So thought the Italian humanist Poggio who was at Constance, and who for all his orthodoxy would seemingly have acquitted Jerome with his learning, humanity, compassion and courage. "Wonderful it was," wrote

Poggio, "to witness the eloquence, the arguments, the bearing, and the confidence with which he confronted his adversaries and brought his plea to an end. So that one must needs grieve that a spirit so noble and lofty should have been lured into the paths of heresy, if indeed those things which are charged against him are true". Jerome was condemned for heresy in Wycliffite and Hussite terms, and burned in May, 1416, at the place where Hus had earlier been martyred.[1]

Such an end for Jerome only deepened national Bohemian reaction and widened the conflict. In view of the country's temper, Wenzel hesitated for a while to accede to the condemnation of Hus by the Council, which was confirmed after 1417 by the new Pope, Martin V. When finally in 1419 he endeavoured to act more decisively, the Hussite movement was already well-developed in organization and power. Among the groups reacting sharply to the execution of the Bohemian leaders, the clergy at Prague as early as August, 1417, formulated four major demands which were to become the rallying cry of the Hussites, but more than this, it was plain by 1419 that Hus's legacy was a divided one. Two leading bodies emerged in competition with each other as much as against outside enemies: the Calixtines or Utraquists, who adopted the symbol of the chalice (*calix*) for communion "in both kinds" (sub *utraque* specie), and the Taborites. The Utraquists were conservative and aristocratic nationalists, unhappy at ideas of breaking away from the traditional Church and anxious not to usher in social and political revolution. Under the teaching of Jacobellus, they followed Hus theologically in his moderation. But the Taborites were composed of lower social groups, the country labourers and urban workers, who not only retained Waldensian ideas but were also engaged in social struggle against the nobles and the Church in southern Bohemia even during Hus's lifetime. After his death, they were inspired to much more radical views by the preaching of John Želivský, a disciple of Hus. They generally adopted Wycliffe's teaching on the Bible as a sole authority for life, on lordship and the Eucharist, and rejected the whole Catholic system of penance, worship of the saints, or the need for any priesthood. Such radicals moreover were millennialist in outlook and became known as Taborites for making their headquarters in 1419 at a mountain to which they gave the Biblical title of Tabor, and where they built the town of the same name a year later.[2] In outlook, the Taborites joined forces with many other similar groups of older lineage in Christen-

[1] Cf. the study by R. R. Betts, "Jerome of Prague", in *University of Birmingham Historical Journal* I (1947), pp. 51–91; and also P. P. Bernard, "Jerome of Prague, Austria and the Hussites", in *Church History* XXVII (1958), pp. 3–22.

[2] Cf. Cohn, op. cit., p. 217 f., and H. Kaminsky, "Chiliasm and the Hussite Revolution", in *Church History* XXVI (1957), pp. 43–71.

dom, and included not only the great Lollard Peter Payne but even "Pikharts" or Brethren of the Free Spirit in Bohemia, whose ideas ran to extremes and contained much that was not properly Christian in content.[1] The Taborites were more truly heirs to Wycliffe than to Hus, and their achievement was unique in Bohemian and European affairs.

In 1419, the Bohemians were therefore already divided among themselves, but they were at one in defence of national Hussitism. Wenzel's belated efforts to check developments led to a rebellion in Prague in July, 1419, when the city councillors were thrown from the town hall windows and murdered. The king died of apoplexy, and his brother, the Emperor Sigismund, who stood as heir to the throne, had to bargain at a distance, whilst the widowed Queen Sophia tried to stay as regent. After further rebellions in other towns and a period when Sigismund was preoccupied with Turkish attacks, the Emperor pressed demands upon Bohemia. In defiance against him, a Taborite nobleman and soldier, John Žižka, seized the capital in November, 1419, and ruthlessly sacked churches and monasteries before leaving to take charge of military preparations at Tabor in the next year. When Sigismund marched into Bohemia and demanded the capital's surrender, Žižka was able to answer the call for help from Prague and defeat the crusading army heavily in May, 1420. In the flush of victory, the Hussites were brought into unified agreement on the basis of the Four Articles of Prague, whose principles had been stated more than once since 1417 in manifestoes against Sigismund. Jacobellus was the architect of these claims which stated that there should be freedom throughout Bohemia for preaching God's Word; that there should be communion in both kinds for all, at least once a Sunday; that the clergy should abandon their riches and simony; and that all mortal and venial sins in the laity and clergy alike should be eradicated.[2] The articles allowed sufficient scope for moderate or extremist interpretations, and they were presented as a basis for settlement with Sigismund. But under papal pressure, the Emperor rejected them, and suffered fresh military defeat that compelled him to withdraw completely from Prague.

Religious fervour was combined with national feeling and military genius where Žižka organized the Bohemian army and commanded it in victory after victory, despite his blindness in one eye and eventual total loss of vision. Žižka himself passed earlier through an honourable career as a nobleman and served King Wenzel before becoming a firm disciple of Hus. His leadership and ability in the Hussite cause indisputably aided its success against seemingly overwhelming dis-

[1] Cf. the discussion of the ideas and rôle of these Brethren by H. Kaminsky, "The Free Spirit in the Hussite Revolution", in *Millennial Dreams in Action*, edited by S. L. Thrupp (The Hague, 1962), pp. 166–186.

[2] Cf. F. G. Heymann, *John Žižka and the Hussite Revolution* (Princeton, 1955), Chapter 10.

advantages, and his great military skill was shown in training the Taborite peasant army, in fighting with wagon formations against superior forces, and in using and controlling the apocalyptic fervour of his troops. The warfare was ruthless, where imperial troops massacred thousands and the Taborites fought to establish Christ's Kingdom on earth, with Tabor itself as the New Jerusalem. In 1421 and 1422, crusades were launched under papal and imperial authorities but on both occasions the German armies were defeated. Within Bohemia, the Archbishop of Prague accepted the Four Articles in 1421 and the Utraquists were able to set up an independent Bohemian Church. Sigismund was deposed by the Diet and his crown was offered in turn to King Ladislas II of Poland and to Duke Witold of Lithuania, who delegated his nephew Prince Korybut to become regent. Korybut served the Hussite cause well for five years after 1422, with Polish forces to aid in their battles, but finally he was deposed for showing himself too willing to intrigue for a compromise with the Catholics. Bitter divisions in religion, meanwhile, led Žižka to crush the Pikharts as heretics in 1421, and brought conflict between Jacobellus and Želivský over the government of Prague and the Church, in which Želivský was murdered. Civil war thereafter flared up between Utraquists and Taborites, in which Žižka dealt harshly with any seeking accommodation with Sigismund, and his death in 1424 left Hussite divisions all the more obvious. Militarily and politically there emerged a new leader in Prokop the Great, who was a priest of gentle birth and who enabled Bohemian defiance of the outside world to continue unabated for a further ten years.

Prokop wanted peace and security for Bohemia in Hussitism, and believed that the only way to gain these ends was to wage campaigns of terror in lands bordering his country. For six years, from 1426 to 1432, Prokop waged war in this fashion, repelling a fourth crusade under Cardinal Beaufort in 1427 and thereafter making sorties successively into Hungary, Germany and other territories. Such a policy succeeded in making Sigismund and other leaders recognize that a settlement had to be negotiated, and the Council of Basel was convened in 1431 pre-eminently to deal with the Bohemian problem. Following the failure of a final crusade led by the papal legate Cesarini, the conciliarists came to terms with the Bohemian leaders at Eger in May, 1432, whereby an embassy was to go to Basel under safe conduct to defend their Four Articles in public debate. All-important for the Hussites in the Compacts of Eger was recognition that they should not be judged by the Council, but that their principles were to be upheld or refuted according to divine law as found in the gospel, the way of Christ, of the apostles and of the primitive Church, with other authorities comformable to this basis. Their representatives attended the Council in 1433 in the position which Hus earlier had believed that he held at Constance, but with guarantees that had not existed for him. The Four Articles were defended by four leaders under Rokycana who had emerged into effective control of the Utraquists after the death of Jacobellus in 1429. Peter Payne was prominent in expounding Wycliffite and Taborite views and was protected by the Council against the English delegates who wanted his extradition for treason. The Hussite case was honourably heard, and further negotiations in Prague led to acceptance of the Council's decrees by 1434, but the Taborites disliked the terms.[1] Civil war broke out afresh and at the battle of Lipany in May, 1434, the Utraquists triumphed and Prokop was killed.

The Hussite menace to central Europe vanished with the death of Prokop and crushing of his Taborite forces, but the Bohemians were able to confirm more general peace on the lines of what had already been agreed at Basel. In religious terms the settlement was incorporated in the Compacts signed at Iglau in the summer of 1436, whereby the Hussites agreed to make peace, to submit and be restored to the unity of the Church. In return, they were to have communion in both kinds and free preaching of the Word of God by those properly appointed. These concessions answered to two of the Four Articles, but nothing was said about ecclesiastical property or its reform. More impressive was the agreement with Sigismund who was at last recognized as King of Bohemia, and who in return promised to forbid the granting of benefices to foreigners or judicial citations beyond Bohemia, and to permit the high ecclesiastics of the Bohemian Church to be elected by the native clergy and people. Sigismund moreover promised specifically to confirm the appointment of Rokycana as Archbishop of Prague, a post to which he had already been elected in 1435 by the Bohemian Diet.

On paper, these settlements appeared considerable, not least where both Council and Emperor recognized the legitimate existence of what they had earlier treated as a heretical movement. Within the framework of a nationally organized church, possessing guarantees about preaching and control, it could be hoped that reform would be consolidated, even in the terms of the earlier programmes of Milič, Janov and Hus. The Four Articles stood as the cherished foundation of Bohemian principles, and the Compacts, however inadequate, were accepted as underlining them. In fact, too little had been positively

[1] For the negotiations and discussions at Basel, cf. E. F. Jacob, "The Bohemians at the Council of Basel", in *Prague Essays*, edited by R. W. Seton-Watson (Oxford, 1949), pp. 81–123; and for Rokycana's work, F. G. Heymann, "John Rokycana – Church Reformer between Hus and Luther", in *Church History* XXVIII (1959), pp. 240–80.

or finally attained by 1436. The Compacts and the other treaty were broadly phrased, and though this made possible acceptance by different parties in Bohemia, too much depended upon their interpretation and the good faith of those who made terms with the Hussites. Neither the Council nor Sigismund planned to keep their agreements. The Emperor quickly showed his hand by omitting to confirm Rokycana's appointment in Prague, whilst the conciliar legates, with no less speed, sought to reimpose Catholic ritual and observance to offset any thought of an autonomous Bohemian Church, save for the bare symbol of the administration of the sacrament in both kinds. The Pope had no part in these settlements, nor did he show that he intended to accept them in the future. It is probable that Sigismund's death in 1437 prevented what would have been a more thorough attempt to undo the agreements of the preceding year, which on any basis represented something less than a full or lasting achievement of reform.

The Hussite movement resounded throughout Christendom as Lollardy never did, and Hus's work was renowned, but the rôle of Hussitism after the 1430's depended as much as Lollardy upon the moulding of events. To a real extent, the two developments illustrated related but differing attempts to grapple with the ecclesiastical and religious abuses of the age. Fundamental ideas were shared to a considerable extent, and the criticisms were entangled in the snares of what was regarded as heresy. In the last analysis, Hus was as radical as Wycliffe in arguing from the concept of the Universal Church as predestinate, even where the Bohemian leader did not seek to probe so deeply or systematically as Wycliffe the antinomian implications of the doctrine. Both men were followed by movements that simplified and modified their principles, with the play of other factors like nationalism and the efforts taken by governments to disrupt them. In the settlements of 1436, with formal reconciliation to the Catholic Church, the Hussite cause can be reckoned to have reached more solid, united ends than Lollardy, which was discredited and driven underground among the lowest social classes at that time. But it is doubtful if the first was so lastingly successful, or the second without continuing, leavening influences in English society, and subsequent developments in Bohemia and England reveal what qualifications are necessary. The significance of the Hussite revolt lay rather in the fact that for the first time the authoritarian claims of the Roman Church had been challenged – and challenged successfully – in the name of religious reform. The full meaning of events was not to be found in the settlements that left the Bohemians with so little gained in substance after twenty years of heroic conflict. It was of far deeper consequence that at Basel and in the Compacts of 1436 they were officially recognized and accepted where previously they had been treated as heretics. Their achievement pioneered the way for all who later in the sixteenth century assaulted papal government of a Church which was visibly united in order and doctrine.

CHAPTER VI

THE GREAT SCHISM AND THE CONCILIAR MOVEMENT

THE ECCLESIASTICAL ABUSES AND CORRUPTION SO FIERCELY denounced by Wycliffe and Hus lay deeply rooted in developments before 1378. Nevertheless, the careers of the two men and the movements fostered by them were closely influenced by the particular crisis provoked in that year with the elections of two Popes, which led in turn to the widespread effort in Christendom to remedy all ills by the instrument of a General Council. What is puzzling at first sight in these affairs is that neither Wycliffism nor Hussitism was welcomed in a common cause by the conciliar reformers, but instead they were condemned as harshly in the councils as by the Popes. The reasons for this reaction are to be sought in the nature of Conciliarism itself – and these self-same reasons help to account for the failure of the movement to bring reformation in the western Church.

The period of the Great Schism was not distinguished by commendable policies or actions on the part of any of the rival Popes, but it was yet significant for stimulating determined efforts to reform the structure of the Church. Thirty-six years elapsed from the elections of 1378 until the Council of Constance met to end the depressing spectacle of warring pontiffs, and this is evidence enough of the personal ambitions, pride and stubbornness ruling each individual in turn who claimed to be the true Pope. The division of 1378 did not arise out of any fundamental theological issue such as had earlier split the Latin and Greek Churches, though initially it was more than merely a matter of personality and involved differing and important views about the government of the Church.[1] The Popes had resided long at Avignon where they perfected their centralized power, but ideologically Rome remained the proper papal capital, the keystone of authority claimed by the pontiffs as Vicars of Christ and successors of St. Peter in the Apostolic Church. Before 1378 more than one Pope had tried to return to Rome: Urban V visited the city in 1367, and stayed for three years, during which time he was visited by the Holy Roman and the Byzantine Emperors. His successor, Gregory XI, finally returned in 1377 and died at Rome in the following year.

[1] Cf. W. Ullmann, *The Origins of the Great Schism* (London, 1948).

Of the sixteen cardinals at hand[1] whose task it was to choose a new Pope, eleven were French, but all united in appointing the Neapolitan Archbishop of Bari from outside the college as the new Pope, and he took the title of Urban VI. Very speedily, however, he disappointed those who hoped to have in him a compliant ruler whom they could control. Quite apart from deciding to stay on at Rome rather than return to Avignon, Urban displayed his authority and vigour in unpopular acts for reform, including reducing the revenues of the cardinals. Personal pique was seen in the developments, for Urban scarcely showed tact or wisdom, but fundamentally there was a conflict of theory between Pope and cardinals over the government of the Church, and Urban drastically cut across well-developed ideas that the cardinals as a body should curb and control papal autocracy. Such theories were important in conciliar arguments by 1400, and bore perennial attraction thereafter, but in 1378 they led the French cardinals to claim that Urban had not been elected as they had voted only under pressure from the Roman mob. Moving to Fondi, they there elected one of their own number as Clement VII. The Italian cardinals, who also went to Fondi out of exasperation with Urban, abstained from voting since they accepted the first election as valid if unfortunate, and the emergence of two Popes was clearly the fault of the French.

Urban VI replied by creating twenty-eight new cardinals, and thereafter, neither he nor Clement VII ever showed the slightest willingness to give way. All too readily the countries of Latin Christendom ranged support behind them, making their choices on political rather than religious or legal grounds, though these were hard enough to discern. Urban's adherents included England, most of Germany, Scandinavia, Bohemia and Hungary, and at first even Wycliffe saluted the new Roman pontiff as the man to break away from the evils of Avignon. Italy shared its allegiances, according to its internal rivalries between princes and leagues, but nearly all France supported Clement VII, together with Scotland, and the various realms of the Iberian peninsula, excepting Portugal. Latin Christendom thus was unedifyingly divided, for the most part according to the animosities of England and France with their respective allies, and it did not help that Catherine of Siena favoured Urban and Vincent Ferrer, the Dominican saint, saw Clement as Christ's Vicar. Each Pope disposed of sufficient support to defy his rival, once Urban had frustrated Clement's first hopes of capturing Rome and had compelled him to retire to Avignon in 1379.

[1] There were twenty-three cardinals in the college at the time, but six were absent in Avignon and one was on a mission, thus leaving the remainder at Rome.

Such a situation, however, had effects more deplorable than the mere partition of Europe, since all too soon there were in each land rivals for appointments and struggles between claimants for bishoprics and abbacies, where both Rome and Avignon asserted rights of preferment. These developments in turn created confusion and corruption additional to what was already known and condemned. Widespread protests were immediately voiced above all in the University of Paris, where two German masters, Henry of Langenstein and Conrad of Gelnhausen, wrote tracts debating the crisis and argued that a General Council alone had supreme authority in Christendom in its representative nature, and should be called to end the schism and undertake more general reform. These arguments were not new, and in recalling what Marsiglio and Occam had earlier asserted they revealed that Paris, in all its prestige and influence in Christendom, was prepared to entertain far-reaching theories of the nature and structure of the Universal Church. At first, indeed, the university refused to accede to Clement VII and thereby sanction the schism. In 1381 it passed a formal resolution stating its preference for the summoning of a General Council to end the impasse, but the French government forced the Paris masters to acknowledge Clement and expelled Gelnhausen and Langenstein with other teachers from the university. In the 1380's therefore both Popes embroiled themselves in political and military intrigues in the efforts to oust each other by force. Urban VI faced political rivals within Italy itself, where he indulged his personal hatred of other Neapolitans and lost much support by his ruthless behaviour. In 1384, he imprisoned six of his own cardinals, allegedly for conspiring against him, and later had them tortured and all executed save one. His relations with Charles of Durazzo, the King of Naples, were volatile and Urban himself for a time suffered the indignity of imprisonment, but more distantly his supporters served him well. The Duke of Lancaster led an expedition to Portugal to confirm it in allegiance to Rome and attempted – though with less success – to invade Castile. On his side, Clement VII hoped to exploit the French political situation in which Charles VI was still only a boy in 1380, whilst the regent was his eldest uncle Louis of Anjou and willing to espouse the cause of Avignon. Louis was showered with titles and privileges by Clement VII in 1379 on the understanding that he should try to reconquer the Papal State in Italy for the French Pope within two years. But his somewhat belated campaign of 1382 achieved nothing because of Charles of Durazzo's effective opposition, and two years later Louis died.

Such Avignonese schemes faltered, but they were revived after Urban's death in 1389 when the Italian cardinals continued the schism by electing another Neapolitan as the next Pope, Boniface IX. Clement gave his blessing to a new military venture led by Charles VI's brother, Duke Louis of Orleans, who was married to the Visconti heiress of Milan and had his own Italian ambitions. A grand scheme of conquest was started in 1390, but failed miserably. Nevertheless, Louis continued his support for Clement, and then for his successor, Benedict XIII, after 1394, whilst he became increasingly powerful in France. His brother went mad in 1392, and thereafter Louis shared the country's government with Duke Philip of Burgundy, who was less happy with the Avignonese claim. Philip did not possess Louis's Mediterranean ambitions, but was anxious rather for compromise in the issue of the Schism as well as in the current war with England. He seems genuinely to have wanted Christian peace and unity, together with ecclesiastical reform, in the greater plan for a crusade against the Turks. Certain it was that in the battle between the Christians and Turks at Nicopolis in 1396, Philip's son John was captured with the Burgundian host. As far as the papal question was concerned, however, Philip's views amounted to criticism of Avignon, and coincided generally with those voiced authoritatively in the same years by the University of Paris.

Meanwhile at Rome Boniface IX proved himself to be far less impossible as a personality than Urban VI, but he made his name synonymous with financial greed, rapacity and corruption in the effort to raise funds for his own power. He served himself well in proclaiming a Papal Jubilee ten years early in 1390, when it was supposed to take place fifty years after the previous celebration of 1350. The occasion was one for pilgrims to go to Rome and secure special indulgences by attendance at the great basilicas, and from the sales Boniface partly replenished his treasury. Indeed, he judged the device sufficiently lucrative to hold a further Jubilee in 1400, but his hopes in that year were disappointed. Boniface showed concern about the Turkish menace to Constantinople, and gave his blessing to a crusade, but he was too much absorbed in money and his own material power, putting up benefices for open sale at Rome and consolidating control over the Papal State with the aid of Charles's successor, Ladislas of Naples. General discontent at such corruption grew, particularly at the University of Paris under its Chancellor Peter d'Ailly and his younger colleague John Gerson. Both men came from Burgundy and the centres of religious reform there, and with their lead, the university in 1394 declared that a General Council should be summoned. The rival pontiffs, it stated, should abdicate, and the reunited college of cardinals elect one Pope who would then convene the council. There were many problems and differing opinions about a General Council, its summoning, composition and authority, but the university's voice gave a lead as to the simplest way in which to re-establish one head of the Roman Church and proceed to a council.

Clement VII curtly rejected these ideas, even when the French king added his authority to the demands, but the Pope died before anything could be done, and the twenty-one Avignonese cardinals decided that a successor had to be appointed. Before the conclave each cardinal promised to resign if elected, were this step thought necessary by a majority of the college. Peter of Luna cheerfully confirmed his promise after being chosen as Benedict XIII, affirming that he would abdicate as easily as take off his hat. He seemed sincere, and Vincent Ferrer was his confessor and placed in charge of the papal palace, but he quickly changed his mind and obstinately refused to yield up his crown when asked to more than once by Charles VI in 1395. The Schism continued in an atmosphere of mutual suspicion between Rome and Avignon. Benedict remained intransigent until and beyond his deposition at Constance, but much earlier there seemed a possibility that the French would permanently abandon him. In 1396 a synod considered withdrawing support from him, and two years later the French clergy were recorded as voting to suspend their obedience; the returns, it has been shown, were falsified, and a majority still held to Benedict, but at the time the decision to withdraw was implemented. From 1398 to 1403 the French Church went its own way – a significant interlude for fostering Gallicanism – and Benedict, deserted by his cardinals, was besieged and forced into surrender at Avignon in 1399. He remained virtually a prisoner until 1403 when he escaped into the territory of the Duke of Anjou, and Orleans was able to bring about the restoration of French obedience. Once again, Benedict promised solemnly to abdicate if his rival did, and he even proposed a conference with Boniface, which the latter spurned shortly before his death in 1404. The Roman pontiff was succeeded in turn by Innocent VII (1404–6) and Gregory XII, who showed more willingness to negotiate with his Avignonese rival, but was in practice no more sincere. Vacillations by both Popes increasingly lost them support on all sides, and Benedict notably was left weak after the murder of his most powerful adherent, the Duke of Orleans, in November, 1407. Yet despite renewed threats from Charles VI and the University of Paris, he obstinately refused to compromise but instead threatened excommunication. As a result, the French Church deliberately stood aside in neutrality between the Popes in May, 1408, after denouncing Benedict as schismatic and heretical. At the same time, eight of Gregory's cardinals deserted him, appealed to Christ as supreme Judge and to a General Council as the highest authority in the Church, and joined with the Avignonese cardinals to summon such a body for compelling the rivals to submit, as they argued, by way of cession.

From this decision came the first of the councils to end the Schism, that of Pisa, which met in June, 1409. Both Benedict and Gregory tried to forestall the meeting by convening their own councils, but without success, and the assembly at Pisa could be claimed as representative of much of the Latin Church. In all some five hundred members attended, amongst them Cardinal d'Ailly, who had received his hat from Benedict XIII but had broken with him in 1408, and Zabarella, the able jurist and future cardinal, whilst Gerson gave his approval to proceedings. In addition, ambassadors came from England, France, Bohemia, Portugal, Sicily and Poland, as well as from many universities, though no approval was forthcoming from Castile or Aragon, Scotland, Scandinavia, Hungary, Ladislas of Naples or the Emperor Rupert in Germany. The Council in fact only met peacefully because of the protection of Cardinal Cossa, whose reputation was that of a pirate. Without any papal summons for its meeting, the Council claimed legitimacy and authority on the basis of arguments developed by d'Ailly, Gerson and Zabarella, vesting power in the cardinals for calling a General Council in the same way that they elected a Pope. Such an assembly, it was declared, fully expressed the unity of the Church in Christ and by divine and natural law possessed supreme power for ending the Schism, electing a single Pope and carrying through reforms. In the event, the Council concerned itself for the most part with the problem of the Schism, although it also tried to deal with heresy in Wycliffism and the Bohemian movement. It deposed the existing Popes as schismatics and heretics, and authorized the cardinals to elect a new pontiff in the summer of 1409. They chose the Greek Cardinal Philargi, who took the title of Alexander V, but although he was welcomed by many in the East as well as the West, the papal results were disastrous: three rival Popes were left clamouring for the allegiance of Christendom instead of two. Benedict and Gregory ignored the decrees, which the Council found itself unable to enforce since it lacked the all-important political and military support of secular rulers in the Christian world.

Events that followed only added to the scandal, for the cardinals chose as Alexander V's successor in 1410 the notorious Cardinal Cossa, who took the title of John XXIII. The new Pope had undoubted ability, but as a politician and military adventurer, not a religious leader. He it was who declared war against Gregory XII's supporter, King Ladislas of Naples, and for his campaigning needs in 1411 authorized the sale of indulgences which Hus condemned. Yet the sight of such a man as Pope stirred leaders into more positive action to end the Schism. For a period there had been scarcely less confusion in Germany, where Wenzel disputed his deposition and the election of his rival Rupert as Emperor in 1400, but when Sigismund followed Rupert in 1410 a more stable situation was re-established. If not so heroic as he imagined himself to be, the new Emperor nevertheless took firm steps that eventually brought the Schism to an end in the meeting of another General Council. He recognized John XXIII as Pope in 1411, and with what prestige this gave, John held a small council at Rome two years later, in which the main work seems to have been the condemnation of Wycliffe's writings. But John also issued invitations for a larger council at the end of the following year, and was unable to abandon his promise as the date approached. After temporary peace in Italy with the King of Naples, the Pope had to ask help of Sigismund when Ladislas seized Rome in the summer of 1413, and the Emperor agreed to give assistance if John gave explicit summons for a Council. The Pope had to comply, ordering that such a body should meet at Constance in November, 1414; and to this agreement he was held, though his immediate peril passed with Ladislas's death three months before the start of the Council.

The assembly which met at Constance at the end of 1414 and continued intermittently in session until 1418 was far more comprehensive and influential than the earlier Pisan body. In some respects it was unique as the last occasion on which the whole of Latin Christendom met as a united body and was acknowledged as such by all concerned, including the Pope. Of the ecclesiastics who attended at some stage or other, three were patriarchs, twenty-nine cardinals, thirty-three archbishops, one hundred and fifty bishops, a hundred abbots, and nearly two thousand were priests, whilst additionally a hundred noblemen and two thousand knights came, each representative of some order, group or nation in the Latin West. Delegates, moreover, came to observe and discuss from the Greek Churches in the East. John XXIII punctually opened proceedings, but others were more dilatory in coming to Constance. Gregory XII only sent an embassy, Benedict XIII merely agreed to meet Sigismund at Nice later in 1415. In the position of honour as Holy Roman Emperor, Sigismund presided over the Council when present, and whatever the final reservations about its aims and work, its achievements as a united body were considerable. Partisan and national currents ran strongly through the Council, but these only highlighted more clearly how remarkable the assembly was, and to what deep feelings for a united Christendom it was able to appeal.[1] By its own declaration early on,

[1] Christendom by 1414 was clearly understood by most as limited to Europe and in urgent need of united defence against the Turks. Cf. Hay, op. cit., pp. 77 f., for views at Constance.

the Council set out three issues above all for its attention – to end the Schism, extirpate heresy, and reform the Church of God in head and members – and the measure of its success or failure lay in what happened with each of these matters.

The urgent task, and the one which had brought the Council into being, was to end the Schism, and methodically and with final success the conciliar leaders pursued this aim. John XXIII was manoeuvred into convening the Council, but thereafter he fought tenaciously to avoid any decision to bring about his own deposition. His supporters tried to suggest that all that the Council needed to do before dissolving was to confirm the Pisan decrees, and to lay down that there should be subsequent meetings of General Councils every twenty-five years. Such transparent efforts to save John's position only sharpened opposition, notably from d'Ailly, who bluntly affirmed the superiority of a General Council to a Pope and that all three rivals should resign or, if necessary, be deposed. John then sought to arrange voting procedures so that he should be favoured with a large Italian support, but this move was foiled by the decision to vote according to four "nations" in which all individuals were grouped. These "nations" were the Italian, the German (including Scandinavia and eastern Europe), the French and the British, and such division automatically excluded any Italian control favourable to John. As a result, he fled from Constance in the vain hope of disrupting or invalidating the Council's work, but proceedings were begun against him, and he was eventually brought back under guard to the city. After trial and conviction on numerous counts, John was deposed in May, 1415, kept in prison until the close of the Council, and he died in 1419. Meanwhile, Gregory XII submitted with grace and abdicated voluntarily in July, 1415, after which he remained as a cardinal until his death in 1417. Benedict XIII was deposed in that same year, but continued to insist that he was the Pope through the remaining five years of his life. In November, 1417, Cardinal Colonna of Hussite fame was elected by the cardinals as the new Pope of unity, and he took the title of Martin V. This event, more than any other, marked the ending of the Great Schism, and ranked as a positive and visible achievement of the Council.

More doubtful, however, were conciliar action and success in dealing with heresy. Challenges to the new practices of the Brethren of the Common Life and the Franciscan Observants were rightly repudiated in the Council, but the great problems of Wycliffite teaching, Lollardy and Hussitism were less fairly handled. Both Pisa and Rome had condemned Wycliffe's works, and Lollardy was a known and measurable threat after Oldcastle's abortive rebellion, but Hus and the Bohemian movement continued to appear intolerable in the eyes of the conciliar Fathers. No less zealous for orthodoxy than for moral and governmental reform in the Church, the conciliarists were overanxious to show their own complete loyalty to accepted dogma in competition with the Pope. The appeal in the teaching both of Wycliffe and Hus to predestination as the essential mark of the Church was potentially disruptive of all authority and order, and this the leaders at Constance could not accept in their concern for a united Christendom. They could only condemn the concept as heresy where the conclusions claimed by Hus for individual responsibility and right in appeal to Christ appeared to threaten the whole structure of faith. The rivalry of philosophical schools only helped to sharpen the issue where it mattered little that Hus so insistently denied many of the Wycliffite points alleged against him; Hus impugned conciliar no less than papal authority for the determination of doctrine, and he could therefore be condemned in terms similar to those used posthumously of Wycliffe. But Hus's condemnation and execution, followed by the same punishment for Jerome, did not bring the end of heresy, nor did the Council's orders for action against the Hussites in Bohemia. After Constance, Popes, Emperors and councils were faced with the militant Hussite challenge until 1436, and after that date, Hussitism, like Lollardy, continued with more subdued but scarcely less pervasive influences for the future. Constance plainly did not root out heresy by executing Hus and Jerome, and by its very treatment of these men possibly discredited the claims and cause of Conciliarism in the eyes of reformers far more completely than by any other act.[1]

Most obviously and immediately, however, Constance failed to achieve its third aim, that of reforming the Church "in head and members". The reasons for this lay in the fact that the aim embodied disparate ideas and that disagreements between groups at the Council made impossible any binding reforms before the assembly dissolved in 1418. Proposals set out in practical terms of authority and organization were tied to a theoretical statement of the nature of the Church and the superiority of a General Council to the Pope. These were essentially two different matters, stated in separate decrees at Constance, but so entangled with each other in the course of events that neither was properly realized.

The theory of Conciliarism was set out most grandly in the decree *Sacrosancta* in April, 1415, which began with these words:

> This holy Council of Constance . . . declares first, that it is lawfully assembled in the Holy Spirit, that it constitutes a General Council, representing the Catholic Church, and that therefore it has authority

[1] Cf. J. H. Mundy's comments in *The Council of Constance*, translated by L. R. Loomis edited by J. H. Mundy and K. M. Woody (New York, 1961), pp. 42 f.

> immediately from Christ; and that all men, of every rank and condition, including the Pope himself, are bound to obey it in matters concerning the faith, the abolition of the Schism, and the reformation of the Church of God in its head and members.

It was precisely because the General Council was meant to represent all Christendom that it claimed to have supreme authority derived directly from Christ. Some leaders at Constance did not go as far as this, and their reservations later helped to undermine conciliar power, but the official statement was uncompromising, and a man like Dietrich of Niem argued the theory through most cogently, copying and elaborating what Langenstein had earlier claimed. The theory essentially was papalism stood on its head with regard to authority and government in the Church. The Popes had progressively elaborated the thesis that the Church in doctrine and hierarchy required government which God had provided through St. Peter, and the Pope as St. Peter's successor and Vicar of Christ. From the Pope as Head of the Universal Church, authority – the only valid authority on earth – was deemed to descend to the priesthood for their exercise, and it was through priestly mediation of the sacraments that God's grace and salvation were brought to the lay order. All secular power was ultimately dependent upon papal grant or validation – shown symbolically in the priestly anointing and crowning of Emperors and kings – and all Christian society was theoretically brought under the Pope's control. This was theory, and medieval practice never properly fitted such claims, but the extreme statements of papalism – as in Boniface VIII's *Unam Sanctam* or Egidius's arguments about lordship – naturally provoked claims to refute them. One way to cut through all papal theories was to assert that the Church in authority and organization was purely spiritual and had nothing to do with material or governmental affairs, and this was exploited by Marsiglio, the Spiritual Franciscans and Wycliffe in his arguments about lordship. More radically, the predestinate nature of the Church could be probed to deny all claims by the Pope or hierarchy, and this too was Wycliffe's way. But the conciliarists argued otherwise. They claimed that in the visible, organized Church there was to be found a supreme, divinely-granted authority for matters of faith, doctrine and order. This authority resided in the Church as a whole, in the Christian faithful as the Body of Christ, and was exercised in that assembly which properly represented all Christians, namely, a General Council. In such a body, the Pope was only one member among the rest: the General Council, not the Pope, possessed final authority over the Church on earth.[1]

[1] The contrasts between papal and conciliar arguments have most recently and sharply been drawn by W. Ullmann, *Principles of Government and Politics in the Middle Ages* (London, 1962).

This was no new thesis in 1414, and ironically enough owed its origin in part to earlier papal ideas. In the Middle Ages generally, the Popes claimed that their summons was the essential factor for constituting a General Council, but to this principle Innocent III added the fruitful idea that such a Council had also to be representative, made up of delegates from all orders and parts of Christendom. This was his thought in convening the Fourth Lateran Council of 1215. In western Christendom more widely after 1200, democratic ideas of representative assemblies or parliaments were also explored and adopted, and conciliar doctrines flourished among the rest. But in the two centuries after 1215 they were increasingly exploited by those challenging papal arguments of authority, and what finally was stated so succinctly at Constance had been claimed during the preceding hundred years by theorists like John of Paris, Marsiglio and Occam, quite apart from Langenstein and Gelnhausen. Conciliarism meant the rejection of any unique power of the Pope as Vicar of Christ and some exponents brushed aside any further thought of papal pre-eminence; others, however, remained willing to allow the Pope an executive leadership under direction and periodic control by the Council.[1] But whatever the precise formulation, the theory generally was weak because its advocates were fighting on terrain chosen by their enemy, in papal terms and with papal arguments. They laid claim to that very same coercive, material control of the Universal Church which they denied to the Pope. They had Hus and Jerome burned for heresy just as any Pope would have done in similar circumstances, and for many, government of the Church by a Council was no more attractive than that by the Pope. In practice, too, the conciliarists were at a disadvantage, for in any likely rivalry between the Pope and themselves after Constance – and it was difficult to suppose that any pontiff would willingly accept Conciliarism – it seemed probable that one person, knowing his own mind, would eventually outwit a whole body of men, who met only infrequently in councils and whose aims would inevitably diverge. This very development was already to be seen taking shape before the end of the sessions of Constance in 1418, and it helped to leave unfulfilled the practical, detailed programme of reform.

In the decree *Frequens* issued in 1417, it was laid down that the next General Council should be held five years after the end of Constance, another seven years after that, and then further General Councils at regular intervals. In association with such provision for continuing conciliar control of affairs, various practical reforms were proposed

[1] Nicholas of Cusa argued in such moderate terms in *On Catholic Agreement*, the magisterial work on Conciliarism, issued in 1433.

or approved at Constance. Care was taken to encourage mendicant concern for rigorous life, and the Franciscans of the Observance were approved, whilst also the undertakings of lay and canonical bodies in the New Devotion were consolidated under conciliar support. The monks by contrast, it seems, ignored and were ignored by the Council, and what reforms came in their orders later were with papal support.[1] More crucially at Constance a series of eighteen proposals for papal reform was drawn up, requiring the "future Pope" to act, but only presented to Martin V after his election. These proposals aimed specifically at curbing papal centralized government, control over appointments, financial abuses, indulgences and appeals, regularizing relationships between the Pope and college of cardinals, and raising general standards of ecclesiastical life and Christian practice. The suggestions were excellent for dealing with outstanding corruption in the Church, and had they all been enacted or guaranteed before the Council disbanded, a major advance would have been made. No such result was achieved. Martin V's election in 1417 brought relief in weariness after years of work and most of the Council's delegates were unwilling for more argument. Sigismund's firm leadership at the start of the Council had been missed when he left shortly after Hus's execution in 1415, and unity among the members was lost before his return in 1417. The very device adopted to outmanoeuvre John XXIII – the grouping by "nations" – impeded progress as it became apparent that different "nations" disagreed about procedures in reform as well as in other rivalries. Quite apart from Anglo-French conflict, which brought Henry V's invasion of France and triumph at Agincourt in 1415, and made Sigismund withdraw from Constance in pursuit of attempts to reconcile the countries, there were internal differences in the Council. The Germans sought binding enactments of specific reform before any papal election, the Italians and the cardinals wanted the election first. After frustrating discussions, the latter course was followed and Martin V then was able to exploit differences in such a way as to avoid any firm decisions about reform during the remaining months of the Council's life. Seven of the eighteen points were embodied in conciliar decrees, but others were accepted by the Pope only in separate agreements with individual "nations", committing him to no overall promises. Martin's fear was of being bound by decree to the theory of papal subordination to a General Council, and he therefore avoided practical as well as ideological reform at Constance. Above all, he carefully refrained from any general confirmation of the Council's statutes, and in his separate concordats was able to prohibit all appeals from the Pope to another tribunal in

[1] Mundy, op. cit., pp. 31 f.

matters of faith and to insist that further action would be carried out under papal control.

The end of Constance therefore saw far less than victory for reform, where so much had to be left dependent upon the promises of the new Pope, rather than upon secure constitutional reorganization of the Universal Church with limited papal monarchy. Martin V's position after 1417, to be sure, was beset with all kinds of problems before any substance could be given to revived papal government from Rome, but he was a man of ability and purpose and the developments of his and his successor Eugenius IV's pontificates showed clearly how the Conciliar Movement was contained and defeated. The terms of Constance meant that Martin could not wholly avoid councils, but the body which met at Pavia in 1423, and moved on to Siena to complete its work in the following year, was poorly attended. Neither the Pope nor the cardinals took part in its proceedings, even though papal legates presided, and little was attained in the deliberations about reform, in the decrees concerning the Hussites or hopes of negotiations with the Greek Church. Pavia reaffirmed the General Council's superiority over the Pope, and decided that the next assembly should be at Basel in 1431, but Martin V was able to end its meeting abruptly and to draw the teeth of complaint about lack of reform by initiating some measures of his own concerning the Curia in 1425, without, it seems, intending to implement them.[1]

The continuing Hussite threats more generally moulded Latin Christian affairs and they thrust responsibility for action back into the Pope's hands, for he proclaimed the crusades against the Bohemians, disastrous though each venture proved to be. Martin made good use of the years between the councils to stave off constitutional reform and quietly and efficiently to begin reconstructing papal power. He was unable to escape the Council scheduled for 1431, and when this body assembled at Basel it was far more vigorous in outlook and purpose than its predecessor, if only because of the Hussite problem. The conciliarists secured Martin's authorization for his legate Cesarini to open and preside over the assembly, and the Pope's death shortly after the start of proceedings seemed to throw power completely into the Council's hands.

The cardinals elected Eugenius IV as the new Pope. He was thought to favour reform, having previously urged the meeting of the Council at Basel and bound himself, with other cardinals in the conclave, to implement precise measures in the Curia and outside if he were elected. But as Pope he acted differently, and in part through mis-

[1] See P. Partner, *The Papal State under Martin V* (London, 1958), for a scholarly appraisal of Martin's ability and work.

understandings, in part because of a genuine determination to maintain and enhance papal prerogatives, Eugenius quickly found himself at odds with Basel and even with Cesarini. The Council began by inviting the Bohemians to come to Basel on their own terms, after the final Hussite victory at Tauss in August, 1431. Eugenius's reaction was to declare the Council dissolved, but his instructions Cesarini and the others defied: they appealed to the precedent of Constance for authority and to the urgent need for negotiating peace with the Hussites, as well as to the wider tasks of reconciling France and England and carrying through much desired reform in the Church. In February, 1432, the Council reaffirmed the decrees *Sacrosancta* and *Frequens*, and the split with the Pope was deepened. For some years it seemed likely that conciliar power would triumph. The Council had the support of Sigismund, the French clergy and most of the cardinals, and until 1434 it vindicated its initiative in coping with pressing problems such as the Hussite threat and ecclesiastical abuses in annates and appointments. At the height of its influence and work, the Council of Basel comprised over five hundred members, mostly French and Germans, but including able leaders like Cesarini, Aeneas Sylvius Piccolomini and Nicholas of Cusa. The Fathers sought to avoid troubles of national divisions such as had so gravely damaged Constance, and for each problem they employed interlocking committees with mixed representation. Unhappily, however, there were fewer high-ranking ecclesiastics at Basel than at Constance, and indeed many were laymen of little standing, though not necessarily the cooks and grooms listed in abundance by Piccolomini. Few were distinguished in scholarship or leadership, and this became all too apparent after the adherence of Cusa and Piccolomini to the papal cause and Cesarini's death in 1444.

Much had been achieved at Basel by 1434, and this was acknowledged most of all with regard to the Hussites, but the years that followed saw control of events pass steadily into the hands of the Pope. Eugenius was able to outbid Basel for securing negotiations with the Greeks and in having them attend a council which he convened at Ferrara in 1438. When it moved to Florence in the following year, the Pope reached agreement with the Greek leaders for reunion of the Churches, whilst at the same period he was able to make his own settlements with the French and German kings regarding the national churches in their own countries. Basel deposed Eugenius in 1439 and elected the hermit Duke Amadeus of Savoy as Felix V, thereby creating a fresh schism. But this strengthened rather than weakened Eugenius IV, for many outside the Council judged that the leaders at Basel lacked wisdom and ability, and the Pope's other achievements left him secure against further conciliar threats. With dwindling numbers and respect, the Basel assembly persisted in session after session through the 1440's, finally moving its headquarters to Lausanne. Eugenius IV died in 1447, and following the election of his successor Nicholas V, the rump of the Council was dissolved two years later and the forlorn anti-pope Felix V given the opportunity gracefully to abdicate.

The tardy and comic conclusion of the Council of Basel, with pressure by the German king on the Fathers to end their sessions, showed plainly that the Conciliar programme, with its constitutional theories and practical reforms, had been defeated. This defeat was confirmed and completed in the following decade, first by Nicholas V who reasserted the major papal claims in practical control of the Church – the claims to reservations and annates – and then by Pius II (the erstwhile conciliarist Piccolomini) in the bull *Execrabilis* at the start of 1460. This proclamation was issued at the Congress of Mantua which the Pope had summoned in the attempt to organize a crusade against the Turks, and Pius II was acutely aware of continuing appeals for a council against papal power. The bull unequivocally repudiated all conciliar ideas of the constitutional government of the Church: as Vicar of Christ and successor of St. Peter, the Pope was declared to be unique and unchallengeable in his possession of full power for ruling the Universal Church. Appeals to any future council from the Pope were denounced as "erroneous and detestable", and the direst penalties of excommunication were set out against anyone who made, or helped to make, such appeals. No General Council met again as at Constance or Basel, and though the threat to hold such an assembly remained and was used many times in the years following, giving anxious moments to particular Popes, there was never again the comprehensive scheme of reform proposed which had inspired the earlier reformers.

The theory itself was defective in failing to advance significantly upon papalism concerning the nature of authority over the Church, but the advocates of conciliar government had many well-conceived and far-reaching proposals to reform abuses and the structure of Christian society. For a time at Basel they attained worthwhile results, but in practice as well as theory, they were never able to bring the Pope to admit his dependence upon the General Council or to determine unquestionably who could summon such a body. They never secured acceptance for any viable alternative to the papal argument that the Pope's order constituted a General Council and his authority made its canons binding. This claim was tacitly allowed in the fact that Constance assembled only at the formal invitation of John XXIII, whatever the pressure from Sigismund, whilst criticism of Pisa was generally expressed because it was convened by the cardinals. Though the later Councils of Pavia and Basel met according to the timetable laid down in *Frequens*, the Popes insisted throughout that their summons alone gave validity to any of these assemblies, and at the same time refused to approve officially any canons beyond most general, unquestioned statements of faith. In this way Pius II was able eventually to repudiate the whole conciliar theory and dismiss the work of the councils, without any effective protest. In 1478, Sixtus IV formally annulled all the decrees of Constance and logically completed the papal victory.

The positive legacy of the Conciliar Movement during the first half of the fifteenth century was intermittent and fragmentary, but negatively it had extensive and harmful results, for the Popes who set their faces against revolutionary ideas of the Church's government turned also against the general demands and needs for material reform. Conciliarism coupled together schemes of democratic, constitutional rule with programmes of practical reform of abuses; in triumphing over the theory, the Popes in consequence refused to consider overall programmes attacking corruption. Some even feared to promote a crusade because it might give opportunity for suggesting that a General Council should be called. Apart from the Fifth Lateran Council of 1512, which was convened solely for Julius II's political ends, the Popes were able to circumvent appeals for any oecumenical assembly until the first meeting of Trent in 1545. But disastrously this dogged rearguard action meant that the Popes almost as consistently refused to deal in any adequate way with the overall abuses in the Roman Church until the middle of the sixteenth century, that is to say, until after the storm of Protestant defiance had split Latin Christendom. The Popes emerging from the Conciliar episode were not predisposed to favouring drastic ideas of reform, though this was long overdue; and the particular influences in Italy that otherwise moulded their actions and guided them through the fifteenth century did not make them the more amenable to such changes.

CHAPTER VII

THE RESTORED PAPACY, ITALY AND THE RENAISSANCE

MARTIN V AND HIS SUCCESSORS DURING THE CENTURY AFTER 1417 had one paramount objective, namely, to restore as far as possible papal authority over the Church. The problems involved in such aims, however, were complex and ranged far beyond the defeat of Conciliarism, essential though that was. They tended to remain constant, even where they were partially surmounted, and in the efforts to deal with them the Papacy developed particular features in structure and tone that took it away from rather than towards fundamental reform.

The key problem facing the Popes of the fifteenth century was the very mundane one of finance, where Martin V after his election found it essential to recover lost papal revenues and to restore a balanced budget for any hope of practical independence and authority. This situation was the product of forty years' confusion in the Great Schism, which had greatly impaired the massive centralized administration of Avignon and had still more disastrously upset the financial basis upon which that organization depended. Despite the complaints of national rulers and churches and the adoption of devices (as in England) to stop papal taxation, the Avignonese Popes drew immense revenues for government and the costs of their lavish court from all over Latin Christendom. But the appearance of two competing Popes, and their rivalries through subsequent years, brought added costs in efforts to maintain two governments and courts, as well as drastic losses in total revenue for any one pontiff. The papal system of collection in different countries was largely destroyed, and in 1417 Martin V found himself with wholly inadequate funds to restore or operate curial administration on the scale that it had known before the start of the schism. His exigencies somewhat paradoxically compelled Martin's return to Rome, which was not necessarily a welcome prospect since both the city and the Papal State were in disorder. The Pope indeed only established himself at Rome in 1420, but it was in this Italian setting that he was forced through poverty to attempt to rebuild papal finances.

Recent study has shown that the reasons for this particular policy were simple.[1] Papal revenues were broadly of two kinds – "spiritual" revenues, derived from the manifold activities of the Curia in its control of appointments, annates, indulgences, and the like through all Christendom, and those "temporal", which were the profits or incomes from territorial possessions and lordships, pre-eminently in Italy in the Papal State surrounding Rome. During their residence at Avignon, the far greater proportion of the Popes' revenues came from the "spiritual" income, whilst Rome and the papal Italian lands fell into anarchy and even became financial liabilities at times. The Great Schism so seriously disrupted the "spiritual" income that in the 1420's it was only a third of its former total, and the obvious difficulty of trying immediately to restore this to any size induced the Pope to turn to Italy, where effective papal government and control could be built up for enlarging the "temporal" revenues. With Martin V, therefore, the Papacy became more Italian than ever it had been before at the very same time as its claims for universal authority and oversight were reaffirmed. What Martin started, his successors were compelled to continue in the following century. The policy was remarkably successful in financial terms, for papal income from the taxes, dues and other revenues in Italy grew proportionately and absolutely in the yearly total, even though the Popes eventually were able to exploit fresh devices for recovering "spiritual" revenues in Christendom and attain wealth beyond what the fourteenth century pontiffs had ever known. But this success was won only at the cost of far-reaching developments in the Papacy.

Curial organization was localized at Rome and in central Italy more completely than in previous centuries, and the results were generally deplorable. Venality became the hallmark of papal work at Rome, so that what had been notorious at Avignon and with Boniface IX in the sale of benefices and appointments through Christendom was extended to include every kind of office, great or small. All curial offices were formally paid for and dealt with financially by the Datary in the Apostolic Chamber or Treasury, and it became well known that a general promotion in papal appointments would be sanctioned for the moneys to be paid over by the persons thus honoured. When Alexander VI created a number of cardinals in 1500, people were scandalized not because the dignitaries bought their hats but on account of the high sums involved and the frankness of the deals. Simony was nothing new in the age. More novel, however, were the orders or bodies of officials "of St. Peter" which proliferated at Rome,

[1] P. Partner, *Papal State;* also, "The 'Budget' of the Roman Church in the Renaissance Period", in *Italian Renaissance Studies*, edited by E. F. Jacob (Cambridge, 1960), pp. 256–78.

with purely nominal functions, where individuals were really creditors of the Pope. Such officials paid for titles and then spent their time at court simply in recovering their deposits at the expense of suitors and litigants, or priests and laymen visiting Rome, who were ensnared in wishing merely to see the Pope. These parasites grew steadily in number so that by 1521, there were some two thousand in the city, representing a valuable invested capital in the Papacy of two and a half million gold florins. This systematic extension of corruption as part of the official policy for financing papal government was a well-marked feature of affairs at Rome through the fifteenth century. Ambassadors and visitors to the city repeatedly commented about the swarms of court officials who surrounded and controlled every function, making it expensive if not ruinous for all unfortunate enough to have business to transact with the Vatican. Moreover, these abuses were coupled increasingly after 1450 to the vast new resort to indulgences, dispensations and provisions in Christendom. These developments were not essentially due to papal concern with Italy, but nonetheless they helped to swell papal income. Particularly useful in these terms were the proclamations of successive Jubilees, which the Popes found so profitable that they ordered the holding of the festival once every twenty-five years – so that Jubilees took place in 1450, 1475 and 1500 – and extended their limits temporally beyond twelve months and geographically to other churches and countries outside Rome to secure the maximum sales of indulgences.

The Pope was the Bishop of Rome, but his direct rule was claimed more widely over territories that straddled central Italy and together comprised the Papal State. This authority had been made real first in the thirteenth century,[1] but had largely lapsed when the Popes moved to Avignon. Papal vicars, who were granted on lease the practical control of numerous cities and duchies in the State, tended to act independently and ignore the Pope's suzerainty. In the 1350's, Cardinal Albornoz was able to rescue something of the Pope's power at Rome and around, but this was no permanent success, and there remained a considerable task for the pontiffs after 1420 in vindicating their claims over semi-independent vicars and military adventurers. Politically and socially, the Papal State was similar to other urban powers in fifteenth-century Italy, where anarchy was contained by rivalries and alliances preserving more general stability. Italy was divided and dominated politically by the towns whose economic wealth had brought them independence from lay or ecclesiastical princes at an earlier age. But in their development, these towns were riddled by faction between social classes – the aristocracy, merchants

[1] Cf. D. P. Waley, *The Papal State in the Thirteenth Century* (London, 1961).

and proletariat – which led usually to alliances of lords and merchants or industrial magnates for controlling the government. Each town moreover fought its neighbour, individually or in shifting alliances with other cities. Freedom to indulge in petty, very local rivalries existed as no stronger power to intervene in Italy emerged until late in the fifteenth century, but something like equilibrium internally was established between five greater States – Milan, Venice, Florence, Rome and Naples – each of which dominated the lands around them and was held in league with other powers. Across this pattern strode the *condottieri*, the military adventurers of fifteenth-century Italy, who fought as professionals and used their armies as mercenaries for any ruler who would employ them for an agreed time and reward. On occasion, such captains were ready enough to found their own dynastic power, like the Visconti and Sforza of Milan, or the Montefeltri of Urbino. Relative confusion could remain as long as the general equilibrium was not upset. The Turks more than once compelled the Italians to halt their local wars and unite against a common foe, but only the intervention of France and Spain in the affairs of Italy in the 1490's ended older opportunities for intrigue and rivalry.

The Popes all too easily took their place as one of the powers competing for political and military supremacy in Italy. Their primary task was to re-establish authority in Rome and the Papal State, and no Pope escaped such preoccupation where in theory and practice alike the Apostolic See needed territorial protection for upholding curial power over the Universal Church. Successive Popes built up the central structure of government, and their State was taken as a political model by other rulers in the work of creating nationally powerful bodies. More successfully than their predecessors, the pontiffs rid Rome of domination by local noble families, such as the Orsini, Colonna, or Savelli, and they dealt ruthlessly at times with mob violence and rebellions. Eugenius IV brought the city under direct papal rule, and both Nicholas V and Pius II later dealt with particular conspiracies. Innocent VIII's reign (1484–92) was notorious as marking a return to urban chaos, where the Pope lacked ability and firmness in control. By contrast, the Romans appreciated Alexander VI's achievement in restoring order after 1492, even though later he allowed too much freedom for private vendettas in the city. Julius II (1503–13) eventually was able to complete this work of freeing Rome from political disorders and turmoil. More generally and with less success, the Popes tried to resume direct power over cities and territories in the Papal State. Their efforts brought a steady restoration of papal revenue from individual rulers and lands, most dramatically with the discovery and working of alum at Tolfa from 1456 onward, but the more permanent military conquest of the State was again only carried out by Julius II.

Beyond the boundaries of their territories, the Popes also sought to gain fresh powers, and they entered fully into the political intrigues, diplomacy and wars of the peninsula in the pursuit of papal ends. Among the rivals in Italy, Venice stood out easily as the most wealthy, able if it wished to dominate all the rest with its maritime empire and trade. But precisely because its commitments were world-wide and it was fighting the Turks, Venice refused to be drawn deeply into Italian politics, and remained happy to make alliances for keeping a balance and preventing any one State from becoming disproportionately strong. This left scope for intrigue among the rest, where the Medici in Florence – first Cosimo who died in 1464, and then his grandson Lorenzo – also endeavoured to maintain a balance of power in their own interests. At Rome the Popes covetously eyed Florence to the north and Neapolitan possessions to the south, where the Aragonese increasingly attracted the attention of many rivals to seize their inheritance. Eugenius IV and Nicholas V both had alliances with Venice, and after the Treaty of Lodi in 1454, which confirmed Francesco Sforza in control of Milan, the peninsula was divided between the Papacy and Venice on one side and Milan and Florence on the other, with Naples an unstable ally in the balance. The Spanish Pope, Calixtus III, was friendly with Naples, since he had made his own career in serving Alfonso V, but the king's death in 1458 split the Aragonese realm: John II retained Aragon and Sicily, but Naples and southern Italy passed to Alfonso's illegitimate son Ferrante, whose weakness invited the interest of everyone else in Italy and beyond. The French thought of invasion, whilst Pius II, who followed Calixtus, intrigued and fought to upset Ferrante's power, but an alliance with Milan held off such threats. Blatant political ambitions took second place to the attack on heresy during the pontificate of the Venetian Paul II (1464–71), but his successor, Sixtus IV, returned avidly to the pursuit of Italian material affairs. In a new alliance with Ferrante, he planned to isolate Florence and overthrow Lorenzo de' Medici, and gave at least tacit assent to the Pazzi conspiracy of 1478 when an unsuccessful attempt was made to murder the Florentine ruler. Lorenzo restored his position by a skilful and dramatic appeal to Ferrante under the menace of imminent Turkish assault on Italy, and the two rivals sank their differences. Sixtus tried next in 1482 to overthrow the small principality of Ferrara, but was halted by the combined efforts of Milan, Florence and Naples. The initiative slipped further from papal hands with Innocent VIII, and when Alexander VI attempted once again to exploit the Pope's position the political situation in Italy was disintegrating: Lorenzo's death in 1492 left no personality strong enough to keep affairs stable, and the rivalry between Milan and Naples opened the door to the French and Spanish to bring their armies and ambitions into the peninsula. Thereafter the Popes were severely restricted in any attempts to intrigue beyond their State, and Rome itself was finally sacked by the imperialists in 1527.

In this political pursuit, the Papacy was strategically best placed of all the powers for hopes of uniting Italy; Dante noted this at the start of the fourteenth century, Machiavelli did so again in *The Prince*. But at the same time, it had a fatal weakness in the Pope's office, and this fact decisively moulded the policies of the fifteenth-century pontiffs as Italian princes. Potentially they each possessed authority in world-wide terms to outmatch any rivals in Italy, but their office was elective, and throughout the century the Popes tried repeatedly to surmount a situation which made impossible that progressive, dynastic pursuit of territorial power seen with other rulers of the peninsula. In all the uncertainties known in holding or transmitting authority, the Medici family of Florence, the Visconti-Sforza in Milan, the Aragonese in Naples, even the Montefeltri in Urbino, all succeeded in enlarging the powers of their respective city-states through their families over two or three generations. But the Popes faced insuperable barriers to any attempt at a continuous dynastic policy, though they stubbornly tried to overcome them.

Dynasticism was nothing new in papal history and struggles went on for centuries before 1400 within the college of cardinals and between the cardinals and each individual Pope. This latter issue had its place in the development of Conciliarism, where the cardinals strove to establish a practical share in papal government and wealth and defended the constitutional theory that collectively they symbolized Christendom and should control the Church. Conciliarism as a general thesis was refuted by the Popes, but the challenge of the cardinals retained considerable force. Each time that a Pope was elected, he was able to assert his claims to divinely-granted monarchical authority and control as the Vicar of Christ, over cardinals no less than other ecclesiastics. Such prerogatives were accepted on each occasion, whatever promises were made in the conclave before an election. It proved impossible to keep Benedict XIII to his agreements once elected as Pope in 1394, but similar situations arose with Paul II, Sixtus IV, Innocent VIII and Alexander VI in the fifteenth century when election capitulations were flouted by the pontiffs newly-established in power. But on each occasion also, the Pope's death automatically thrust all issues into the melting-pot and enabled the college to act. As ecclesiastics of the Roman Church, the cardinals had been constituted in the eleventh century to exercise one vital function above all, and this they continued to do even when their wider ambitions of government were frustrated – to hold the reins of power in the Roman Church when a Pope died and to meet as a college to elect his successor. In the disputes between Popes and cardinals that went on throughout the later Middle Ages, the latter were able again and again to use their elective rôle as a weapon – their sole effective one – to disrupt dynastic ambitions and try to bind the Pope-to-be by election promises. And though the capitulations were generally repudiated after the conclave, the new Pope's task was always politically daunting, since invariably he was of a different family from his immediate predecessor, and had usually to dismantle an existing dynastic structure in papal affairs before starting again at the bottom to build up his own position.

In the century following Martin V's election, therefore, individual Popes in turn sought to advance their families like other Italian rulers, and had their work partially or wholly shipwrecked at their deaths. The same families indeed more than once occupied St. Peter's throne – the Colonna, Barbi, Piccolomini, Rovere, Borgia and Medici – but never where a Pope was related to his immediate predecessor. Martin V belonged to the Colonna dynasty and had the primary task of recovering any semblance of power at Rome after Constance, but he managed to staff the government so well with his relations that Eugenius IV afterward was harassed for years. Calixtus III came from the Spanish Borgia family and systematically brought his nephews into the hub of Roman affairs after 1455; two were made cardinals, a third was created the commander of the papal army, and many lesser relatives gained employment throughout the curial organization. But Calixtus's early death in 1458 was the signal for popular anti-Borgia feeling at Rome that ended any immediate dynastic hopes. The general died of heart failure in his flight and Cardinal Rodrigo Borgia, who was already head of the papal administration as Vice-Chancellor, judged it best to make his peace with the new Pope, Pius II; his patience was rewarded much later when he became Alexander VI in 1492. Both Pius II and Paul II looked after their nephews in papal government less ostentatiously than had Calixtus III, but Sixtus IV blazed a yet more lurid trail in his determination to use his family to the full for dominating Italy and leaving the Rovere in power after his death. Two nephews were made cardinals, two more were married into leading Italian noble families, but yet the machinations and hopes of Sixtus's reign were disastrously interrupted by his death in 1484, and it was only nearly twenty years later that one of the nephews became Pope as Julius II. Innocent VIII lacked the ability to exploit family fortunes like his predecessor, though he advanced his relations in numerous offices and had the distinction of being the first Pope openly to acknowledge his sons. In this Alexander VI copied him, but otherwise the second Borgia Pope made the most logical and cold-blooded attempt to create a dynastic papal power, albeit unsuccessfully. He used four of his children to extend control over the Papacy and to link it and his family through marriage and public offices with other rulers in Spain and France, no less than in Italy. In addition, he promoted as many of his relatives as he dare to the college of cardinals. Yet once again death destroyed such hopes for consolidating a more permanent political structure in the Papacy, and after 1503 there was neither the opportunity nor the purpose to attempt this solution. Julius II's work lacked family complications and was confined to the Papal State insofar as it lasted.

Their Italian preoccupations thus led the Popes after Constance steadily into deeper and deeper political and dynastic schemes of very localized nature. Though this development can be understood it cannot easily be excused, and at the time, the criticisms made about papal corruption were not answered. Individual pontiffs were able administrators and sincerely concerned to ensure that curial machinery ran smoothly and with efficiency, but this was concern to make a corrupt system work, not to introduce genuine reforms in meeting wider complaints. Meanwhile, the fact that they were Italian princes meant their involvement in all that engaged the peninsula in the fifteenth century – the great age of the Renaissance. Two contrasting movements in particular – Italian spiritual life and the pursuit of Renaissance ideals – demanded reactions from the Popes, and how they responded further illustrates what was weak or wrong in their work.

Italy knew a popular religious life that flourished and swept through the country every generation irrespective of political troubles and before the luxury and corruption of the later fifteenth century came to give specific causes for condemnation. The ideals held out gained strength from the Black Death and behind that from the whole Franciscan movement, with particular stress upon poverty and service. As early as the time of Catherine of Siena, a Franciscan was given permission by Gregory XI in 1373 to found a convent of strict observance – according to the rule of Francis – and though the community took long to grow, yet the number of reformed convents was large enough by 1415 for the Council to legislate in protecting the Observants against the Conventuals in the order. The Observant movement brought renewal of spiritual life and purpose among Franciscans who were all too justly criticized for laxity and wealth, and the man who gave inspiration to the development was Bernardino of Siena, the greatest preacher of his age. Bernardino, born in 1380, became a friar in a strict convent, and, inspired by the Dominican Vincent Ferrer in his evangelistic work in North Italy, he gave himself to preaching after 1404. His tours of the following forty years through Italy captured the hearts of the people, as he sought to turn them back to simple faith and Christian living. His preaching was compelling and balanced, and avoided the extremes of apocalyptic vision and the plea for asceticism. For Bernardino the rules of the Observance did not lead to the excesses found by some of the earlier Fraticelli, and he sought more widely to remedy the faults in greed, illiteracy and worldliness so frequently alleged against the mendicants. He refused bishoprics on three occasions, preferring to stay in control of the Observants, first in Tuscany and Umbria, then over all Italy after 1438, and he was joined by other great preachers like John of Capistrano and Albert of Sarteano.

The Observance did not remain confined to Italy; at Bernardino's death there were over four thousand reformed convents, and the movement spread more extensively through France, Spain and Germany, and to other mendicant orders. In Italy itself, an even stricter group of hermit Franciscans was started by Francis of Paolo in 1436, and the fame of the leader grew so great that later in 1483 the French king Louis XI sent personally for him to come to France. Eventually in 1493 Francis had his houses constituted as the new Order of Minims, with membership that included other Mediterranean countries and Germany as well as Italy. The Popes were not unaware of these tides of enthusiasm, popular and ascetic: Martin V was prominent in trying to reconcile Franciscan Conventuals and Observants with a new rule in 1430, whilst Eugenius IV was himself an Observant and greatly encouraged Bernardino and Capistrano in their missions and more directly at times in papal service. Pius II was deeply influenced by Bernardino as a young man, and both Francis of Paolo and Catherine of Genoa in the second half of the century were respected and listened to at the papal court. But how far the Popes more generally responded even to spiritual needs in Italy is doubtful, and Sixtus IV, who was General of the Franciscan Order before his papal election, showed what could be abandoned in the material pursuits of power, even where he tried to bring internal peace in the Order. Their other interests allowed the Popes little room to embrace and direct those movements for religious reform which had an important place in Italy in the fifteenth century.

Far more plainly the Roman pontiffs were moulded as Italian princes of the Renaissance in its ideals and achievements. It is impossible to give any short, satisfactory definition of such a kaleidoscopic movement as the Renaissance, but it can be isolated primarily as an Italian phenomenon which only in its later phases spread more widely through Europe, undergoing important modifications in the process. Despite interdependence of Italian and non-Italian ideas and developments, the Renaissance in Italy can be defined in recognizable terms that found their clearest expression in the fifteenth century. Central to these features was the reappraising of Man as of unique value in the world: Man was the measure of all things as in Greece, in his work and in his control of Nature, and he was created by God. This ideal was broadly comprised under the title of Humanism, and it developed in the context of all kinds of influences from centuries before 1400 – urban economic prosperity, political independence, and the opportunities for the individual to make his personal fortune and gain rank and power within a lifetime, all helped to foster the spirit of enterprise, self-sufficiency and pride characteristic of Renaissance outlooks. The ideas and the particular pursuits to which they gave rise took long to mature, but from the start of the fourteenth century Dante reflected newer interests in and appreciation of the classical world. He gave attention to ancient Rome, even where much of his attitude was still conservative. Petrarch, who died in 1374, more completely epitomized early Renaissance reactions in his adulation of writers like Cicero or Livy and his desire to recreate in spirit what the Roman age was like since he could not live in it. His interests he related very closely still to the Christian framework of thought, but Boccaccio was more open in applauding pagan virtues and copied classical themes and ideals in his *Decameron*. Before the close of the fourteenth century, an extensive cult of letters was already flourishing in Italy, and for a time it also knew encouragement and support at Avignon and in Bohemia at the court of Charles IV.

This attachment to the classical past reached out in enthusiasm as well for study of the language and writings of the Greeks who seemed to be closer in spirit to the Italians of 1400 than their own immediate forebears. In Latin Christendom, both the Greek language and many of the writings of Plato and Aristotle were known in different centres through the later Middle Ages, but the Italian scholars at the close of the fourteenth century discovered such knowledge as a breath-taking key to unlock new and untold treasures. When the Byzantine ambassador, Manuel Chrysoloras, came to the West from Constantinople to seek help against the Turks in 1396, he was persuaded to stay on teaching in Florence so that the Greek language and writings could be more widely known. Through him, the young Humanist, Leonardo Bruni, was inspired to take up Greek studies, and he later attained eminence both for his translation of so many Greek classics into Latin and as Chancellor of Florence under Cosimo de' Medici. Such reverence for the classics and the past grew in various ways through the fifteenth century in Italy and was mirrored most powerfully in painting, sculpture and building. These developments had their early origins in the work of Giotto of Florence, who was contemporary with Dante and set the pattern for observing and painting Nature as a real world in his Christian subjects, rather than in traditional, wholly stylized forms. He was followed by nobody of similar ideas or genius until the start of the fifteenth century, when the full tide of Renaissance art flowed in, with the delight in naturalism, man, perspective and colour, and the schools of painting in cities like Siena, Venice and Milan as well as Florence. Renaissance painters and sculptors continued to draw their themes predominantly from Christian history, above all from the Passion of Christ, but their debt increasingly was to classical, non-Christian forms and interest in the natural world rather than the supernatural. To an ever-growing extent, they copied what they saw as beautiful in itself rather than as the symbol or vehicle of expression of the Christian faith. Individual wealth and patronage made possible the artistic and cultural achievements of the movement, and the great families of the cities added politically to their prestige at the same time as they beautified their surroundings in employing men like Donatello, Fra Angelico, Botticelli, Leonardo da Vinci or Michelangelo.

Beyond these primary interests there developed more positive attitudes in thought and philosophy where study of Greek ideals inspired widespread discussion and formulation of principles for education and Christian argument. Guarino of Verona (died 1460) taught and worked out his theories of education in Ferrara, and his pupil, Vittorino da Feltre, carried them further in instructing the children of the Gonzaga family at Mantua. Their concern was with an all-round discipline for developing personalities to the full in culture, manners and devotion to basically Christian principles; and their ideals were nurtured at Urbino, which was made by Federigo the great cultural centre of Italy in the latter part of the fifteenth century. There Castiglione developed his talents and placed the setting of *The Courtier* at the start of the sixteenth century, giving in that work full expression to the ideals of Renaissance education and training. Meanwhile, an advanced intellectual enterprise was started in Florence under the patronage of Cosimo and with the inspiration of Gemistos Pletho, one of the Greek delegates to the Council of Florence in 1439. The aim was to have a centre of Platonic studies, and Marsiglio Ficino was trained under Vittorino's system eventually to lead such studies. At the age of twenty-nine, Ficino was given a house and manuscripts by Cosimo in 1462, and thereafter he dedicated himself to work and teaching about Plato until his death in 1499. A distinguished and cosmopolitan group gathered round Ficino at the Academy, and Medici patronage remained constant, but most brilliant and disturbing in his speculations was Pico della Mirandola who came to Florence at the age of twenty-one in 1484. He believed that Plato and Christianity could be reconciled with the aid of Jewish teaching, and to show this he learned Hebrew and all that he could of writings like the *Cabbala*. In 1486, he published a long series of conclusions which he was prepared to defend, but was condemned by the Pope and imprisoned in France whither he fled in 1488. Following his release on Lorenzo's intercession, Pico returned to Florence where he continued in his studies and wide-ranging speculations during the last six years of his life. Under the influence of Savonarola, he renounced the world on his death-bed and adopted the Dominican habit.

Alongside these developments, there spread more corrupting ideas and practices, with murder, immorality and a general breakdown in traditional standards of behaviour. Fifteenth-century Italian politics were treacherous, but they were also accompanied by social changes that directly challenged Christian ideals. Two features stand out and can be taken as illustrative of the tone of Italian Renaissance society – illegitimacy and respectable prostitution. In that age, illegitimacy was counted as no impossible bar to social standing or office, and though such an attitude was enlightened, the situation which made it necessary was reprehensible. Moreover, it was in Italy generally after 1450 that the title of "courtesan" came into use to describe wealthy prostitutes who were accorded high social standing at the courts of different princes, notably in Venice, Florence and Naples.

As Renaissance rulers, the Popes were deeply influenced by Quattrocento culture quite apart from sharing in the political attitudes and rivalries of Italy. From the fourteenth century they inherited the Avignonese traditions of luxury and splendour, but in the end they far surpassed such achievements at Rome. For a period this development was hardly evident, since the city was in disorder and impoverished, and both Martin V and Eugenius IV were fully occupied in trying to restore papal power in central Italy. Nevertheless, in and around the Papacy, Renaissance influences made themselves strongly felt before 1450 with the challenge to many Christian assumptions and conclusions. Classicists like Poggio were contemptuous of ecclesiastical Latin, whilst more widely in the study of texts Humanistic scholars queried Christian sources, particularly some of those buttressing papal claims. Lorenzo Valla developed principles of textual and Biblical criticism, and in 1440 demonstrated that the Donation of Constantine – the grant of territory and local power to Sylvester I allegedly made by Constantine in the fourth century – was a forgery of much later date; and about the same period, both Piccolomini and the English bishop Reginald Pecock similarly rejected the Donation in papal argument. Somewhat later, Nicholas of Cusa in 1464 declared that the Isidorian Decretals, upon which so many other papal theories stood, were ninth-century forgeries, not a genuine collection made before 600 by Isidore of Seville; and the value of these decretals was impugned as strongly by Cardinal Torquemada, although he was prepared to champion papal authority afresh to defeat Conciliarism. Such criticisms, indeed, did not lead to any fundamental abatement of claims by the Popes, and the enquiring attitudes of Humanistic study led elsewhere later into the work of Erasmus and other Christian Humanists at the start of the sixteenth century. There was some truth in Piccolomini's claim that, on becoming Pope, he gave up a life of Renaissance luxury for a more austere religious pursuit, but his Humanism he also directed into the uncompromising rejection of Conciliarism in the bull of 1460.

By that date, however, Renaissance interests were already flourishing at Rome, and Nicholas V is generally regarded as the Pope who deliberately embraced the movement and brought it into the Papacy. It was clear by the middle of the century that the Popes could no longer ignore the Renaissance development as completely as they had hitherto tended to do; its disturbing social effects and challenges to Christian morals were obvious in Italian life around. The Popes could only oppose or accept such changes, and Nicholas chose the latter course with the genuine aim, it seems, of capturing the movement for Christianity and exploiting the enthusiasms in learning and culture for Christian ends, rather than permit a reviving paganism to harm the Church. Events, it can be judged, worked out differently, even if all was not to be condemned in Renaissance activity. Nicholas was the patron of artists like Fra Angelico and sculptors such as Alberti, and he appointed Valla as a papal secretary to work with other scholars – Poggio, Filelfo, George of Trebizond – in collecting, editing and translating many Greek works into Latin. He rebuilt in part the Vatican Palace and Library, stocking the latter with classical writings for study, whilst more widely he restored older churches and began building new in Rome. Nicholas's own tastes were very liberal, and on this account he incurred criticism in reading such scurrilous books as Filelfo's *Satires*, which he defended for their style and wit. Where Nicholas led the way, later Popes and cardinals generally followed, with their patronage of art and letters and in their building of splendid palaces and monuments in Rome. Exceptions there naturally were to such interests, and these included Calixtus III who immediately followed Nicholas in 1455. Calixtus was an austere Spaniard, and he enraged popular opinion in Rome by rejecting Renaissance aims and splendour; he dismissed all the Humanists, apart from Valla, sold Vatican treasures and even stripped the library doors of their gold leaf in order to finance his crusading ventures. His faults lay, as has been seen, in his dynasticism. The Venetian Paul II later was sweeping in condemning luxury and corruption in Renaissance life and refused to allow the Humanists to continue in their literary studies, but he nevertheless stood out as a patron of architecture and an art collector, leaving the magnificent Palace of St. Mark as the monument of his interests and achievement. More generally the Popes followed similar paths in building, commissioning works of sculpture and painting, writing and poetry, to beautify Rome, whilst wealthy cardinals such as d'Estouteville, Rodrigo Borgia or de la Grolaye (who commissioned Michelangelo's famous Pietà), vied with their colleagues in spending lavishly to built their own palaces and churches. Alexander VI is said to have used the first supplies of gold brought back by Columbus from the New World in 1494 to decorate the roof of the Church of Santa Maria Maggiore in Rome. But the climax in this development only came with Julius II in the sixteenth century when the Pope had Michelangelo complete the internal decorations of the Sistine Chapel (commenced earlier by Sixtus IV), and in 1506 began the building of the new Basilica of St. Peter.

In this manner, Rome became one of the great Italian Renaissance cities, perhaps the greatest in the full tide of the movement, where Florence had been supreme in an earlier stage. By some it has been reckoned that the finest papal achievement in the age was to transform a city of poverty, squalor and disorder, such as Rome had been through the centuries before 1400, into a leading cultural and artistic centre in Christendom by the early sixteenth century. But in all this there was a darker side to be condemned, quite apart from any general criticism at such material preoccupation amongst those who claimed to rule the Church. The Papacy came to share in the corruption and lax attitudes of Renaissance society no less than in higher cultural aims. So often politically corrupt as Italian princes, the Popes frequently became morally corrupt as well or sanctioned practices which accorded ill with their assertions of spiritual leadership. Some stood apart in their attempts to keep high standards: Pius II was renowned for changing his mode of life, Paul II was exemplary in his attitudes and behaviour. But otherwise the Popes became too tolerant in accepting Renaissance practices. Apart from papal nepotism and the open acknowledgement of mistresses by pontiffs, it was significant that courtesans had become so numerous and wealthy in Rome by the

1480's that Sixtus IV profitably taxed the profession, and in the following decade they comprised seven per cent of the city's population. It was little wonder therefore that pilgrims who came to Rome for the Jubilees of 1450, 1475 and 1500 were often astonished at what they saw, and expressed disgust at corruption in the official court and general social life, which was frankly pagan and encouraged by the Popes.

Whether through necessity or choice, the Roman pontiffs of the fifteenth century became all too completely imbued with Renaissance ideals, in politics and moral issues alike. As an institution the Papacy became patently Italian and Mediterranean and increasingly lost its close ties with other peoples. It is noteworthy that in the age Cusa was possibly one of the last North European members of the Curia, certainly the only influential one.[1] But the Popes' involvement in the Renaissance was deeper and even more disastrous where it became clear to many before 1500 that so far from capturing and leading the movement for Christianity, they had become its prisoners. The Popes were too obviously of the world as well as in it, and the discrepancy was glaring between their claims to universal authority over the Church as Vicars of Christ and what they did as rulers of a petty Italian State. Criticism became loud and was sharply crystallized in the turmoil of Savonarola's career. Yet for years after the defeat of Conciliarism, the Popes remained largely untroubled, able indeed to foil further suggestions of action and to make their office more splendid than ever before. That they could do this was chiefly because national rulers were confirming control of their own churches apart from effective papal authority and did not worry about it. But at the same time the Popes continued to retain no little support and they did not forget all responsibilities in their work. Outside Italy in the fifteenth century, Christendom had contact with a still wider world and other spiritual currents flowed through the Church. Such features help to show more fully the Papacy's rôle at the time and to account for the fact that the Popes could for long avoid fundamental challenge to their positions.

[1] Cf. Mundy, op. cit., p. 47; and J. P. Dolan, editor, *Unity and Reform: Selected Writings of Nicholas de Cusa* (Notre Dame, 1962), p. 39.

CHAPTER VIII

CHRISTENDOM AND THE NON-CHRISTIAN WORLD

FOR MOST OF THE FOURTEENTH AND FIFTEENTH CENTURIES, Christendom was divided into two communions, where the Pope's headship reached over the Latin Church, and the Eastern Orthodox bodies recognized the Patriarch of Constantinople as preeminent. And though this division appeared to be of decreasing consequence in an age when the Byzantine Empire was finally overthrown with Constantinople's capture by the Turks in 1453, relations between the Churches absorbed, and continued to absorb, the attention of Latin Christians. The ideal of a crusade remained to stimulate schemes for aiding hard-pressed brethren, and the Orthodox Churches were not all brought under Turkish control with the Ottoman advance. Western Europe was not closed to wider influences or responsibilities in Christian terms, and despite the internal problems of reform and government, its leaders continued to attend to wider religious issues outside the lands obedient to the Pope.

These developments were generally disadvantageous to the cause of Christianity, since from about 1300 to the early sixteenth century there was the steady contraction of faith in one part of the world, which was offset only by the initial steps of an expansion that took the Latin belief to new lands and continents. Where European Christians looked eastward to Asia, or even the eastern Mediterranean, their focus was progressively narrowed by Ottoman attack to the waging of wars against the infidel, first to help Constantinople, then more directly to defend the Latin world itself against the assaults of the Turks. This development contrasted markedly with the earlier missionary expansion of the Franciscans and Dominicans, who had travelled through Asia in the thirteenth century and established their own centres alongside the Russian Orthodox churches and more widely-scattered Nestorian bodies of the Mongol Empire. Such expansion with communications and exchange of knowledge across the countries of Asia to China was brought to a decisive end in the fourteenth century for two main reasons – the wide resurgence of Islam and the Black Death. The Frankish crusaders were driven from Acre, their last stronghold in Syria, in 1291 by the Turks who became champions of a more intolerant Islam; they were joined by the Mongols after 1295 in the adoption of the same faith. Individual khans as Moslems were not necessarily unfavourable to Christian churches or missionaries, and for a period in the fourteenth century the Nestorian communities expanded in China,[1] and Roman missionaries remained in central Asia until 1362.[2] But Tamerlane's accession to power in 1363 and his gradual conquest of the Mongol world cut off Christian activity across the continent, for apart from being generally ruthless in subduing his enemies, he was also a fanatical Mohammedan and obliterated Nestorian and other Christian churches in Asia. Added to this was the disruption of life and economy brought by the Black Death from the 1340's onward which affected the world east of Europe no less than Christendom itself. For over a century, the organization and missions of the friars in Asia were halted, even though they continued active elsewhere in north-west Africa.

Turkish attacks and conquests brought the collapse of Byzantium, which never reached far beyond Constantinople in the two centuries following the overthrow of the short-lived Latin Empire in 1261. The city remained imposing and Christian, but outside its walls its empire was only ever fragmentary. By contrast, the Turks were formidable, and when the Seljuk dynasty lost control in 1299 under Mongol attack, a new leader – Othman – emerged in Asia Minor, and his own State was well established at his death in 1326. It was these Ottoman Turks that conquered at the expense of Christendom through the following centuries. As early as 1308 they set foot in Europe, but more permanently they subdued all Asia Minor in the first half of the fourteenth century before landing on European territory again in 1352; Gallipoli fell in 1354 and eleven years later they made Adrianople their capital. Constantinople was surrounded, if impossible to take. Thereafter the Turks pressed on into the Balkans, successively overwhelming the Serbs at Kossovo in 1389 and the Bulgarians in 1393. Serbia remained in dependent alliance upon the Turks but Bulgaria was occupied and the Greek churches there were tolerated only as far as the sultan wished. In 1396 the Turks won the battle of Nicopolis against the Hungarians and their allies, but Hungary under Sigismund stayed independent and in the forefront of continuing resistance. Further to the north, the countries of Poland and Lithuania were united dynastically in 1386 when Jagiellon accepted Christianity for the Lithuanians; he became King of Poland as Ladislas II and relinquished the Duchy of Lithuania to his cousin, Witold. Both

[1] N. Zernov, *Eastern Christendom* (London, 1961), p. 121.

[2] K. S. Latourette, *A History of the Expansion of Christianity*, Vol. II (London, 1939), pp. 337 f.

Ladislas II and Witold were long-lived, and their States played important rôles as Christian and Orthodox barriers to aid the defence against the Ottomans into the fifteenth century. But Sultan Bajazet I brought the eastern Mediterranean largely under his control and left Constantinople so isolated that in 1400 its fall appeared imminent. The city was besieged two years later but was saved as Bajazet himself had to meet Tamerlane's Mongol assault and suffered defeat and capture at Ankara in 1403. Constantinople was again besieged in 1411 and 1422, on each occasion escaping capture because of dynastic struggles in the Ottoman State, and in the end it only fell in 1453 after a long but inevitably successful assault by Mohammed II.

These developments did not take place without profound repercussions in Christian Europe, even though they did not all threaten particular countries. They provoked response in two ways – first, in the continuing attempt to mount crusades, and secondly, in concern to bring reunion of the Latin and Greek Churches so as to combine resistance to the Turks. The two issues were closely interwoven, for the relations of the Latin and Greek worlds were at stake in both, but the crusade and the crusading ideal extended beyond preoccupation with the defence of Constantinople. There is much truth in the argument that the crusades had lost their spirit and force as well as their connection with the Holy Land before the close of the thirteenth century – national and commercial motives had come to dictate largely what was done, the crusade itself had been used against the Pope's political enemies and heretical Albigensians within Christendom, and Acre had fallen in 1291. But in the more general terms of a Christian war against Islam, the ideal stubbornly persisted and retained its appeal, cynical though Europeans could be in considering or ignoring it. In the twelfth century the crusades had above all given expression to the religious unity of medieval Christendom, and they became increasingly impossible to conduct as that unity vanished. Yet as early as the Second Crusade of 1147 the ideal was disintegrating, whilst in 1500 there still remained some response to the call for such a venture by Alexander VI.[1]

Though Syria no longer remained in Christian hands in the fourteenth century, there were constant efforts to stem Turkish advance and to bring aid to Constantinople. The Knights of St. John took possession of Rhodes in 1310 and used it as their bastion for expeditions against the Turks for over two hundred years. Despite their materialistic pursuits the Avignonese Popes often showed deep concern for organizing a crusade. John XXII failed in his hopes of engaging the French

[1] A. S. Atiyah, *The Crusade in the Later Middle Ages* (London, 1938), shows how important crusading ideas and actions remained after the thirteenth century.

nobility *en masse* in an expedition, where the Hundred Years' War quickly absorbed the interests of England and France, but Clement VI was able to achieve more success in aiding the capture of Smyrna in 1344 in alliance with Venice, the Hospitallers and Cyprus. This foothold was only lost to Tamerlane in his brief but extensive sweep into Asia Minor at the start of the following century. In the 1360's, Peter I of Cyprus and his Chancellor de Mézières campaigned for a combined assault on the Turks, and though there was no general response the king terrorized the coasts of Syria and Egypt until his assassination in 1369. De Mézières thereafter sought by himself to bring united Christian action to stem Ottoman threats, but it was only in the closing years of the century that the attempt was made at such an enterprise. Under pressure from Turkish attacks in the Balkans where only Montenegro and Ragusa remained free, Boniface IX preached a crusade in 1394, and a combined force of Hungarian, French, German, English and other knights under King Sigismund of Hungary marched to fight the Turks. In the ensuing battle of Nicopolis in 1396 the Christians were overwhelmingly defeated, and the calamity was seen as a great blow in religious terms; chroniclers spoke of a hundred thousand men in each army when in fact the numbers were only a tenth of these estimates. Sigismund was fortunate to escape to Constantinople and thence back to western Europe, whilst many French nobles, including the son of the Duke of Burgundy, were captured and later ransomed from Bajazet.

Yet Nicopolis revealed how confused issues had become: the Greeks would not join with the crusading army from the West, Venice was careful not to upset its commercial relations with the Turks, and Bajazet's force contained not only Janissaries – the sons of Christians converted to Islam and trained up as a special fighting group – but also in alliance the Christian Serbs, whose action in the battle probably won the day. The ideal, however, remained in part, and when the Byzantine Emperor Manuel II in 1399 visited Western countries in a desperate bid to recruit help, he did not go completely unrewarded. The great French knight Boucicaut, ransomed from Nicopolis, returned with twelve hundred French men-at-arms to Constantinople and served the cause of Byzantium well for a year. Longer reprieve for the city, however, came through Tamerlane's victory, whilst increasingly the appeal for a crusade met response only as rulers and countries themselves were directly threatened. Popes and councils alike remained active in efforts to counter the Turkish menace at any point, but too often the answer to a summons was piecemeal. Moreover, in the years leading to the fall of Constantinople, the issue of a crusade was further confused by the attempts to reunite the Churches.

Developments before 1300 had left the Latin and Greek Churches split over doctrine and personalities, but in addition there was on both sides a legacy of justifiable distrust. The extreme pressure of circumstances in the century before 1453 did not suffice to break down these attitudes, though the question of reunion was seriously raised more than once. In Latin Christendom the Great Schism made leaders ponder deeply the older schism with the East and ask if that could not be healed; but in Constantinople the Greeks seemed rarely sincere for renewed unity beyond what could be gained in immediate political and military advantages in any agreement. Every approach that they made contained reservations to enable them to repudiate settlements if necessary, and proposals that were accepted by Greek envoys were invariably rejected in Constantinople. It must be noted, however, that the Popes on their side never offered terms conceding any points of value to the East. Views about authority differed radically – the Popes were prepared only for the subordination of Greek ecclesiastical rulers to their supreme Petrine authority, the Orthodox leaders sought in reunion for recognition that the great churches were all independent, even if acknowledging a papal pre-eminence in the succession to St. Peter at Rome. Between these two attitudes there could be no lasting compromise, as events plainly showed, but the Conciliar episode had some importance in developments. The reunion negotiated in 1274 had been quickly rejected by the leaders at Constantinople, but in 1356, Emperor John V found himself in such straits from Turkish attack that he visited the West to make a treaty with Innocent VI. He undertook a second visit in 1365 to Urban V at Rome, and on this occasion made a personal submission to the Pope and the Latin Church. Although John's actions were those of an Emperor, not a Patriarch, his authority in the Byzantine Church was paramount and a grave view was taken of what he had done. The Church leaders in Constantinople refused to accept the Emperor's decision, nor did anything come of papal appeals for aid to Byzantium at this juncture. Suggestions repeatedly made for a General Council of West and East always foundered on the fact that the Popes insisted that the Lyons Council of 1274 had been universal and had negotiated reunion, whilst the Greeks as adamantly denied its oecumenical character since only their envoys had attended.

The circumstances, however, which drove Manuel II personally to tour the West at the close of the century stimulated fresh discussion about reunion. Wycliffe had castigated the schism of West and East as one of the greatest faults in the Church, and the Lollards took the opportunity of Manuel's brief appearance in England to cite (somewhat in ignorance) Eastern organization and practice as purer than those of Rome. But concern for reunion was more widespread and was fed by the election of the Greek Pope Alexander V at Pisa in 1409. Alexander's election was welcomed by the Eastern Emperor as by other leaders, and though his early death cut short immediate hopes, interest remained: the Greeks took note of conciliar developments, whilst the Lithuanian and Polish rulers made their own moves to unite communions. Embassies of the Greek Church went to Constance in 1415 and were honoured in the Council's proceedings, but nothing came of their participation. It seems likely that they were disillusioned at the discord in the Council which made them the more willing subsequently to negotiate for some agreement with the Pope. Manuel allowed discussions to go on with Martin V for a time, but his aim was political, to impress the Turks with his potential allies, and in 1425 he made a treaty with the sultan himself to gain temporary security for Constantinople. But the years following saw more genuine attempts in different quarters to reunite the Churches. So seriously were Turkish threats to Constantinople appreciated in 1429 that Witold of Lithuania convened a conference at Lutsk, which was attended by the German Emperor Sigismund and Ladislas II of Poland as well as by representatives from all the different churches. Some of the Greek leaders, notably Bessarion, the Archbishop of Nicaea, and Isidore, the Metropolitan of Moscow, made sincere efforts towards a compromise in other approaches. But no agreements were made, and more decisive steps were only taken in the West in the rivalry of Eugenius IV and the conciliarists at Basel after 1431.

Both Pope and Council wanted the Greeks to negotiate with them separately in these circumstances, and ironically enough the fateful decision of the Orthodox leaders to accept Eugenius IV's invitation in 1437 was made because they were prepared to go to Italy but not as far as Basel. Their choice was crucial both for hopes of reunion and for papal victory over a discredited Council. Eugenius convened his assembly at Ferrara in January, 1438, but because of the plague it soon moved to Florence where its work was completed in the following year. The Council of Florence fully represented Greek as well as papal leadership, and apart from Isidore and Bessarion, envoys came from the Patriarchs of Alexandria, Antioch and Jerusalem. The Roman delegation was led by Cesarini who worked carefully to reach agreement with Bessarion and Isidore. A Formula of Concord was produced and signed on five main issues in July, 1439, but it revealed too complete an acceptance of papal principles for any hope of satisfying all the Orthodox leaders. Doctrinally, the Greeks assented to the *filioque* clause in the creed, that is, that the Holy Spirit proceeds from the Father *and* the Son, but it seems that the Eastern leaders did not understand the Latin scholastic formulations in the arguments beforehand. Both sides agreed on their diverging practices and views about the bread of the Eucharist, the words of consecration and Purgatory. But most ominously the Greeks accepted a formula declaring papal supremacy, with the proviso that patriarchal privileges should remain unimpaired. "We recognize," they stated, "the Pope as Sovereign Pontiff, Vice-Regent and Vicar of Christ, Shepherd of all Christians, and Ruler of the Churches of God," but their concern was to preserve their own independence from papal power, and this was not what the Pope's agents meant. In fact, the agreement at Florence, which also incorporated unions with the Armenians and Jacobites, was notable chiefly for strengthening Eugenius IV's hand against Basel, and, for their part in producing the Formula, both Bessarion and Isidore were created cardinals. Even with qualified reading, it appeared a hollow capitulation by the Greeks, made out of dire necessity by the Emperor and the Patriarch, and some of the delegates at Florence refused to sign.

When the Greeks returned to Constantinople, popular resentment against the terms was plain, but the Emperor John VIII insisted on clinging to them and obedience to Rome. His hope was in papal promises of aid which Eugenius IV honoured by preaching a fresh crusade in 1443. The expedition which marched against the Turks was led by Cesarini, the able general John Hunyadi of Transylvania, and young King Ladislas III of Poland, who had succeeded his father in 1434 and had also been elected to the Hungarian throne in 1440. The crusading army gained a resounding victory over the Turks who agreed to a truce of ten years, but Cesarini broke the peace on the pretext that no terms could be kept with the infidel. In renewed fighting, it was the Turks who triumphed at Varna in 1444, and both Cesarini and Ladislas were among those killed in the rout. Thereafter the path was left open for the sultan to take Constantinople when he so desired. John VIII's death in 1448 did not end the unpopular union, for his successor Constantine XI still hoped for military aid against the Turks. The city was rent by factions that reached their climax at the end of 1452 when it was besieged and close to surrender. The Emperor had the union proclaimed and the Roman Mass celebrated in the Basilica of St. Sophia, but the population refused thereafter to worship in the church as a profaned building until the very moment of the city's fall in the following May. Constantine XI died fighting in the final Turkish assault, but the union was not preserved; many of the Greeks in Constantinople spoke openly of their preference for rule by the Turks to that of the Pope, and saw in their city's ruin God's just punishment for treachery by the Emperor and the Patriarch.

The capture of Constantinople by the Turks in 1453 was in some respects not so important or decisive as has sometimes been judged. The catastrophe only resulted in additions of Greek knowledge and manuscripts in the Latin West where classical interests were already long-established, whilst politically, the city had for several decades rested *en prise* to the Turks, and western Europeans showed little consistent interest in maintaining Constantinople as a bastion. In the developments, both Venice – which judiciously betrayed its commitments at Varna and in 1453 – and the Popes were prepared to accommodate themselves to the Turks on different occasions. But in religious terms, the event was deeply significant. It completed the rupture in attempts to frame any reunion of Rome and the Orthodox Church, and the consequences flowing from this were far-reaching. Extinction of an independent Patriarchate of Constantinople and of a free Orthodox Church more widely through the Balkans brought particular hardships to Christians there, and positively opened the way for the Russian Church to assume leadership of these communions. Mohammed II and the Turks generally were relatively kind in treating the Orthodox since they recognized them, with the Jews, as "people of the Book". As already in Bulgaria and Serbia, they allowed them to continue practising their religion, though with hindrances involving exclusion from citizenship. The Christians in Constantinople were divided by their new masters according to their confession – Greek Orthodox, Coptic, Armenian, Nestorian – and each was allowed a hierarch approved by the sultan to govern them. In this way, the Patriarch of Constantinople continued in office as the only officially recognized spiritual ruler of the Orthodox, and other leaders were subordinated to him. But the situation for Christians was precarious, for no new churches were allowed to be built and the boys of Christian families were taken away for conversion to Islam and training as Janissaries after the age of eight.[1] Yet the Turkish treatment had its appeal, not least of all in contrast to papal policy which viewed Orthodox adherents in the Balkans too often as heretics. The Bosnians, for example, happily turned to Islam, where earlier they had known Bogomilism, welcomed Wycliffite ideas and suffered persecution by Rome.[2] In the fall of Constantinople, some Greeks preferred to flee to the West, and Cardinal Bessarion enjoyed a distinguished career as a scholar and high-principled ecclesiastic at Rome until his death in 1472. But the fugitives were exceptional; the great majority of Greeks remained to accept Turkish rule and even Islam and came to serve the Ottoman sultans. Papal pride and intransigeance were in no small measure responsible for such an outcome.

[1] Zernov, op. cit., pp. 134 f.

[2] Brandt, op. cit., pp. 66 f.

Meanwhile the Russian Church emerged into leadership of Orthodoxy though there were few wider repercussions from this advance before the start of the sixteenth century.[1] The reunion agreed at Florence by Isidore was never accepted in Moscow by Grand Duke Vasili or the people. Isidore himself had to flee from Russia and in 1448 the Moscow leaders appointed their own metropolitan Iona without reference to the Greeks, an event marking the "emergence of the new national Russian Church".[2] At the time the Russian Duke still recognized Mongol overlordship and seemed of less significance than the Jagiellon rulers of Lithuania and Poland, where Orthodox believers were numerous, but developments after 1450 made Church and State at Moscow uniquely important. The downfall of Constantinople was seen by the Russians as divine punishment for Greek betrayal of orthodox faith, and it left the Church at Moscow in a position of ecclesiastical responsibility where there could be no thought of renewed dependence upon the Byzantine Patriarch. The Grand Duke of Moscow became the leading sovereign ruler of Orthodox adherents, and this position was enhanced after 1480 when Ivan III finally threw off allegiance to the Mongols. His previous marriage in 1472 to Sophia Palaeologus, the niece of the last Byzantine Emperor and a ward of the Pope, gave Ivan dynastic ties to the Roman ideal as well as contacts with Western leaders, who hoped vainly that he would favour Catholicism in Russia as well as oppose the Turks. By the start of the sixteenth century, and in particular after 1492 when the Russians had fearfully expected the end of the world, the idea was firmly held that Moscow was heir to the imperial and religious traditions of Constantinople. Just as Constantinople had been the second Rome, so Moscow became the third after 1453, and would, it was believed, remain as the last guardian of Orthodoxy or true Christian faith.[3] Ivan III on occasion used the title "Czar", equivalent to "Caesar" or "Emperor", though it was only formally assumed in 1547 by his son Ivan IV, and not until 1596 did the Metropolitan of Moscow become a Patriarch.

These steps followed logically upon the assumption of religious leadership by the Russians after 1453, and they reflected their deep consciousness of Christianity and its importance. In this formative period that saw the consolidation of Russian Orthodoxy, religious issues were fiercely debated in forms strikingly reminiscent of the earlier Wycliffite controversies. Over questions of Church and State, the concern of the clergy with secular affairs, their possession of

[1] Cf. G. Vernadsky, *The Mongols and Russia* (New Haven, 1953), pp. 311 f.
[2] Vernadsky, op. cit., p. 325.
[3] Zernov, op. cit., pp. 140 f.

property, and freedom for the individual to believe as he wished, there developed two parties – the Possessors and the Non-possessors – which remained balanced in argument and conflict until 1522. Before that date, religious life in Russia flourished and contacts were retained with leaders in the West, but the Possessors then secured direction of ecclesiastical affairs in the State and imposed rigid forms in belief that tended to isolate the Orthodox bodies from Latin Christendom during the Reformation age.[1]

Meanwhile, in the West, Nicholas V spoke of the events of 1453 as calamitous and called for a crusade, but this and subsequent appeals by the Popes provoked pitifully little response. When they did bring action, it was because of the alarming need to halt further Turkish advance rather than to attempt the recovery of Constantinople. Piccolomini in 1454 lamented that the Popes' universal appeals counted for so little, where many were apathetic and the rest interested only in their own safety. "Christianity," he wrote, "has no head whom all will obey . . . . There is no reverence and no obedience; we look on Pope and Emperor as figureheads and empty titles." Calixtus III was deeply concerned to fight the infidel, but his very zeal embarrassed contemporaries, and they hardly responded with more enthusiasm to Pius II's efforts to organize a European expedition against the Turks. Pius was disappointed at the lack of interest in the Congress of Mantua, and though he rejoiced at the discovery of alum at Tolfa in the Papal State for crusading funds, he himself died at Ancona in 1464, where his legates were trying unsuccessfully to assemble a fleet and army. The Turks were more effectively checked by national leaders like John Hunyadi, who with Capistrano defeated Mohammed II at Belgrade in 1456, or the Albanian Scanderbeg who contained attacks along the Adriatic coast until his death in 1467. Hunyadi's son, King Matthias I of Hungary, similarly campaigned to hold the Turks in the Balkans during his reign lasting to 1490. Popes like Paul II and Sixtus IV endeavoured to add to this resistance, the former by subsidizing Skanderbeg, the Venetians and the Hungarians, and the latter in promoting alliances among the Christian States. Venice reluctantly became embroiled in a series of wars with the Turks to defend its Mediterranean empire, and following the end of the first conflicts in 1479, Mohammed II a year later launched an attack on Rhodes and seized Otranto in southern Italy. This landing abruptly cut short domestic Italian bickerings, but the assault was called off in the same year with the sultan's death and onset of civil war in Turkey.

The new sultan, Bajazet II, lacked his father's qualities but he was able to defeat the challenge for supremacy by his brother Djem. The

[1] Zernov, op. cit., pp. 142–3.

latter fled for refuge to the Hospitallers at Rhodes in 1481 and thereafter, until his mysterious death fourteen years later, Djem was the prized and honoured hostage of different European rulers. Part of the time was spent in French hands, but from 1489 until the start of 1495, when Charles VIII took charge of him in Italy, Djem was held by the Popes in princely custody at Rome. Diplomacy and blackmail replaced military effort where Innocent VIII and Alexander VI contained Bajazet with the threat of loosing Djem against him at the head of a Christian and rebellious Turkish army. The sultan willingly paid the Pope an annual subsidy for his brother's safe keeping, trying more than once to have him murdered, but additionally in this curious arrangement Innocent VIII secured a fragment of the Holy Lance from Bajazet which his father had taken in capturing Constantinople. Contemporaries criticized the Popes for their actions, even suggesting that Alexander VI was willing to make a bargain with the sultan against Christians, but through these years papal custody of the Turkish prince helped to check further onslaught on eastern Europe. In the 1490's, Bajazet renewed his struggle with Venice, but gave his main attention to the conquest of Syria and Egypt. Only when these new conquests had been consolidated in 1517 by Bajazet's son, Selim I, and the Caliphate established at Constantinople, was the Ottoman drive into Europe vigorously renewed. Papal concern in the intervening years brought only temporary relief, not least where many were justifiably cynical at Alexander VI's appeal in 1500 and saw money for a crusade diverted into Borgia coffers for the local Italian campaigns of the Pope's son, Cesare. The lull in Turkish pressure allowed Julius II to ignore the question of resistance, and the initiative for organizing the defence of Christian Europe passed later to Charles V and the Habsburgs. He it was who had to meet the crises that brought successively the fall of Belgrade and Rhodes in 1521, the Hungarian defeat of Mohacs in 1526, and the siege of Vienna three years after.

The ideal of the Christian war against the infidel remained, but scarcely under papal leadership or without political compromises that allowed enemy rulers to co-exist and have their faiths tolerated. Whilst the Ottoman advance went on into south-eastern Europe, however, the advantage further west lay with the Christians, both in recovery of territory from Islam and in the new developments of naval exploration across the oceans. At the close of the fifteenth century came the climax of struggle against the Moors in the Iberian peninsula, when the Spanish overthrew the Kingdom of Granada in 1492. The Reconquista to drive the Moors from Spain and the western Mediterranean had been fought continuously from the 1050's, and by the fifteenth century the small Moorish principality remaining in the peninsula had long ceased to threaten the Christian kingdoms, but nevertheless the conquest of Granada was acclaimed in religious terms fitting the larger context of conflict against Islam.

It was also with the peoples of the Iberian peninsula – first the Portuguese and then the Spanish – that ideas of missionary enterprise and action against Islam were included with many other motives in explorations into the Atlantic, around the coast of Africa to India, and to the Americas in the fifteenth century. Earlier expansion for missionary as well as commercial or political objectives had been across Asia, and though these links were almost entirely severed from about 1360 for two hundred years,[1] knowledge of the world beyond Christendom remained stimulating. The Portuguese and the Catalans were best placed for sailing into the Atlantic and led the way in exploration by sea. Their primary purpose was to examine the African coast, and already by 1350 there existed an Italian map of Africa in recognizable outline, the product of brilliant guesswork rather than practical knowledge. It took over a further century of effort by the Portuguese to establish their trading stations and navigate around Africa into the Indian Ocean, but in the process the islands of the Canaries and the Azores came into their hands. The first part of the fifteenth century saw this enterprise patronized by Prince Henry the Navigator, a younger son of John I of Portugal and Master of the Military Order of Christ. Henry's share was severely limited to encouragement from Portugal, but he fostered all kinds of technical developments and knowledge, and at his death in 1460, ships had explored as far as the Cape Verde Islands. In the following quarter of a century they ranged further south along the African coast before Diaz rounded the Cape of Good Hope in 1486, and Vasco da Gama eleven years later sailed by this route to India. By that time, Columbus had already returned from sailing westward under the Spanish flag in search of the route to the Indies in 1492; he touched on the islands of central America, and returned safely to Spain in 1493. As a consequence, Alexander VI issued a bull dividing the New World between the two Iberian powers, and this settlement was modified by them – without further papal arbitration – in the Treaty of Tordesillas in 1494.

Though in later years Columbus's exploit came to be seen as fundamental for European affairs, both in the 1490's and for twenty years after what the Portuguese had achieved appeared more consequential than the discovery of America. The voyage of da Gama

[1] Indicative of the ending of older missions was the fact that the Dominicans and Franciscans closed down their special departments for controlling them in the 1450's (Latourette, op. cit., p. 324).

was the logical end of a long-developing venture to restore communications and trade with India, to turn the flank of Islamic power in the eastern Mediterranean, and to open up fresh sources of wealth. Throughout this development, religious and economic motives were entangled in fine confusion. Hopes of wealth in trade certainly counted primarily with the Portuguese adventurers who were concerned to set up trading stations and bring back profitable dividends in their exploring. Their African ports tapped not only the gold of Guinea but also a source of slaves in the Negroes, whilst success in reaching India brought to their hands the coveted spice trade from the Far East. Thereby they were able to cut through the older Venetian and Arabic monopolies of the Indian Ocean. But besides purely economic factors in Portuguese ambition there were religious aims and hopes, above all to alter the balance between Christendom and Islam. The Portuguese showed little of that strong missionary concern which developed in Spanish American expansion in the sixteenth century, but they took their Christian faith with them, for their own nationals at the stations and for the natives with whom they had dealings. More positively they hoped to cut across the advance of Islam in Africa by linking up with the Christian ruler and church in Ethiopia. Prince Henry's plans contained such an objective,[1] which drew upon older ideas when knowledge of Ethiopia had been hopelessly confused with that of Asia, and the thought of a Christian priest-king, Prester John, had repeatedly fired Western enthusiasm. On different occasions, and in relation to different leaders in Asia, through the twelfth and thirteenth centuries, Christian rulers had looked to such a person for aid against Islam, but none had ever come.[2]

More enduring were links with Africa, where the Coptic Christians of Ethiopia remained in tenuous contact with Latin Christendom, in part through the Ethiopian Convent left at Jerusalem whose representatives accepted the Formula of Union agreed at Florence.[3] Though this action was later repudiated from Ethiopia, the Popes despatched legates and embassies more than once in efforts to reach the African State, and possibly with success in one instance. But these ties were hazardous and not much could be made of them, even though the Turks found them threatening. Greater promise, however, lay in Portuguese expeditions sent from west Africa with envoys accredited to the Ethiopian court of "Prester John", as they styled the ruler in harking back to the older tradition of a Christian Emperor in the heart

[1] Cf. E. Prestage, *The Portuguese Pioneers* (London, 1933), pp. 29 f.

[2] Nestorianism in Asia provided the general basis for such hopes, and the garbled news of the careers of local chieftains and then of Jengis Khan's conquests seemed to give specific illustration of Christian attack against Islam.

[3] Latourette, op. cit., pp. 326–7.

of the continent.[1] These contacts were consolidated when the Portuguese passed the Cape of Good Hope, explored the east African coast and were able from that quarter to send ambassadors more directly to Ethiopia. In these developments, monks and friars took their part as missionaries and envoys, and the religious contacts of the fifteenth century had their sequel in later attempts by the Ethiopians to secure help from Portugal against the Turks. But the connections remained very slight and never brought the success hoped for by the Popes or the Ethiopians.

Meanwhile, the early stages of Spanish exploration and settlement in the West Indies and Central America brought problems of religious and social policies, where the ruthless behaviour of explorers and governors like Balboa and Pedrarias in exploiting natives was strongly criticized as early as 1511. In that year the Dominican Montesinos condemned current colonial policy and was sent home from the West Indies to put the case for the natives before King Ferdinand. As a result, the Laws of Burgos were issued in the following year, setting out a remarkably enlightened policy for dealing with the natives, inadequate though the Dominicans found it to be. Indians were to be treated as free men and converted to Christianity in peaceful evangelism, not by force, whilst they were able to work within defined limits for their protection. These principles were not properly to be honoured in the further growth of the Spanish Empire in South America, but Montesinos was followed by a greater advocate, missionary and writer – Las Casas – who fought long and with great effect to uphold rights for natives, not least in extending missions and teaching amongst them.[2] But such advances merged with fresh concern for converting heathen in Protestant as well as Catholic churches in the sixteenth century. The nature of achievement in the hundred years before was in promise of what might be accomplished in new lands as they were glimpsed from Europe rather than in work already completed. Until the start of the sixteenth century Christendom was on the defensive and closely beleaguered under Turkish attack: it scarcely appeared to be on the threshold of fresh missionary expansion which was to take the Christian faith into new as well as old worlds.

[1] Prestage, op. cit., pp. 32 f.

[2] Cf. J. H. Parry's account in *New Cambridge Modern History*, Vol. I, pp. 433–8; also the same author's *The Age of Reconnaissance* (London, 1963), Chapter XIX.

CHAPTER IX

THE WAY OF THE MYSTICS AND THE NEW DEVOTION

REFORM IN CHRISTENDOM WAS DEMANDED FROM MANY QUARTERS in the fourteenth and fifteenth centuries, and each of the attempts already considered – by Wycliffe and Lollardy, Hus and Bohemian national defiance, and Conciliarism – made its mark, even if the consequences were not always as anticipated. But interwoven with these developments, there was suggested another way of spiritual and ecclesiastical revival, that of mysticism in its Christian sense. In this approach, individuals were primarily concerned not with comprehensive or radical schemes of reform but to renew personal spirituality in withdrawing from the world in contemplation; more active work would only follow thereafter in teaching and attacking corruption in the Church at large. Christian mysticism thus understood directed attention to the soul's immediate communion with God, but it was not new in the fourteenth century, nor could it be contained simply within one definition. Its manifestations ran through all the grades of belief from orthodoxy to rank heresy, and from the ideal of the hermit's solitary meditative life to that of communal lay activity in Bible reading and study, possibly approved but more generally condemned by the Church. The tradition in Latin Christendom could be traced back to Bernard of Clairvaux and the Victorines of the twelfth century, and behind them to the early Christian Fathers; whilst it included groups like the Beghards and Beguines (condemned at Vienne in 1311), the Spiritual Franciscans, or the German Dominicans and the Friends of God, who occasionally suffered persecution by the Inquisition in the fourteenth century. Contemporary with Wycliffe and through the following hundred years, distinctive developments in England and on the Continent showed both what the mystical outlook could contribute towards reform in Christian life and organization, and wherein its limitations lay.

England in this period saw a succession of remarkable figures whose mystical writings as a whole bore comparison with no other age.[1] Though the temper and direction of thought in their works was far

[1] Cf. W. A. Pantin, *The English Church in the Fourteenth Century* (Cambridge, 1955), Chapter XI; and at greater length, the brilliant study by D. Knowles, *The English Mystical Tradition* (London, 1961).

different from the scholastic, urgent tone of Wycliffe's tracts, they shared many criticisms and enriched each other's arguments. There were five writers in this tradition of mystics – Richard Rolle, the author of *The Cloud of Unknowing*, Walter Hilton, Dame Julian of Norwich and Margery Kempe – and they were all essentially solitaries, ordained or not; they are known almost entirely through what they wrote. Rolle was born in Yorkshire in 1300 and went to Oxford where he studied for three or four years; however, he never took orders but later retired to his birthplace, Pickering. There he adopted a hermit's life and wrote and taught before, in his final years, becoming the spiritual director of a group of Cistercian nuns; it was on a visit to Hampole in 1349 that he died of the plague. His life almost completely antedated the age of Wycliffe, but the influence that he exerted developed concurrently with the spread of Lollardy and continued into the fifteenth century. Rolle became the most well-known and revered of the English mystics and his writings in Latin and the vernacular remained popular, probably because he did not withdraw entirely into contemplation but combined practical exhortation and criticism with his passion for the love of God. Apart from the translation of the psalter which he produced, Rolle wrote much in English as well as Latin, in no way confining himself strictly to instruction for other hermits. He issued commentaries on the Bible and practical tracts for reform of parish life and clerical behaviour, and he roundly condemned the corruption and lack of spirituality in the clergy, particularly in the monasteries. His sharp denunciations at times seemed to fit oddly with contemplative ideals, and they made it easy later for Lollard writings to be included with his works criticizing religious life, but Rolle was highly individualistic and simple in appeal rather than deeply skilled in exploring mystical experience.

Many of his formal ideas came from the Victorines, and his concern above all was with love of Christ and devotion to His Holy Name and Passion. In *The Mending of Life*, written in Latin but soon translated into English and later the most popular of his works in the fifteenth century, he stressed conversion and that Man should desire to love Christ truly and turn from the world and sin. "If thou desire to come to the love of God," he wrote, "and be kindled in thy desire for heavenly joys, and be brought to the despising of earthly things, be not negligent in meditating and reading Holy Scriptures; and most in those places where it teaches manners, and to eschew the deceits of the fiend, and where it speaks of God's love, and of contemplative life." Love of Christ he defined in terms of fire and song, reflecting his own ecstatic experiences, and he divided it into three progressive degrees, where the last made "Jesus . . . all your desire, all your delight, all your joy, all your solace, all your comfort". Rolle was a poetic writer of great power, and in these terms his religious arguments evoked a ready response among all classes in England. The Lollards approved of his works, adding their own comments at times in his treatises and passing manuscripts abroad to their friends in Prague.

The author of *The Cloud of Unknowing* cannot be identified, but the high quality and technical skill in its argument suggest that he was probably a priest, well trained theologically and aware of contemporary ideas in Germany. The work itself was written in part to correct some of the implications in Rolle's teaching, possibly some years before 1380, when Hilton knew of it.[1] Its author's indebtedness to earlier mystics was plain, above all to Dionysius the Areopagite and Richard of St. Victor, but at the same time it was possibly the most original in purpose and presentation of all the English works, with claims to be the most perfect treatise on the life of contemplation. Written in the vernacular, the book gave direct, practical instruction about the mystical life for a person seeking advice how to begin on such an experience. The "cloud of unknowing" lay between God and Man and could only be pierced through by God in His love; this love was made accessible to Man in contemplating Christ and in prayer. "Lift up your heart to God with humble love," was the advice, "and mean God Himself, and not what you get out of Him. Hate, indeed, to think of anything but God Himself, so that He alone occupies your mind or will." Only those with the proper vocation were to follow the path using love to beat down the "cloud of unknowing" and set up instead the "cloud of forgetting". "When thou hast forgotten all other creatures," the author explained, "there will remain between thee and thy God a naked knowing and a feeling of thine own being. This knowing and feeling must always be destroyed before the time thou mayest feel truly the perfection of this work." By this path, the contemplative life in prayer could more completely be pursued and the soul's experience of God more closely realized. These precepts contained warnings against dangers inherent in Rolle's teaching, where too much stress could be placed on bodily feelings and struggles at the expense of those spiritual, and *The Cloud* remained balanced and clear as a manual for those suited to its temper. For this very reason, it seems, it was by no means so popular or influential as the writings of Rolle in the England of the fourteenth and fifteenth centuries.

Walter Hilton's *The Scale of Perfection* was in many ways similar to *The Cloud* in spirit and criticism. Little is known of Hilton himself apart from the fact that he was an Augustinian canon at Thurgarton

[1] Knowles, op. cit., pp. 68–70.

in Nottinghamshire, and that before his death in 1396 he had probably known of local Lollard activities. His study was divided into two parts, the first of which set out principles for guiding an anchoress through the early steps of the mystical path, whilst the second was designed to describe some of the more advanced, though not final, experiences of such a life. Hilton attempted to outline the characteristics of the whole spiritual life as a long journey to a heavenly Jerusalem with particular incidents on the way, and the major distinction which he drew was between the "reformation in faith", the active ascetic life, and the "reformation in feeling", which more truly was the life of contemplation. "Faith" in his understanding ordinarily meant holding truths incapable of intellectual perception or apprehension, but "feeling" went beyond this as a mystical or supernatural experience, the product of the second reformation within the soul when a person had come to possess knowledge of God in Himself and was possessed by God. Everything had to be done in Christ's love, "for Christ is door and He is porter . . . . No man may come to the contemplation of the Godhead, but he be first reformed by fulness of meekness and charity to the likeness of Jesus in His manhood". A spiritual experience in cleansing, insight and contemplation was held out by Hilton as the goal of the soul's pilgrimage, and this he claimed was to be found in Christ Himself. Although the tone of much of his work resembled the aims of the Lollards, Hilton was critical of the tendencies in Lollardy, and above all differed from Wycliffe as also from Rolle in showing no concern to attack existing abuses and institutions. Supremely and positively his task was to instruct the individual for the highest life of contemplation, and from this, he implied, outward reformation would flow. His argument was methodical and sane, and his book became widely known as a manual amongst the religious in the following century, meriting distinction as one of the earliest works to be printed in England in 1494.

Another form of mystical outlook and experience was presented by Julian of Norwich, who was born in 1343 and at the age of thirty asked for three favours or "shewings" from God. One of these "shewings" – a profound illness – was granted, and it opened her way in visions and mystical insights into her subsequent life as an enclosed solitary attached to St. Julian's Church at Carrow. Her experiences she recorded in the one work by which she is known, *The Revelations of Divine Love*, and they ranged widely in subject and conclusions. Particularly prominent in her thoughts were the Love of Christ and the Motherhood of God, but her "shewings" were each of Christ crucified and they probed many basic theological issues of God, Man and salvation. Though in fact Julian did not argue systematically, clear principles underlay her insights concerning God's activity in instructing her and the fact that at best the visions were distorted insofar as they could be received by the human senses. The *Revelations* combined a deep faith in Christ, His Passion and Cross with optimism for triumph over sin, and a homely passion which found widespread response in the attitude of many people. "Our courteous Lord," Julian counselled, "willeth that we should be as homely with Him as heart may think, or soul may desire. But beware lest we take recklessly this homeliness, so as to leave courtesy. For our Lord is sovereign homeliness, and as homely as He is, so courteous He is." Yet elsewhere she could reveal profound mystical insight in speaking of seeing God in a point, and like Hilton show concern with sin and evil only in passing in the all-consuming experience of Christ's love.

Standing apart from all these writers, and far less of a contemplative in her work, Margery Kempe was yet significant in her experiences and what she showed of currents of thought in England in the early part of the fifteenth century. She was born about 1373 of a well-to-do family at Bishop's (King's) Lynn in Norfolk, and at the age of twenty she married John Kempe, by whom she had a large family. Her life was erratic, worldly and marked by nervous breakdowns in child-bearing, but in 1413 she took a vow of chastity and persuaded her husband to do the same before Bishop Repton of Lincoln, the erstwhile Lollard. Repton treated her with respect, though her personality was not easy or calm. She had earlier sought instruction from Dame Julian about the contemplative life and following her vow she travelled extensively through Europe to Rome and Jerusalem. On returning to England, Margery was suspected of Lollardy and interrogated by Arundel, whom she personally rebuked for his clergy's conduct, whilst before the Archbishop of York, she roundly repudiated reports that she was a bad woman and answered arguments that she should stop preaching or leave the diocese. From her autobiography, *The Book of Margery Kempe*, it seems at first sight as if her contribution to mystical discussion was not unlike that of Julian, since both women wrote personally and set down the visions or messages which they had received. But there were profound differences, for Julian's book became a discussion of doctrines rather than an account about herself, whilst Margery Kempe gave a survey of her life over about forty years, with conversations or monologues that had no systematic programme or arrangement, and only the occasional vision. In comparison with other writers in the tradition, Margery Kempe, in Professor Knowles's words, was "more homely, perhaps, and even more comprehensible, but of an altogether coarser mould". She was a strange mixture of recluse, self-abasing mystic and exhibitionist, typifying the popular religious and spiritual enthusiasm of many in fifteenth-century England, and with her came to an end that stream of English mystical experience and comment that had flowed so strongly through the preceding hundred years.

These writers illustrated a reaction to religious conditions that was complementary to the attack made by Wycliffe. At times they joined with that attack in criticizing ecclesiastical corruption and lack of spirituality, but at times too they were highly critical of Lollardy, much as Wycliffe on his side scorned the "feigned contemplative life". In their individualism and anti-intellectual attitudes, and with practical arguments expressed in the vernacular, they gained steadily in reputation from the fourteenth century onward. Rolle and the others built widely upon a common body of knowledge and lay religious literature that came to include Langland's *Piers Plowman* and many of Chaucer's poems with their social and religious comment. Some of the ideas led to developments condemned by the Lollards – worshipping of images or concern with pilgrimages – but they could also issue in attitudes which were as much applauded by Wycliffe's followers, for example, a love of the sermon in services or emphasis on the laity in religious life. Doctrinally, the mystics remained within orthodox limits, and unlike Eckhart and some of the Germans of the fourteenth century did not become lost in pantheism or philosophy. Even Margery Kempe was able to deny accusations that she was a Lollard. This orthodoxy in part stemmed from the fact that the English writers constantly emphasized fundamentals of belief where there was no dispute, they kept Christ and His Passion central in all their visions and arguments. In part, it was the product of an attitude looking for reformation in the inward, spiritual relations of the soul with God, rather than in challenge to the external system of religion. Lollards, by contrast, were condemned as heretics on specific charges, their movement in the fifteenth century made synonymous with heresy.

Rolle, Hilton and Margery Kempe were energetic in grappling with everyday problems around them, even though their mysticism posed the solitary life as the ideal to follow. Yet, important as their writings were in leavening piety in England, they lacked any systematic following or legacy. This was equally the case in many contemporary developments on the Continent, where women like Bridget of Sweden and Catherine of Siena were notable in their own lives rather than for any organized movements. Bridget certainly founded a monastic order for men and women – the Brigittines – in Sweden in 1346, but her later renown came through her residence at Rome after 1349 and efforts to bring reform before dying in 1373. Catherine appeared as Bridget's younger disciple, not least of all in seeking to persuade Gregory XI to leave Avignon, and she championed Urban VI's cause after the start of the Great Schism. In her visions and life she gathered a great following in Italy, and had links with some of the English mystics of the day. Nevertheless, both Bridget and Catherine were remarkable individuals, not the leaders of more enduring and widespread traditions, and a similar situation tended to develop even in the Observant movement of the following century. Bernardino, Capistrano and others were dynamic leaders, but the impacts again largely remained personal, where enthusiasms aroused by the preaching and lives of particular men all too easily subsided at their deaths. It was in and around northern Germany by contrast that a more organized and influential movement arose in the age.

From the start of the fourteenth century, the Dominicans in Germany fostered mystical studies and teaching, with Meister Eckhart and his disciples such as John Tauler, Henry Suso and Rulman Merswin, and with the associated activity of the Friends of God. In fundamentals this movement seemed to have been strictly orthodox in devotion to piety, asceticism, introspective study and visions, but Eckhart himself was condemned and later in the century the Friends of God suffered censure, some of them, like Nicholas of Basel, being executed. Many of the Friends were recruited from the older Beghard groups and aimed to bring spiritual renewal in devotion and Bible study amongst laity and priests outside the existing ecclesiastical structure. In this there were echoes of older attempts at independent lay organizations, and also similarities to the Lollards in England, but in further activities there came a fresh spiritual awakening in Flanders through the mystic John Ruysbroek, himself a follower of Tauler and one of the Friends of God. Ruysbroek combined both active and contemplative lives in his career, for he was a secular priest at a church in Brussels until aged sixty in 1353, and thereafter he became an Augustinian canon to write and work. His efforts at Brussels were to counter some of the more excessive practices and teaching of Beghards, Beguines and Lollards in the area, whilst his writing showed a return to much of Eckhart's teaching, particularly his pantheism, for which Gerson later criticized him. But Ruysbroek's place was all-important in helping to bridge the gap from the more formal monastic mysticism of the age to a religion increasingly popular in its mystical form. This influence he most clearly exercised in his teaching of Gerard Groote during the last years before his death in 1381.

Groote was born of wealthy parents in 1340 and enjoyed a fine career as a scholar for most of his life. He became a professor at Cologne where he came probably under the influence of the Friends of God, and was converted eventually in 1374 through the ministry of a Carthusian and Ruysbroek himself. He remained a layman, and after a period of preparation preached as a lay-evangelist through the Rhineland and Low Countries in 1379. The success and popularity which he gained were unequalled at that time, but so fierce was he in condemning ecclesiastical abuses that his license was withdrawn and he was compelled to give up such preaching. But this setback only turned his thoughts into a fresh direction, and on the advice of his friend and follower, Florent Radewyns, he retired to Deventer in 1381 and planned out the idea for a community of Brethren of the Common Life. His death in 1384 came before these ideals and methods had been put into practice, but Radewyns continued in organizing the community and its expansion through the years that followed. Groote's vision was for increased devotion and spirituality among the laity as well as the clergy, and this he hoped could be realized in the life of houses of lay Brethren or Sisters of the Common Life, as at Deventer itself, or of Augustinian canons, which Radewyns and other Brethren established at Windesheim near Zwolle in 1386. Neither Groote nor Radewyns was concerned if people were lay or cleric, nor did they intend that any should adopt strict orders and monastic vows for spiritual reform. Indeed, their whole attitude was against monastic withdrawal from the world or necessary obedience to traditional rules of the orders. In the "New Devotion", as it was called, the aim was for men and women to live ordinary lives still very much in contact with the world, but organized communally in houses with study, Biblical devotions, teaching and preaching. The Brethren were to follow a spiritual life without vows, and the whole movement was a protest against the decadent monasticism and ecclesiasticism of the age.[1]

Such a venture not unnaturally provoked criticism, and in the closing years of the fourteenth century, as their centres at Deventer and Windesheim flourished and spread, the Brethren were accused of Beghardism or heresy by the mendicants. Boniface IX officially approved the Augustinian house at Windesheim in 1395, but the lay community in Deventer fell foul of the Inquisition and in 1398 had to set out a series of "determinations" to refute these attacks.[2] A major issue concerned the lawfulness of community life for laymen and women without monastic vows, but also important was the question of lay use of vernacular Scriptures. The doctors who pronounced on

[1] For Groote and the Brethren of the Common Life see A. Hyma, *The Christian Renaissance* (New York, 1924); and E. F. Jacob, "Gerard Groote and the Beginnings of the 'New Devotion' in the Low Countries", in *Journal of Ecclesiastical History*, III (1952), pp. 40–57.

[2] M. Deanesly, *Lollard Bible*, pp. 89 f.

the articles for the Brethren were from Cologne. Most of them were probably influenced by earlier teaching from Waldensians and the Friends of God and were therefore antagonistic to the Inquisition and even the views of the Parisian masters who were prominent in reform at the time. They upheld the organization and life of the Brethren and also the lay reading of vernacular books of Scripture and devotion. But important qualifications were accepted that compared interestingly with Lollard ideas about reading and the Bible. Both Wycliffe and his followers contended for translation of the whole Bible into English and for its use by laity as much as clergy, but on the Continent, vernacular "Scriptures" and reading meant far less than this. Even Janov, for example, with his deep concern for the Bible, limited knowledge of its text to theological students, and Hus had to advance noticeably upon such views. Individuals certainly could possess vernacular Bibles, but these were ecclesiastics or the qualified literate reader, and all too frequently what were read were selected passages, as in England before the Lollard translations. Similarly, preachers used Scripture in their sermons and were required to instruct the congregations in the elements of faith, as with Peckham's Constitutions in England, but the Bible as a whole was not officially employed in the ordinary tongue or encouraged for copying.

With these attitudes the Brethren generally agreed, and in their concern for vernacular writing and to copy books into Dutch or other languages they had in mind popular devotional books of the day, which contained Scriptural excerpts rather than the whole Bible. The findings of 1398 had their meaning in this context, when the doctors categorically rejected arguments that unlettered lay people could not suitably study Scripture or that it was illegal to have the Bible in the vernacular. This judgment was very different from that of the friars concerning the Bible in English in the 1390's and came much closer to Lollard affirmations. But there were important qualifications made, in particular that the books had to "treat clearly of plain subjects", and on this basis many parts of the Bible (for example, the prophetical books) could be banned where such was not the case. Nevertheless, the provisions enabled the Brethren to evade inquisitorial condemnation of their life, reading and teaching and to surmount subsequent clashes with the friars.

From the 1390's onward, the movement developed in two main ways led respectively by Windesheim and Deventer in their differing organizations. The Windesheim house represented the more strictly ordered side of the New Devotion, since its original purpose was to provide a permanent refuge for members who sought a more retired life and a temporary sanctuary for the lay workers at Deventer. In adopting the rules of the Augustinian canons for its members, Windesheim set out general principles and aims for monastic reform, and already by 1400 a number of houses had been founded from the community or had joined it through the missionary work of individual members. Its influence, and that of the sister body for women at Diepenveen, spread rapidly in the fifteenth century. In places, older established monasteries of the Augustinians were reformed and more closely a great many became members of the congregation. Windesheim was not particularly favoured by papal or episcopal grants, but the ideals incorporated in its life and presented for spiritual reform and revival were appeal enough to many monastic foundations where all sight of proper service to God had been lost. Local ecclesiastical authorities and monasteries on occasion opposed thoughts of reform, but far more remarkable was the welcome widely given to these missionary efforts through the Netherlands and north Germany. Under John Vos (1391–1424), the second Prior of Windesheim after Radewyns, the initial and greatest period of expansion took place. Of forty brethren invested before Vos's death, half of them became rectors or priors of monasteries built or reformed under their supervision. One or two Dutch houses joined Windesheim at the start, then after 1400 German Augustinian monasteries in increasing numbers, until in 1430, the great chapter of Neuss, with thirteen houses, was added to the congregation. By 1464, the Windesheim body contained eighty-four houses, and in 1500 over a hundred, scattered through the Netherlands, Germany and into Switzerland, whilst many more foundations accepted reforms without joining a specific group. Outside Augustinian houses, the Windesheim principles were introduced into Cistercian, Premonstratensian and Benedictine foundations.

One of the most energetic figures in this work was John Busch (1399–1480), who was a native of Zwolle and saw his vocation in preaching spiritual revival and return to personal faith in monasteries across north-western Europe. He eventually spent some years following 1447 in the wealthy monastery of Neumark, attracted Nicholas V's attention and led the Pope to send Cusa to Germany in 1451 with authority to reform all the Augustinian houses in Saxony, Meissen and Thuringia. Cusa reorganized Neumark and its dependents into a new chapter so that it should join Windesheim, but this the latter did not wish because Neumark was so rich; in consequence, the new chapter continued as a centre of reform outside the older congregation. Meanwhile, Busch's zeal had inspired the Abbot of Minden to deal with abuses in his community before taking charge of Bursfelde in 1433, when he set on foot a parallel movement to bring revival and fresh spiritual life in the German Benedictine foundations. From

Diepenveen, missionaries similarly went to preach and introduce reforms among communities of women far and wide in Holland and Germany. This achievement of monastic reform compared favourably with efforts to recall the mendicants to strict principles on Observant bases, for despite their spread to the Augustinian order into which Luther was introduced, they had brought considerable confusion and discord in various bodies by 1500. It seems clear that the Windesheim movement diverted much criticism about the whole purpose of religious life and provided moreover important principles later for reformed monasticism in countries like Spain and France.

The members of Windesheim were famed for their practical attention to revival in spiritual life, but their contribution in discussing ideas and principles was no less striking. The Brethren drew upon the teaching of Groote and Radewyns, but to these were added Hendrik Mande (1360–1415) and Gerlac Petersen (1378–1411) who provided manuals for the reformers in their journeys to monasteries through north-west Europe. More notable still was Gerard Zerbolt who until his death in 1398 dominated developments as scholar, student and apologist of the New Devotion. He provided the detailed defence of the Brethren's life for the Cologne doctors, but in addition wrote *The Spiritual Ascensions*, a treatise setting out briefly and clearly the deeper arguments of the movement and exploring mystical experience. His thesis was that Man was involved in three falls or descents – the first fall of Adam from innocence in Eden, the second the consequence of individual sins on earth, the third where Man continually commits mortal sins, like the prodigal son in going among the swine. Correspondingly there were three ascents, each divided into several steps. In the first ascent, Man left godless ways and began confessing his sins and showing repentance; in the second his repentance brought God's forgiveness, but as well he had to gain the fear of the Lord, a hope in future joy and ability to love. Thus began the third ascent, with the proper exercises for purification and the progressive acquiring of perfect love which could only come through Christ. In this process, Man had to go as far as was humanly possible in cleansing his heart from the evil taint and consequence of Adam's fall, always remembering his final purpose and end, to know Christ, follow and love Him in purity of heart. Zerbolt placed considerable stress upon Man's effort in salvation, even though he balanced this by discussing Christ's Person and Work. The manual deeply influenced all the followers in the New Devotion and later at the close of the fifteenth century it was used by Mombaer in France and Garcia of Cisneros in Spain. Not least of all, it provided the basis for Loyola's *Spiritual Exercises* in the 1520's.

But the most celebrated representative of the Windesheim principles and pre-eminent as a mystical writer of the age was Thomas à Kempis. Born about 1380 at Kempen near Cologne, he was taught entirely by the Brethren, first at Deventer, then after 1399 in the Augustinian house at Mount St. Agnes, a daughter foundation of Windesheim set up by his own brother. Thomas himself became a canon in 1412 or 1413 and stayed at the community for nearly all the remaining sixty years of his long life. His experience in consequence fitted more into the pattern of monastic withdrawal than that, say, of a Francis of Assissi, but even so he used his time in practical tasks and wrote homilies, poems and biographies of the leaders of the Brotherhood alongside works of more ascetic or mystical nature. Supremely his views were expressed in *Of the Imitation of Christ*, which came into circulation about 1418 and seems to have been composed in part, if not entirely, by Thomas. Ideas and phrases in the work so closely echoed those common to all the members of the movement, most of all Groote and Radewyns, that much of it could have come from their hands, and disputes about authorship raged from the fifteenth century onward. But there appears to be little doubt today that Thomas completed and issued the book, which sublimely reflected the spirit of the New Devotion and subsequently became the most widely read and treasured of all writings in the Christian world, apart from the Bible itself.

In many places, the *Imitation* was little more than a collection of Scriptural verses, whilst fundamentally it urged on all men the way of discipline for knowing God, and knowing Him in His love. Man was a pilgrim or prisoner on earth, Thomas argued, and his need was to fight against the flesh and overcome sin in order to reach towards God's appointed goal. Human nature was depraved, for "through Adam the first man, Nature being fallen and corrupted by sin, the penalty of this stain hath descended upon all mankind". Only in self-renunciation, obedience to God, humility and willing service to others could Man attain communion with God and fellowship with Christ:

> "The Kingdom of God is within you," saith the Lord. Learn to despise outward things, and to give thyself to things inward, and thou shalt perceive the Kingdom of God to come in thee. Christ will come unto thee, and show thee His own consolation, if thou prepare for him a worthy mansion within thee.

Vices were to be rooted out, and on the pilgrimage there was no place allowed for mirth, let alone gossip, curiosity or concern for reputation. Above all, Man was to know himself in subjecting the flesh to the spirit and willingness to "lead a dying life". Thomas allowed that Man as created in God's image was not wholly depraved – he preserved a divine spark in his heart that could be fanned by God's Holy Spirit to burn sin away and leave the mansion for Christ's dwelling and God's pure love. The initiative for salvation lay with God, and Man's response could only be in stretching out a hand to receive the offer in faith. This approached Luther's understanding of justification by faith, but remained sufficiently different where faith for Groote and Thomas – as for Erasmus later – could not be imagined apart from works. Christian living was praised against barren scholastic and philosophical debate, and though Thomas did not claim that books and their study as ordained by God were wrong, he supposed God as saying, "In a moment I can lift up the humble mind, and make it enter more deeply into the principles of Eternal Truth, than if one had studied ten years in the schools".

In some respects, it can be claimed, the *Imitation* was mystical only within narrow limits, for though containing the steps of contemplative life, it presented no search for the Absolute; it was a disciplined manual to show men how to know Christ, to "imitate" the human Christ in their lives. Nevertheless, the work fell fully into the tradition of mystical writings whose aim was to lay bare the purposes and principles of true Christianity, and in this way it was certainly the finest product of the New Devotion, with influences that were profound later among the Reformers of the sixteenth century. The Windsheim activities and the message of the *Imitation* did not, however, comprise all that the Brethren achieved, and though Thomas himself showed little interest in it, work amongst laity figured obviously and more positively for spreading ideas of reform in the fifteenth century. The Brethren living at Deventer fostered this development, and with others in a similar community at Zwolle and in Sister houses, they devoted themselves to simple living, works of charity and aid for the poor and the copying of books for some income, whilst sharing in Bible reading, discussions and meditation. Until 1400, they lived under Radewyns's leadership at Deventer, though from that centre and Zwolle other houses were established in neighbouring towns as early as 1395. Eventually there were about forty-five Brethren houses and twice as many Sister houses scattered through Holland and the adjoining countries. It was laid down that if possible each house should have four priests and some other clergy in attendance, but no limit was set to the numbers of laymen who could live in each community. They were only admitted into residence if they loved reading and could write, and had to remain as novices for a period to test these qualifications.

From the start, the Brethren were interested in education apart from their practical good works, for Groote himself had been impressed by the value of teaching and had taught. Reform of the Church, he and his followers felt, could only come more widely with right instruction of the young, who in time would grow to be priests and leaders in ecclesiastical affairs. The houses of the Brethren of the Common Life therefore became renowned in the fifteenth century, their influence ranging through all movements because of the individuals who were taught at their hands. Not all the schools, strictly speaking, were owned by the Brethren, nor was it possession so much as their teaching and provision of hostels with any school that gave them their influence. There were never schools at Deventer or Zwolle belonging to the Brethren, but from the start they had hostels where students like young Thomas à Kempis lived. The Brethren never systematically formed a body of teachers like the Jesuits of later date, and indeed most of them were not teachers but copyists until after 1450, when the introduction of printing began to make manuscript copying unrewarding for meeting expenses. But their work in individual friendship and instruction was of incalculable value all through, where their expressed aim was to serve God and to bring those with whom they had dealings to seek salvation and purity of heart. In this, their copying had its place, since they translated Scriptures into the vernacular for arranging passages and verses in their manuals of instruction.

The Brethren early crossed paths with the conciliarists, and in particular were influenced by and helped to influence in turn two men – John Gerson and Nicholas of Cusa. Gerson, the great French conciliarist and Nominalist and Chancellor of Paris University after 1393, was in many ways a man of contradictions. He urged Hus's condemnation at Constance, and yet could be sympathetic and tender, a great preacher and beloved pastor of a church in the last ten years of his life after 1419. Moreover, he stood out as a mystical writer in traditional forms, following the Victorines and Bonaventura, as much as the theorist of Conciliarism. In general terms, he eschewed extremes, posing a midway course in thought, and despite admitting to no mystical visions or insights, he mapped out the scheme for progress in such understanding. He stood firmly against the Nominalism leading into arid and academic discussion, but on the same philosophical bases argued for the unknowability of God except by the intuitive or "affective" faculty, which enabled the individual to have communion with the Deity. Human reason could not give this knowledge, nor was it necessary to resort to pantheism or the Neoplatonism favoured by many. Gerson's stress was laid upon the fact that the human mind by intuition could receive supernatural truths in a direct way. His position meant that he condemned radical groups like the Brethren of the Free Spirit, or the Flagellants championed at Constance by Vincent Ferrer, but on the other hand vigorously defended the Brethren of the Common Life in 1418 against Dominican criticisms. For their part, the Brethren admired and copied his mystical writings, and for long Gerson was considered to have composed *Of the Imitation of Christ*.

The Brethren were troubled by attacks more than once and in 1431 secured official approval for their organization from Eugenius IV. But they also had further ties with Conciliarism in Gerson's younger friend, Nicholas of Cusa, whose thought and career bestrode the fifteenth century. Cusa was born in 1401 and spent his schooldays at Deventer before going on to study in turn at Heidelberg, Padua and finally Cologne after 1425 in order to gain his doctorate in canon law. His early instruction in the New Devotion moulded his outlook where later he placed great stress on an inner personal devotion to Christ and supported monastic reforms deriving from Windesheim, alongside his enthusiasm for the new Humanistic learning in Europe. Though the Brethren abandoned scholasticism and were popular in their simpler, more practical stress in piety and Bible study, they were not Humanists, nor was their teaching in accord with Italian educational principles. Their concern was hardly with the classics, certainly not before 1450. Nevertheless, their mode of teaching, their attitude of enquiry and care for texts, could develop and blend with other interests in Renaissance Humanism, and this possibility Cusa pre-eminently realized in his attempt to synthesis ideas. At Heidelberg, he was trained under the influence of Occamism deriving from Marsilius of Inghen, but in Padua he met Italian mathematical speculation and enquiry, and these disciplines gave a complex and stimulating foundation for his further studies at Cologne and his diplomatic career in the Church. His participation at Basel was notable since he wrote *On Catholic Agreement*, the outstanding defence of Conciliarism in the age, and though he followed Cesarini in 1437 to join Eugenius IV at Ferrara and to persuade the Greeks to accept the papal invitation, he always argued that the Pope should be restricted in his authority. Cusa secured still greater renown in papal service by helping to negotiate the settlement with the Germans, and after receiving his cardinal's hat, he was appointed as papal legate in German lands. Even more striking was his work for religious peace, for by tact and understanding he paved the way for the reconciliation of the Bohemians with Rome, though this work was destroyed afterward by Capistrano's intemperate and arrogant Hussite mission. Cusa's other work in reform coincided with that of Busch, to whom he gave support, but as Bishop of Brixen he himself met opposition from Duke Sigismund of Saxony and was forced to abandon his schemes.

He died in 1464 with his practical aims largely frustrated, but having written copiously and profoundly in terms that showed how far apart he stood from general apathy in Rome and what was the range of his ideals and hopes. Philosophically he was Nominalist in the belief that Truth was one and unknown in rational terms, and that God, far beyond man's intellectual apprehension, could only be understood by intuition. Seen in such a context, human knowledge was relative, complex and approximate, what Cusa termed "learned ignorance", and it was in exploring what he meant by this in contrast to Truth that he probed more deeply and positively than Gerson. His protests against attempts to marry Aristotle with Christianity, and appeal to "learned ignorance", did not imply anti-intellectualism or scepticism as to man's possibilities. Rather they expressed his profound attempt to underline the relation of the finite to the infinite, where reason could accept its own inadequacy and allow that Man in his intuition should be open to God. Such an intellectual evaluation Cusa found in the outlook that he met at Padua, in mathematics as the highest study and the means for revealing ultimate Truth. In work after work, he explored the practical, philosophical and theological implications of mathematical enquiry in which, for him, geometry and symbols held the key. But at the same time he appreciated that these schemes would not solve the problems in the Church and its life so much as a renewed spirituality in seeing Christ in His Incarnation, in His creative and human activities, and as the One who sustained the world and brought all things into harmony in the universe.[1] Cusa in the end was able to find every issue resolved in Christ as the Mediator bringing God and Man together and bridging mystical and scientific attitudes. Herein he revealed ideas from the teaching of the Brethren of the Common Life, whilst in his appreciation of Christ's humanity and His oneness with men in their lives, sufferings and needs, he also drew close to Wycliffe in his insights. Officially, Cusa remained a papalist, with a clear conviction of the superiority of the Pope and priesthood over the laity, and he was therefore more conservative than the Brethren as well as opposed to Wycliffite doctrines. But he showed profound appreciation of what was needed and how conflicting tendencies of thought could be reconciled in an outlook spanning all

[1] Cf. J. P. Dolan (editor), *Unity and Reform: Selected Writings of Nicholas de Cusa* (Notre Dame, 1962), pp. 42, 43; also E. Cassirer, *The Individual and the Cosmos in Renaissance Philosophy*, translated by M. Domandi (New York, 1963), Chapter 1; and E. F. Jacob, *Essays in the Conciliar Epoch*, second edition (Manchester, 1952), Chapter IX.

views. His abiding concern for peace and his theories made him enemies and he did not escape the criticism that he was pantheistic. But his conviction of the reality and work of Christ in creation and salvation kept him from unorthodoxy and made him stand out among papalists in his search for doctrinal and practical reform.

The school of Deventer had its part in shaping Cusa's outlook, but it also opened the way more specifically to Humanistic studies and even radicalism in northern Europe.[1] Its greater days as a school came later in the fifteenth century at the time when Windesheim's work was spreading widely into many parts of western Christendom. Repercussions from the movement came to be found in the lives and work of men like John of Goch, Hegius and Gansfort, Mombaer, Lefèvre and Erasmus in their hopes of reform, more faintly with Luther and Calvin, and not least of all in Loyola when he had to meet the needs of the Roman Church in its crisis. Only in the course of the sixteenth century were the Brethren's houses and influence largely destroyed, but their service was immeasurable in bringing revival and preparing the path for reform through the preceding hundred years.

[1] See Chapter X, p. 161 f. below.

CHAPTER X

GERMANY, EASTERN EUROPE AND THE HUSSITES AFTER 1436

FOR NEARLY TWENTY YEARS BEFORE THE SIGNING OF THE COMPACTS of Iglau, Bohemian wars dominated central Europe and made the name "Taborite" one of terror. After 1436, the situation changed substantially in that never again did the Hussites threaten the world outside Bohemia as they had under Žižka and Prokop, whilst at the same time they stood by a formal settlement safeguarding their religious and ecclesiastical claims. More widely, as the Pope triumphed over the many voices of Basel, he reached agreements with different countries, including Germany, and Bohemia continued to develop within that same framework of the Holy Roman Empire. Nevertheless, its path in religion and politics through to the age of Luther remained distinctive, and can be traced out by itself, even where it no longer appeared as a beacon trail for the rest of Christendom.

The settlement of 1436 was pre-eminently the triumph of Rokycana and the Utraquists whose position was secured at the expense of the more radical Taborites in Bohemia, but hopes for a national church in communion again with Rome and at peace under imperial rule were fruitless. Neither Emperor nor Pope was prepared completely to tolerate the Utraquist Church on the basis of the Compacts, whilst through the following century, Bohemia had neighbouring Catholic States in Hungary and Poland, and their internal fortunes became intimately involved in dynastic successions. In the event, it mattered little what the German Emperors sought, for Sigismund's successor, the Habsburg Albert II, ruled for only eighteen months, and was in turn followed by Frederick III, crowned at Rome and recalling the earlier Hohenstaufen Fredericks, but ineffectual in government for forty years. His son, Maximilian I, was far more able politically, but he only attained effective control of affairs in the last years of his life when already Luther was challenging the Church's authority. More consequential for Bohemia were the struggles of local families for control over Hungary, Poland and Lithuania as well, and these moulded and blighted the high hopes of the Utraquists. For their part the Popes never acknowledged the Compacts and in 1462 Pius II denounced them. Rokycana was never officially recognized as Archbishop of Prague, and neither he nor his successors were able to take possession of Prague Cathedral, which remained in the hands of Catholic canons. Concern to retain communion in both kinds and to have a continuing validly ordained ministry were issues that beset the Utraquist leaders through the century, and what success there was came through Rokycana's faithful control, but Utraquist developments were also organically tied to Bohemian political affairs.

Albert II's brief reign as King of Bohemia left the situation troubled in 1439, for a son, dubbed Ladislas Postumus, was born to his widow and accepted as the new king, with a regency council effectively in charge over a number of years. The council split over the religious question and Ladislas, as he grew up, increasingly favoured the Catholics, not least because he also became King of Hungary in 1444 at the death of Ladislas I. Decisive control of Bohemian government lay, however, in the hands of a young nobleman, George of Podebrády, who was broadly Hussite in sympathy and in 1448 seized Prague in conflict with the Catholics. Four years later George was elected sole regent of the country and he remained in charge of administration when Ladislas was crowned in 1453; his concern pre-eminently was for Bohemian national unity and prosperity at the same time as he was prepared to uphold Utraquism. At first George worked well with Ladislas but relations gradually worsened over religious issues, and the young king gained in popularity after sharing with Hunyadi in the defeat of the Turks in 1456. Further dispute in Bohemia, however, was averted as Ladislas died of the plague a year later, at which point Frederick III could claim to inherit the kingdom or to approve its next ruler. The Bohemian Diet rejected Frederick and other candidates for the crown and in March, 1458, chose George as their new king. He was well known for his patriotism and Utraquist leanings, and the election was significant in that Rokycana used all his influence to secure it. In earlier years Rokycana had hoped for direct negotiations with Rome to consolidate Bohemian privileges, but by 1458, it seems, he had come to believe that the best safeguards for the national Church with its Compacts were to be found in a Bohemian king like George. The latter took care to be crowned according to ancient Bohemian rites and publically swore to preserve the liberties of the land, in particular the Compacts of 1436. In normal Roman coronation he enjoyed the traditional royal privilege of receiving communion in both kinds but nevertheless could be regarded in the realm as a Hussite. This left ambiguity, especially where he promised secretly at the same time to uphold obedience to Rome, which papally could be interpreted as condemnation of the Compacts. George's aim was for agreement with the Pope to gain peace in

Bohemia, and this meant that he and Rokycana did not always look on issues similarly,[1] Utraquist though both were. In 1461, the king even took action against the new religious body – the Unity of the Brethren – as well as against Taborites from whom it arose, to attempt to have the Compacts recognized and avoid outside Catholic condemnation and attack. Through the first part of his reign, George brought prosperity to Bohemia with his policy and earned wider respect with his statesmanlike hopes for a European coalition to defend Christendom. But he failed to bring more lasting resolution of the religious dispute with Rome. Pius II flatly condemned the Compacts in 1462, thereby driving George into the single-minded defence of Utraquist principles and close alliance with Rokycana. This in turn brought renewed civil conflict in Bohemia in 1465, papal excommunication of George in the following year, and attacks by his enemies outside, notably the Emperor and Matthias Corvinus, who had become King at Hungary in 1458. Bohemian military strength had waned since the 1420's, for the free peasantry which had been the backbone of resistance was steadily declining with the growth of serfdom, but nevertheless in 1467 George defeated both his Catholic rebel subjects and the Emperor. Reverses against Corvinus in the following year compelled him to agree that the Hungarian king should succeed him and to seek peace with the Pope on the basis of the Compacts. But no papal reconciliation followed and in 1469 the Catholics in Bohemia elected Corvinus as king. Renewed civil war broke out and in the effort to preserve the Hussite heritage, George recognized as his heir Prince Ladislas, son of the Jagiellon Casimir IV of Poland. The succession was still to a Catholic ruler, since the Jagiellon family had moved away from its older Orthodox and Hussite sympathies, but this settlement blocked Corvinus's claims.

On George's death in 1471, Ladislas II became the new king although Corvinus for some years disputed the title. In the end, indeed, the crowns were united in reverse fashion, for Ladislas succeeded Corvinus as King of Hungary in 1490. Thereby all the States of eastern Europe were brought under the control of the one Jagiellon family; Ladislas continued to rule Bohemia and Hungary until his death in 1516, while his brothers in turn governed Poland and Lithuania after Casimir's death in 1492, and the system was only disrupted when Ladislas's son, Louis II, was killed at Mohacs in 1526. This dynastic structure held hopes for political and military stability in eastern Europe, but in religious terms it spelt danger for Bohemian Hussitism. The year 1471 was critical, for Rokycana died shortly

[1] Heymann, "Rokycana", restores Rokycana's reputation, and pp. 253 f. outlines George's difficulties and the differences with Rokycana.

before King George, and it was he who had kept the Utraquist body strong and attached to the Compacts even where he was unwilling for a complete break from Rome. No one of comparable ability could take his place, and Ladislas's policy favoured the Catholics and communion in one kind, as in Poland and Hungary. Intermittent civil conflict followed throughout his reign. His actions led the Utraquists after 1482 to employ an Italian bishop temporarily for maintaining their clerical ordinations, whereby they could avoid complete rupture with Rome and yet maintain adherence to the Compacts against Catholics and the king. Riots in Prague in 1483 brought municipal legislation reaffirming Hussite principles that included not only communion in both kinds for adults and children but also vernacular hymn singing and other Scripturally based claims. The people appealed to older privileges about the Cup and expelled Catholic monks and priests from the city. Ladislas finally had to give way to Utraquist demands and at the National Diet in 1485 at Kutna Hora he agreed to a treaty whereby, for thirty-two years, both Utraquists and Catholics undertook to observe the Compacts and Sigismund's decrees about them. Both sides were to continue in their respective churches with separate practices and complete freedom for individuals to receive communion as they wished. The Catholics thus abandoned their uncompromising opposition to communion in both kinds, whilst the Utraquists allowed Catholics to return to the city and positions which they had held. The settlement left the Utraquist Church predominant in the capital, with a greater degree of toleration and respect for the Compacts by Ladislas than before. But the Utraquists did not achieve reconciliation with Rome, and after their bishop's death in 1493 they remained in isolation amid surrounding Catholic churches.

Utraquism and its fortunes through the fifteenth century were not the only developments from Hussitism, nor were they necessarily most significant for the future. Alongside controversies involving Utraquists and Catholics there was the legacy of Taborite and radical Hussite ideas. The military power of the Taborites was broken at Lipany, and Tabor itself was eventually taken over in 1452 in George's policy to break sectarianism, but extreme ideas continued to flourish among the lower classes. In the circumstances of George's election as king in 1458, a new society – the Unity of the Bohemian Brethren – was formed. All kinds of groups were included in the movement, Waldensians as well as Taborites and other individuals, and they were inspired by Peter Chelčický, the Bohemian squire and thinker.[1] Born

[1] For Chelčický, see M. Spinka, "Peter Chelčický, The Spiritual Father of the Unitas Fratrum", in *Church History* XII (1943), pp. 271–91.

in 1379, Chelčický became a devoted disciple of Hus and learned Wycliffe's doctrines through the Taborites, but he remained unschooled, without Latin or academic theology, and depended more completely and radically than his masters on Scripture alone. To the Bible he ultimately appealed for all his ideas, so that he rejected the whole system of the Roman Church, and any homicide or thought of crusades. From his first appearance in 1420, he preached pacifism and in his many writings thereafter attacked Utraquists as well as Rome, in particular criticizing Rokycana and even the Taborites for their involvements in war. Most of his later years he spent in south Bohemia, where he gathered disciples around him and practised a primitive, communal life. In his *Net of Faith* he argued against the actions of Emperor and Pope in their attempts to impose religious conformity; they were, he said, like two great whales, destroying the "net of faith" and unity for salvation, thereby allowing ordinary people to be lost. His hope was for Hussitism reconstituted in "apostolic" terms, with complete separation of Church and State, and not long before his death, he was brought by Rokycana into contact with a group led by the archbishop's nephew, Gregory. Together, they formed a religious community in 1458 at Kunvald, and under Gregory's guidance fellowship was extended to other groups; but the attempt to unite with Waldensians – from whom Chelčický drew many of his ideas – was unsuccessful, chiefly because they found that they had departed from apostolic poverty.[1] In 1467, the Kunvald Brethren took a decisive step in setting up a church separate alike from Rome and the Utraquists, and at this point they adopted the title of "The Unity of the Brethren". They had one of their number, Matthew, ordained bishop by a local priest possessing both Roman and Waldensian ordination, and the new bishop in turn consecrated priests for the new body. The principles adopted were for complete separation of Church and State, extending to a ban on oaths, military service or participation in municipal life. The Brethren held all possessions in common and went so far in their exclusiveness that they rebaptized all converts, even from the Utraquist communion.

By instituting its own order of priesthood, the Unity became "the first reformed Church which consciously and expressly renounced the Catholic principle of the apostolic succession".[2] The opposition of its members to the Utraquists earned Rokycana's disapproval as well as that of King George, and they were later actively persecuted by Ladislas II as disturbers of the peace. The Brethren took their authorities from the Bible and Chelčický's writings, and at Prague

[1] Cf. G. H. Williams, *The Radical Reformation* (London, 1962), pp. 210 f.
[2] K. Krofta, in *Cambridge Medieval History*, Vol. VIII, p. 103.

University in 1478 defended their strict views in debate against the Utraquists. Later, however, they modified some of their ideas, and grew even stronger in support. The original communalism of the Unity was that of an agrarian party, and this was drastically altered in 1490 at a synod in Brandys so that, with Bishop Matthew's agreement, members were allowed to join in civic and national life. These new ideals were confirmed in 1495, and at the same time the works of Chelčický and Gregory were condemned. Such actions split the Brethren into Major and Minor parties, where the latter remained conservative and agrarian and complained that the others – the burgher members – had broadened the "strait gates" and were like rogues and thieves "who come not in by the door".[1] Efforts made to reconcile the parties failed and in 1500 Amos, the leader of the Minor Party, ordained a separate priesthood for his followers. Despite the rancour that developed between the two bodies, however, both continued to flourish in their zeal for evangelism and spiritual life. The Amosites resembled many other contemporary groups in Germany and Switzerland and merged later in Anabaptist bodies, but the Major Party was of vital importance for its ties with Luther.

It was under the leadership of Luke of Prague that this body prospered. Luke, born in 1458, had begun as a Utraquist but joined the Unity in 1482 before the appearance of divisions. His work and teaching were both of moment, for he had dealings with Orthodox Christians in the East and Waldensians in Italy, and sought to make the Unity's position publicly known. In 1511, he issued a Latin defence of his party's faith and orthodoxy for Ladislas II, and his arguments and expositions directly influenced Luther during the years when he changed from attempting to decry Bohemian heresy to the point in 1520 at which he proclaimed that he was a Hussite.[2] But beyond this, Luke's theology came close to much that was Lutheran afterwards. His rejection of an outright, exclusive stress on Scripture for the appeal to God's voice and witness in the Word realized in preaching and life, fitted Luther's argument, even though at the same time he retained some Taborite ideas denying the Real Presence in the Eucharist. Until Luke's death in 1528, the Unity moved along its own path, at variance with the new German developments; thereafter, its members adopted Lutheran ideals, and were later persecuted and suppressed in the seventeenth century before the movement was revived as the Moravian Brotherhood, that body which was to have such profound influence upon Wesley. On the eve of the Lutheran

[1] Williams, op. cit., pp. 212 f.

[2] For Luke's influence on Luther, see S. H. Thomson, "Luther and Bohemia", in *Archiv für Reformationsgeschichte* XLIV (1953), pp. 160–81.

Reformation, however, the Unity of the Brethren was only one of three bodies into which Hussitism had divided in the fifteenth century and where the vision of a Bohemian national church had scarcely been achieved. By 1500 in Bohemia alone there were between three and four hundred congregations of the Major Party, and it was supported respectably by the urban classes, but the older stock of independent peasant allegiance to Hussitism had greatly disappeared in the growth of feudalism and serfdom. With this change had also vanished much of that strength which had given community of purpose and achievement for Christ's cause in Hussitism at the death of its original leader.

Bohemian reform movements lost much momentum and potential for success in their divisions, but the Hussite victories and the privileges of Utraquism and the Unity of the Brethren were considerable by comparison with what took place more generally in Germany. They showed what possibilities there were in a national objective, and this Luther well noted, despite his early aversion as a German to Bohemian achievements. It was not hard to observe in Germany that various developments – in the organized church and its working with papal or princely control, in ideas and in popular devotion – conflicted rather than came together, and tended to confirm corruption and disorder rather than aid reform in the land. In the Hussite wars, Sigismund found his German imperial power desperately weak, whilst the princes, ecclesiastics, towns and leagues which held much local control were confusing in the extreme. But the results of settlement with the Hussites and the Pope still further accelerated the dissipation of political and ecclesiastical power in fifteenth-century Germany. Until his death, Sigismund was the mainspring for reform in the German Church, but from 1434 onward he was increasingly dissatisfied with Basel, and his successor Albert II declared in 1438 that the Empire would be neutral in the dispute between the Council and Eugenius IV. This proposal the Pope accepted at Mainz in the following year, and during the next decade of official neutrality the Emperor, princes and Popes alike negotiated privately for a more stable concordat. In 1445, two of the imperial electors – the Archbishops of Cologne and Triers – declared for the anti-pope Felix V, for which Eugenius somewhat rashly deposed them. Wider divisions, however, were avoided by the able diplomacy of Cusa and Piccolomini, by then the Emperor's secretary, and following an assembly at Frankfort and a Concordat of the Princes in 1447, a more lasting settlement was signed at Vienna in 1448 with the new Pope, Nicholas V.

This agreement restored to the Pope wide and effective control over the German Church, greater control than over other national churches, but it also confirmed local princely authority in clerical as much as secular affairs. Reform of any meaningful kind was conveniently ignored alike by Pope and princes. Before his death, Eugenius IV had secretly absolved himself from binding arrangements made at Frankfort and the subsequent terms at Vienna had significant omissions securing papal prerogatives. Nicholas V remained willing to underwrite vaguely the older pact with the German "nation" made by Martin V in 1418, but nothing was said about specific reform, the college of cardinals, or matters of papal jurisdiction and control. In theory the Pope's authority over provisions, justice and finance was left intact and in practice many abuses continued in ecclesiastical organization. Even where Nicholas V showed interest in Windesheim reform and Busch's work, and was prepared to support Cusa in attacking corruption, the evil effects of the settlement were soon apparent in the decisive opposition of Duke Sigismund and other princes to such measures. Papal patronage remained extensive, and in 1474 and 1475 Sixtus IV bestowed on the Emperor presentations to no less than three hundred benefices in Germany. But this transfer of control entailed no reform, even where appointments passed into non-papal hands. Little substance in German terms remained in the threat of appeal to a General Council against the Pope, for power was divided between Emperor and princes, and many were willing to appeal to the Pope against Frederick III whom they considered unfit to rule. More solid authority lay with the secular and ecclesiastical princes, and by the time of the Vienna Concordat political rivalry and strife were widespread in Germany. Families like the Wittelsbachs and Wettins had their own domestic feuds, whilst the conflict that started in 1449 between Albert Achilles of Brandenburg and the south German towns became notorious for the damage that it caused.

But apart from these disturbances, local rulers consolidated control over ecclesiastical matters, governing the churches in their own lands and ensuring that they shared the profits in clerical taxation, appropriations and the workings of justice. The Pope certainly asserted his authority in these matters and made heavy financial demands upon the German clergy, but the princes and nobility generally retained their powers and grew wealthy from abuses in the system. Each ruler, it was said, went his own way and behaved as "Pope in his own lands", and nothing officially remained of the hope for a German reformed Church, such as had been glimpsed at Constance and in the writings of Cusa. Ecclesiastical confusion and demoralization naturally followed, even where attempts were made in the orders to deal with spiritual laxity and corrupt life. The Windesheim missionary efforts among the older monastic bodies and the extension of Observant principles in German mendicant houses revealed awareness of many failings, but they also suffered from the conflicting authorities and demands of princes and Popes that made more general reform impossible to achieve. The Observance was adopted with great zeal by the German Augustinian friars after 1477, and early in the following century the Vicar General John Staupitz applied such principles in the hope of reviving spirituality more widely. It was as an Augustinian friar under Staupitz that Luther learned both what was possible in these reforms and how far they remained from touching abuses in the German Church or reaching people's needs. Anti-papalism and anti-clericalism both grew apace where the local prince was stronger than the Emperor, and papal demands were not as effectively countered as in countries with strong national monarchies. Apart from reforms in the orders, these feelings were voiced in other developments, above all in the growth of scholarship and teaching and in movements of popular unrest.

Universities in Germany had generally been established only after 1300, but they developed steadily under princely patronage, and individual scholars became famous in the fifteenth century. Nominalist in traditional philosophical terms and nationally antagonistic to the Bohemians, they provided little sympathetic support to Wycliffite ideas, but John of Wesel was an exception and of consequence in influencing Luther. Wesel was born about 1400 and studied at Erfurt where he became a doctor of theology and rector in 1456. He later taught at Basel and in 1464 was appointed cathedral preacher in Worms, but his sermons and writings brought his deposition in 1477 and trial by the Inquisition two years later. In his views he attacked current practices of penance and indulgences, advocated marriage of the clergy and communion in both kinds and denied transubstantiation. Moreover he strongly defended the Wycliffite principle that the Church was composed of all the predestined and was alleged to deny any doctrine of original sin. For his views he was condemned to imprisonment for life and he died in 1481. But more widely in the growth of German scholarly studies the New Devotion gave inspiration, both in helping to consolidate older attitudes and for blending with new themes in Humanism. Contemporary with Wesel, John of Goch was possibly schooled by the Brethren of the Common Life before studying at Paris, and thereafter spent most of his career in Mechlin until his death in 1475. His life was that of a secluded theologian and scholar, and he escaped the official criticisms and censure accorded to Wesel, though he shared many of his ideas in attacking abuses, upholding the authority of Scripture and arguing for a doctrine close to justification by faith.[1] Meanwhile, the last great Nominalist and disciple of Occam, Gabriel Biel, was born in 1420 and educated at Heidelberg and Erfurt before joining the Brethren of the Common Life. He was appointed to the charge of Urach Church in 1479 and shared in founding the University of Tübingen, of which he became and remained until his death in 1495 the first Professor of Theology. Biel's philosophy most sharply presented the Nominalist view of God's relationship to Man and to his fundamental teaching on the place of faith Luther owed a great deal, even though he turned from Biel in his scholastic expositions.

At the same time the New Devotion became deeply influential in other ways, especially where the school at Deventer was placed in 1485 under the control of the well-known classical enthusiast and former protégé of Cusa, Alexander Hegius. He introduced reforms into the school to lay weight on classical principles and writings, and with such changes moved on far from the original ideas of the Brethren. In his pride and scholarly ambition, Hegius seemed a great contrast to the earlier teachers in the school, but many of the older principles remained as under him Deventer became a renowned centre for training German classical scholars. Before his death in 1498, his pupils had reached a total of over two thousand. At the same time the school at Zwolle attained no mean reputation, and from it came John Wessel Gansfort, one of the most important thinkers in the New Devotion and in German Humanism, supplying one more link to Luther and other reformers in the sixteenth century.

Gansfort was born about 1420 and spent most of his life until thirty at Zwolle and Deventer, where he knew à Kempis and studied and taught in the community. In following years he travelled widely through Europe, making the friendship of Bessarion and the future Pope Sixtus IV, as well as that of Goch and the young Reuchlin. But Gansfort's contacts with Italian Humanism for the most part confirmed his critical feelings about contemporary clerical corruption which he castigated as worse than the evils of the Pharisees and scribes in the time of Christ. He learned Greek and Hebrew and for a period returned to Heidelberg to teach, but theologically he argued fiercely for reform, particularly for a renewed spirituality and attention to Scriptural principles. Much of his criticism was in form familiar to Groote and other Brethren, but he brought out strongly the themes of predestination and faith like Wesel and Goch before him and Luther afterward. Indeed, Luther thought that his enemies could have accused him of borrowing from Gansfort had he read his works earlier than he did.[2] "Faith", Gansfort wrote,

[1] Cf. C. Ullmann, *Reformers before the Reformation*, translated by R. Menzies (Edinburgh, 1863), Vol. I, Bk. I.

[2] Hyma, op. cit., pp. 191 ff.; Williams, op. cit., pp. 30 f.

. . . is not the cause of our justification, but its proof . . . . "The just shall live by faith" . . . . Hence in unbelievers, their unbelief separates them from life. But "he that believeth on Him hath eternal life". Therefore our goods works nourish and strengthen our faith, but do not make it alive, yet they strengthen the bond of life, namely our faith. For only Christ and the Spirit quicken us . . . . It is not our faith, whether it be in Christ or in God who delivered Christ over to be a sacrifice, nor is it the sacrifice of Christ that constitutes our righteousness; but it is the purpose of God, who accepts the sacrifice of Christ, and who through Christ accepts the sacrifice of Christians.

These arguments came close to those of Luther and Calvin later, but Gansfort went further, and apart from denouncing abuses he opened the way to radicalism in discussing the nature of the Eucharist. Whilst affirming a doctrine of transubstantiation, he strongly emphasized that the sacrament was inward and received by faithful Christians as a commemorative feast. This spiritual sacrament had been possible before the Incarnation and remained possible for Christians without essential dependence upon any bread: St. Paul alone in the desert after his conversion, and hermits having no contact with priests demonstrated this fact. In the statement that "those who believe on Christ are they that eat His flesh", Gansfort dismissed the need for bread or priest in communion, or the thought that it had to be bound in time or space. Such commemorative ideas suggested by Gansfort passed on to the more extreme Protestant groups after 1500 who refused to remain content with the conservative understanding of Luther or Calvin about the Eucharist.[1]

Gansfort's legacy for the sixteenth century was therefore involved; but for Humanism it had a direct and valuable meaning, since he founded a school at Münster and influenced Rudolf Agricola (1442–85), the most respected of German scholars in the age and reputed "father of German humanism".[2] For a brief period, Agricola followed Gansfort at Heidelberg, and though he wrote little, his learning was immense and he championed the newer studies against scholasticism in Germany. More widely in the Rhineland, Humanistic ideas grew under the influence of Conrad Celtis (1459–1508), who gained distinction in his Latin writing, was honoured as poet laureate by Frederick III and at Heidelberg in 1491 founded the "Literary Society of the Rhine". Within this circle came to be included Jacob Wimpfeling, the historian Trithemius, Abbot of Spontheim, John Reuchlin, and at greater distance scholars like Peutinger at Augsburg

[1] Williams, op. cit., pp. 31–3.
[2] Cf. L. W. Spitz, *The Religious Renaissance of the German Humanists* (Harvard, 1963), Chapter II.

and Pirkheimer in Nuremberg.[1] In this spread of studies, it was notable that scholars travelled all over Europe, above all to Italy, for their classical Latin and Greek knowledge, but on return repeatedly stressed their national outlook against that Italian. Celtis spoke of the "ancient hatred" that could "never be dissolved between Italians and Germans", and this sentiment was shared by others who rejected much that was Italian despite their enthusiasm for learning. With memories of the older Hussite wars, these German Humanists also condemned everything in Bohemia in terms of nationalism and heresy,[2] but they none the less concerned themselves with ecclesiastical troubles in Germany. They gave attention to Hebrew and Greek for textual studies in the Bible, and more positively than the Italian Humanists were sensitive to what was wrong in the Church and in religious life as well as in society and politics. From early years in German Humanistic studies, teaching was more directly focussed on remedying the world around than was the case with the Italians, who looked supremely to the education and training of men to be responsible in society as they found it.

The use of printing, known in Holland in the 1440's but effectively the discovery of Gutenberg and his associates in southern Germany after 1450, similarly revealed the differences between German and Italian studies. Printing spread rapidly in the closing decades of the fifteenth century, most noticeably into Italy, where scholars and Humanists generally delighted in having classical works made available in such form. But significantly, its contribution to German Humanistic studies remained comparatively small until about 1500, partly because competition from Italian printers was fierce, but in part because Gutenberg, Fust and Schoeffer printed theological works – Bibles, psalters and devotions – rather than the ancient writings of Greece and Rome. Wider classical interests were only more fully catered for in the production of books by a man like Koberger of Nuremberg in 1500. Throughout, German Humanism was orientated to reform of Church and State, far more so than the movement in the Italian Renaissance, and it was illuminating that the issue between scholasticism and the New Learning in the German universities was fought out in a celebrated religious dispute over the study of Hebrew. Reuchlin became famous in Europe not only for his knowledge of Greek and Latin but also as a Hebrew scholar, and he made a critical study of the language of the Old Testament alongside the New. In his work he met opposition from a convert from Judaism, Pfefferkorn, who violently attacked Jews and in 1509 secured from

[1] For Celtis, Wimpfeling, Reuchlin and Pirkheimer, cf. Spitz, op. cit.
[2] Thomson, "Luther", p. 161.

Emperor Maximilian an edict to confiscate all anti-Christian Jewish books. Reuchlin protested, chiefly because of the value of the Talmud and other Jewish writings for the study of Christianity, but also because he considered such action unjust. Thereby he aroused attacks from Pfefferkorn and the Dominican Inquisitors, and the argument flared into a general dispute between the New Learning and the Old. Reuchlin eventually was accused of heresy and in 1513 was cited to appear before the Inquisitor-General in Germany at Mainz. He refused to go, appealing instead to the Pope, who exonerated Reuchlin and confirmed this decision when his enemies tried to reverse the judgment. The victory for Reuchlin and Humanism was vindicated, and the academic and theological follies of the scholastics were ridiculed, in *The Letters of Obscure Men*, a series of fictitious epistles written by the Humanist Ulrich von Hutten and others, who lampooned their opponents' casuistry and pedantry.

Reuchlin's dispute resounded through Europe, and all could see the folly of his enemies, but yet much of what the scholars voiced in Germany for long had little effect beyond their university centres. They were given the patronage of the Emperor and the secular princes and bishops, who were anxious for prestige in learning but generally took too little interest in dealing with social and clerical evils. As in Italy, cultural pursuits claimed much wealth, and German churches and religious art were famous before 1500, but they went hand in hand with oppression and discord that stimulated popular religious and social movements without exact contemporary counterpart in Christendom. Lack of any strong central authority hamstrung official demands for reform even though later it left Luther adequately protected by one prince, the Elector of Saxony. But more than this, weak monarchical power in Germany accompanied social developments that formed a distinctive part in the Reformation with Luther and after him.

The political situation in Germany in the last part of the fifteenth century stopped short of the anarchy which had prevailed earlier because the princes were consolidating direct control over their territories. This development was reflected in the declining work and terror of the Holy Vehme, the secret judicial organization which had its origins in Westphalia and dominated Germany more widely in its work. The tribunals in this organization claimed to administer God's justice in dealing with morals of all kinds, popular superstitions and witchcraft, and they conducted nocturnal trials, with compurgations and ruthless judgments irrespective of class. Their membership was secret and any betrayal of their activity brought death. They were a feature in society where royal and imperial government had lost its power and even the Emperor could be cited before a court, but the Vehme was a declining force after 1450 as effective control was being drawn back into the hands of princes who could police their own States. Paradoxically, however, this growth of princely power brought greater, not less, oppression in localities and stimulated religious demands with complaints against political, social and economic injustices. More than once these movements were tinged with apocalyptic or millennial ideas, which sprang in part from older general hopes – such as were found in the French Jacquerie or the Peasants' Revolt – but in part also from specific Taborite missionary activity after the 1420's. Hussite congregations flourished later in Franconia and revolutionary Hussite ideas could be traced in disturbances at Eger in 1467; such ideas were embedded in thoughts that Frederick III would be a deliverer from tyranny and in the hopes centred on Sigismund's agreements of 1436, which were published several times in the 1480's and 1490's as *The Reformation of Sigismund*.[1]

In 1476 there occurred the episode of the so-called drummer of Niklashausen, which most notably illustrated the growth of Hussite and other influences.[2] Niklashausen, in the Bishopric of Würzburg, lay close to Bohemia, and in the 1470's was the centre of disputes between the ordinary people and the bishop whose government was crushing in its financial demands. A young shepherd and drummer, Hans Böhm, declared that the Virgin Mary in a vision had ordered him to preach the end of the world and its salvation at Niklashausen, and in his preaching he rapidly began denouncing priests and governments. The new State of the Millennium was at hand, he proclaimed, where all were equal and to have possessions in common; all lordships were abolished, no more tolls or taxes were to be paid and the clergy in particular were to be deprived of their material goods and amend their lives. Such preaching was popular in its anti-clericalism and peasants from all over south Germany flocked to Niklashausen, where the worship of Mary was extended to Böhm as a saint. The Prince-Bishop of Würzburg became alarmed and arrested Böhm, but his supporters marched to the city to release him from prison. After unsuccessful efforts by the bishop and other authorities to have the insurgents peacefully dispersed, they were scattered with cannon-fire, Böhm was tried, found guilty of heresy and sorcery, and burned. Though his ashes were scattered, Böhm's influence lived on, and in 1477 the church in which he had preached in Niklashausen was demolished to end his cult more completely. The rising was checked, but it showed that feelings of religious and social discontent ran deeply

[1] Cf. Cohn, op. cit., pp. 113 f., 249. [2] Cohn, op. cit., pp. 240 f.

in Germany underneath the burden of corrupt ecclesiastical and princely rule. Böhm himself seemingly was little more than the tool of men known as Hussites or Beghards in the region, and though he was quickly dealt with, the other movements persisted and had their consequences in the multiplying of radical religious and social groups through Germany in the following century.[1]

More widespread and less tinged with chiliastic ideas were the peasant "Bundschuh" disturbances, so named after the clogs or laced shoes of the common man who joined with his fellows in seeking to have grievances redressed. The programmes of such groups repeatedly urged that all intermediate powers should be cut out – princes, bishops, knights, all regarded as oppressors – and that the Emperor and Pope with overriding authorities should act to bring justice. Until the early years of the sixteenth century, these appeals were essentially conservative and directed to restoring peasant rights under old German "common" law – village rights over woods, pastures and stock – which so often had been usurped by local lords. But ominously these demands became more extreme where peasants in Carinthia and Würtemberg and then more widely spoke of the justice of God, and appealed to divine or Biblical law for ordering society. In addition the earlier struggles were fragmentary and localized, but the disturbances after 1500 had support and organization throughout Germany, and blended peasant grievance with plans for religious reform. In these developments, a radical minority worked to band groups together, particularly in south and west Germany, and presented programmes that were increasingly sweeping in their scope – there were schemes for killing nobles and priests, seizing control of the government, distributing possessions among the people and giving justice to all. Joss Fritz appeared as a leader of the "Bundschuh" in numerous risings around the Rhine between 1493 and 1518, and despite repeated failures the general movement gained in support and responsibility with its hopes for reform. For the most part, such hopes had little chance of success but they were nevertheless indicative of conditions in Germany in the early sixteenth century. Moreover, they formed the basis of Luther's appeal to the German nation in 1520 and of the revolutionary aims of Thomas Müntzer and his followers in the Peasants' War. Unrest and open struggles after 1512 also disturbed the towns, and together with the other factors in social, religious and Humanistic developments, helped to provide the setting for that general response to Luther's individual challenge in Germany in 1517.

[1] Williams, op. cit., traces through these connexions in the abundant growth of extreme groups in the sixteenth century.

CHAPTER XI

THE ENGLISH CHURCH AND LOLLARDY AFTER 1431

WITH THE SUPPRESSION OF THE DISTURBANCES OF 1431 BY A government possibly over-anxious about political or social rebellion, Lollardy in England passed into its third phase, where neither intellectual leadership nor political involvements had any formative part in the movement. Lollardy went underground as the creed of unlettered or semi-literate laymen who placed their trust about everything in the Bible. Thereafter in the fifteenth century, Lollards only occasionally attracted public notice, and though they continued to be of more consequence for the sixteenth century than has sometimes been thought,[1] their part in events leading on to the Reformation crisis can best be viewed in the perspective of English ecclesiastical affairs as a whole. These developments showed continuing and close interaction between politics and religion, where to a large degree England went its own way in practice if theoretically still a country in Latin Christendom, and the break with the past only came in revolutionary action in the 1530's, as the full tide of Lutheran and other Protestant struggles swept across the English world. Despite, however, earlier demands for action, the same factors continued to mould English religious affairs through the whole century that led to Henry VIII's summoning of Parliament in 1529.

Chief amongst these factors was the English Church in its organization and working, where king and Pope competed for control and the hierarchy attended to politics as much as religion. At times it seemed as if ecclesiastical issues were less open to reform than in earlier years. Though in theory continuing to be fully part of the Latin Church and governed by Roman canon law and papal authority, the English clergy fell far more certainly under royal control than before 1400. Because of Lollard problems, the English kings and bishops were always anxious to show themselves completely orthodox, but they also agreed in keeping papal authority at a distance. On occasion, royal and episcopal aims merged, at other times the kings brought

[1] Cf. A. G. Dickens, *Lollards and Protestants in the Diocese of York*, 1509–1558 (Oxford, 1959), pp. 8 f., revaluing older conclusions summarized in J. Gairdner, *Lollardy and the Reformation*, Vol. I.

pressure to bear on the bishops to make them act against the Pope. It mattered little that royal government during the century experienced the vicissitudes of minority and regency rule, the struggles of barons and dynasties, and the strong hand of individual monarchs. Henry VI was a boy when he succeeded to the throne in 1422, and though he began to rule personally from 1437 onward, his later madness opened the door to noble quarrels before he was deposed in 1461. The Yorkist kings who followed – Edward IV (1461–83), Edward V (1483) and Richard III (1483–5) – and the first Tudors after them – Henry VII (1485–1509) and Henry VIII (1509–47) – all knew the political, social and dynastic uncertainties of continuing faction and possible overthrow, vigorous though they might be in controlling the country.

Irrespective of changing political leadership, however, all the English rulers behaved similarly to the Popes and bishops in their single-minded concern to uphold royal power. The second statute of Provisors in 1390 extended and made more effective the earlier legislation against papal authority and laid down severe secular punishments for anyone making or supporting illegal appointments by the Pope to English sees. Boniface IX's attempt to annul this law led to the third statute of Praemunire in 1393 which set out penalties for anybody involved in buying or distributing papal bulls, sentences of excommunication or instruments of any kind infringing the king's rights. Such measures were partly the product of special circumstances in the Great Schism, and only five years later Richard II made concessions in a fresh compromise with Boniface, but the statutes remained operable all through the following century and they deeply irritated the Popes. Martin V's complaint that "it is not the Pope but the King of England who governs his church and his dominions" was echoed frequently by later pontiffs. In 1428 the Pope browbeat Archbishop Chichele and granted legatine powers and a commission to act in England to Cardinal Beaufort, a great-uncle of Henry VI. Despite Beaufort's position, however, the government protested at what it considered an illegal infringement of ancient right. The council, it was stated, had not asked for the visit of a legate, and Beaufort's claims and actions were therefore disallowed.[1] At a later date Pius II's demand for a crusading subsidy was met with the clergy's argument in Convocation that the King of England had to approve and raise taxes, whilst at the end of the century, Henry VII was no less high-handed in disposing of similar appeals from the Popes. In 1489, Innocent VIII's request for money met with the low response of a collection of eleven guineas at the royal court,[2] and when Alexander VI in 1500

[1] Gee and Hardy, op. cit., No. XLIV, pp. 139–41.

[2] H. M. Smith, *Pre-Reformation England* (London, 1938), pp. 23 f.

made his plea for a crusade, Henry allowed Canterbury Province to hand over twelve thousand pounds whilst explaining that he could contribute nothing himself. Individuals like Beaufort, John Kemp, Bourchier, Morton and finally Wolsey could all gain papal advancement and become cardinals, but only as the kings permitted or wanted such rewards for their servants, and these they could flatly disallow if royal rights were being infringed. When Wolsey showed himself eventually too conscious of papal honours and authority as a cardinal and legate, his behaviour brought anti-papal feeling to a head in England as well as his own disgrace by Henry VIII. Royal control over episcopal appointments was in practice final, not least as the Papacy appeared increasingly as an alien, Italian power and protests about annates or payment of any moneys going out of the country were made regularly by Parliament and Convocation.

More completely even than in the fourteenth century, the English bishops were royal civil servants, administrators and members of the government, sometimes laymen who were trained in civil law, not theology, and in consequence took holy orders and became bishops solely for the revenues of the office.[1] Chichele as Archbishop of Canterbury until 1443 brought many able men for government on to the bench, but there were few who were spiritual or religious in outlook. Partly because of the effects of the statute of Provisors of 1390, which stopped papal funds for poor students at the universities, and in part because of Arundel's Oxford constitutions, scholarship was to a real extent at a discount. Only towards the close of the fifteenth century was such a trend checked as Humanistic interests spread in England, so that the English bishops after 1500 numbered more with scholarship and spiritual concern. Throughout the period the bishops generally were non-resident and possessed of plural livings, whilst their work of a pastoral nature was carried out by assistant bishops or bishops *in partibus infidelium*, who had no proper responsibilities otherwise; Kemp scarcely ever visited his primatial seat of York from 1426 to 1452 as archbishop, and Bourchier in charge of Canterbury for thirty-three years never made a metropolitan visit. These men became notable for their patronage in learning and building, in founding schools and colleges. Bishop Waynflete of Winchester founded Magdalen College at Oxford, Alnwick of Lincoln assisted Henry VI in instituting Eton and King's College at Cambridge, whilst later in Henry VIII's reign Fitzjames of London and Bishop Fisher were known for their gifts respectively to Christ's and St. John's Colleges also at Cambridge. Wolsey's splendid foundation of

[1] Cf. A. H. Thompson, *The English Clergy and their Organization in the Later Middle Ages* (Oxford, 1947), pp. 42 f.

"Cardinal's" College, later Christ Church, at Oxford only followed in a well-established tradition by 1520.

Such leadership was valuable, even indispensable, in government and for promoting intellectual pursuits, but no more than in the fourteenth century was it the best for meeting criticisms about abuses and initiating reforms. Alongside anti-papal sentiment which could bind king and bishops together, there was strong criticism of the Church's order and a current of anti-clerical feeling which was not necessarily Lollard in content. For all his neglect, Bourchier did issue a comprehensive commission in 1455 for the reform of the clergy, and he singled out as evils the decay of monastic rules and practices and the corruption of secular clergy,

> . . . who . . . neglecting and scorning the cures of souls to which they are bound, like vagabonds and profligates run about through the kingdom and apply themselves to worldly gain, to revellings moreover, to drinking bouts, and to wicked adulteries and fornications . . . .[1]

Bourchier in addition condemned illiteracy among the priests and lay immorality or the refusal to pay tithes, and he authorized his officers to act severely in correcting failings. But the commission had little effect, expressing pious hopes rather than leading to determined action, and Bourchier himself soon became absorbed in government at the expense of pastoral duties. His concern as a bishop was exceptional, but sharp criticism was voiced by other influential men of the day.

Amongst these critics was Thomas Gascoigne, who became a priest in 1427 and thereafter refused almost all preferments in order to pursue his academic career, in which he became Chancellor of Oxford University.[2] No friend of the Lollards and their ideas, he was nevertheless scathing in condemning the faults of the clergy and attacked not only papal corruption but specific practices and abuses in England. Appointments of wholly unsuitable men as bishops brought Gascoigne's censure, as when George Neville, the Earl of Warwick's brother, was made Bishop-elect of Exeter in 1455 at the age of twenty-two for purely political reasons. Gascoigne judged that Neville "was licensed at Rome to gather the moneys of the Bishopric of Exeter, not to gather the souls of that bishopric to God". He was equally irate about the scandalous promotion of John de la Bere by papal bull to the see of St. David's in Wales at royal request in 1447, even though the Chapter of Wells Cathedral had already rejected him as incapable for the deanship in that diocese. Although Gascoigne denounced

[1] Gee and Hardy, op. cit., No. XLV, p. 141.

[2] For Gascoigne, see Gairdner, op. cit., pp. 243 f.

annates and pluralism, he reserved his gravest criticism for the practice of appropriations which grew steadily worse in the fifteenth century. Where these rights of appointment fell into the hands of a monastery, the community could neglect the living, perhaps putting in a poor vicar at a pittance to say the services and having the tithes collected by a lay officer. As much as pluralism, costs in litigation or the appointments of foreigners, these practices brought decay in church life and the whole care of the people, and Gascoigne was deeply conscious of the loss of faith and of general moral standards with appropriations. He addressed a prayer to the Pope for him to act in ensuring that endowments were properly administered and that spiritual pastors should be appointed to stay and work in their parishes. His criticisms revealed some measure of what was wrong, and he felt strongly enough to see in the natural calamities of 1457 God's judgment on contemporary society. But remedies were not then forthcoming and this is illustrated by the fact that on becoming Bishop of Lincoln in 1521, Longland found all the livings in Buckinghamshire appropriated.

Apart from general laxity and worldliness of the clergy – which was not as bad in the fifteenth century in England as in Germany or Rome – there were specific issues where reform was sought. One concerned the work and power of the ecclesiastical courts, whose costs could be ruinous and whose growing interference in all matters of life was deeply resented. The civil courts naturally disliked such interference, but so also did ordinary people without professional interest. Heresy naturally became a prominent subject with Lollardy, but issues had only to involve minor matters of life for the archdeacon's court to deal with blasphemy, drunkenness, lechery and the like. As these courts flourished, they were served by official proctors with legal qualifications in the higher courts, or by summoners in the lower, where the latter, already condemned in Wycliffe's day, were regarded as parasites or blackmailers in society. The chantry priests, who also multiplied in the fifteenth century, helped invaluably in providing information since they possessed neither parish nor cure and were able to spend their time as scandalmongers and spies, reporting faults and crimes to the archdeacon's court. Attempts to eradicate this abuse had been made from Thoresby's time onward by bringing chantry priests under some corporate discipline, but it was not until Warham became Archbishop of Canterbury in 1503 that more general steps were taken to check the scandals in ecclesiastical jurisdiction. Warham limited the numbers of proctors, had his own special officers appointed for pleading poor causes free of charge, and tried to bring all cases into his own reformed court. But there was protest from his episcopal colleagues, and Wolsey's efforts later as Lord Chancellor to aid litigation with his own poor man's court in the 1520's conflicted with Warham's work, and little therefore was done to mitigate criticism on this score before the storm of major reformation in England.

More effective and positive steps, however, were taken to deal with two other matters – benefit of clergy and sanctuary – which grew beyond all reasonable bounds in the fifteenth century. These issues involved the question of royal power over subjects, clerical as well as lay, and in consolidating their central government the English kings were able also to deal with such abuses. Benefit of clergy dated from William I's reign when ecclesiastical and secular courts and jurisdictions were separated, and it entangled Becket in his dispute with Henry II in the twelfth century. Criminous clerks in practice were favoured where bishops could not impose the death penalty and were loath to degrade a priest convicted in an ecclesiastical court and hand him over to the civil power. As a result, convicted clerics were repeatedly only confined in the bishop's prison, even for very grave crimes. Moreover, anybody who was tonsured and could recite the first verse of Psalm fifty-one was allowed to claim clerical privilege, and such a provision included all who were literate for schoolboys received the tonsure. Barring high treason, after 1351 there seemed no limits to claims of benefit, and in 1400 it was made possible for women – though they were not tonsured – to assert similar privileges. A parliamentary petition of 1455 to restrict benefit of clergy was refused, and later Edward IV secured clergy against arrest in civil as well as criminal cases. The system was only tackled more forcefully by Henry VII and his son after 1485 when it was clearly seen as an abuse to treat the clergy as a separate and privileged corporation. Careful distinctions were made by statute in 1489 between those in orders, those who were not and clergy who had already claimed benefit. Three years later, military deserters were barred from such rights, and in 1510 Henry VIII deprived minor clerics of any claim if guilty of murder or robbery. The Popes confirmed royal action at each stage and in 1516 Leo X legislated that minor orders should always be taken all at once by those who were *bona fide* candidates for the priesthood, and not just for immunity in committing crimes. Such steps were salutary, but benefit of clergy was not swept away until after the Reformation in England. As it was, the combination of severe punishments for crime and the protection claimed by clergy helped notably to strengthen anti-clerical feeling before 1530.

Through these same years, the privilege of sanctuary was notoriously abused even though the incidents at the time of Wycliffe had shown it to be an uncertain claim.[1] Where strict limits were placed as to the

[1] See p. 31 above.

time during which a person could have sanctuary before abjuring the realm, little scandal followed, but some rights were less innocuous in providing more permanent refuge for debtors and felons, and certain centres became renowned as headquarters of crime. Westminster and the Church of St. Martin-le-Grand in London achieved this dubious notoriety, and in 1457 regulations for reform and control were introduced at the latter institution. At St. Martin's, it was stated, rogues "have at divers times issued out of the sanctuary and committed many riots, robberies, manslaughters and other mischiefs", and to remedy this state of affairs a register of inmates was to be drawn up, their arms removed and sureties taken, the gates were to be locked at night, and gambling and entertainment of mistresses were forbidden.[1] Plainly a few clerics would have found these rules difficult to enforce if the sanctuary men were a sizable company, and later reports suggested that the reforms had little effect. In addition there remained great areas in England, such as the Earldoms of Durham, Chester and Lancaster in the north, where exemptions from royal justice remained and were given ecclesiastical colouring on the ground of sanctuary. By his actions and legislation, Henry VII limited the abuse of such privilege, and after taking the rebel Humphrey Stafford from santuary for execution in 1486, he secured three successive bulls from the Popes in 1487, 1493 and 1504, to end the right for various groups. But again it was only in the Reformation that much of the substance of sanctuary disappeared with parliamentary acts in 1536 and 1540 and the concurrent dissolution of the monasteries.

During the century before their destruction, the older monastic foundations steadily decayed, both in numbers of inmates and in spirituality. The conflict with France isolated many of the houses from their governing institutions on the Continent, and though this helped English monasteries to avoid the disasters that overtook communities in French and German fighting (and the Wars of the Roses brought no such widespread destruction), yet they also missed the great reforming movement associated with Windesheim and other bodies in the fifteenth century. Henry V initiated his own monastic reforms and founded two new communities – the Charterhouse of West Sheen and the Brigittine house of Syon – with rich endowments in 1415,[2] and some later bishops like Bourchier were anxious about the decay in the monasteries, but generally too little control was or could be exercised. The Benedictines were exempt from ordinary episcopal oversight and owed allegiance to superiors abroad, but the

[1] Smith, op. cit., pp. 70 f. Cf. also I. D. Thornley, "The Destruction of Sanctuary", in *Tudor Studies*, edited by R. W. Seton-Watson (London, 1924), pp. 182 f.

[2] Knowles, *Religious Orders*, II, pp. 175–84.

Cluniac communities, similarly placed, were separated from direct allegiance to the French mother house in the Schism, and after 1417 were kept by Henry V on a national basis as "alien priories". Abortive efforts were made in 1432 and 1458 by representatives from Cluny to have the houses restored, but only later in the century was foreign control directly under the Pope again permitted.[1] At the start of his reign, Henry VII established a convent of Franciscan Observants in England and encouraged efforts by Morton as Archbishop of Canterbury to reform the monasteries. Morton secured papal authority in 1490 to begin this work and proceeded vigorously to deal with the great Abbey of St. Albans, where corruption was said to be rife. But this project faltered and monastic problems were not methodically taken into hand until Henry VIII's reign. Wolsey in the 1520's dissolved twenty-one smaller foundations to endow his new college at Oxford and as a preliminary to more drastic action, whilst others like Fisher and Alcock suppressed individual institutions, but the wholesale sweeping away of the monasteries came only with the Reformation developments after 1530. On all sides in the early sixteenth century, there was feeling that the monastic bodies were no longer serving their proper functions where they were often nearly empty, held too much wealth in land and property and were failing even in social and hospital work to fulfil older ideals. Exceptions to such sweeping criticisms there were, but by 1500 the monasteries had become too powerful and prominent in their possessions to escape condemnation and the envious eyes of those who wanted their wealth. What Wycliffe had urged on theological and practical grounds much earlier was directly and progressively carried through by Wolsey and Thomas Cromwell. But resentment against the monasteries was sharpened in wider anti-clerical feeling, where England had too many churches and clergy around 1500. As high a proportion as one in twenty-five of the whole adult population were nominally clerics and in some places this figure was higher; in York, where admittedly clergy were attached to Minster services, there were forty-one parish churches and five hundred clergy for a population of eleven thousand.

The clergy were criticized but popular piety continued to flourish. People of all classes devoutly attended Mass, went on pilgrimages and were serious in their lives and prayers; the vast multiplication of chantries reflected evident concern for the individual soul. Ambassadors and travellers in England were struck not only by the wealth of the Church but also by the religious behaviour of the people. "They all," wrote the Venetian Trevisan in 1497, "attend Mass every day and say many Paternosters in public. They give liberal alms,

[1] Ibid., pp. 159–61.

because they may not offer less than a piece of money . . . nor do they omit any form incumbent on good Christians." Against this general religious background the continuing place and development of Lollardy after 1431 can be measured. Proscribed as heresy, Lollardy figured officially, if at all, in the records only of trials, recantations and burnings produced by the bishops and civil authorities through the fifteenth century. Echoes of revolutionary teaching from Wycliffite arguments lasted on until 1431, but in later popular understanding Lollardy was no longer politically and socially subversive. The movement became pietistic, the Lollards themselves could boast no leaders of intellectual standing to add to Wycliffe or Purvey, and in Jack Cade's rising of 1450, which voiced anti-clerical feeling with other grievances and led to Bishop Ayscough's murder, there was no suggestion of Lollard participation.[1]

But Lollardy did not disappear, and though most of those who came within the arm of the law preferred to abjure rather than burn, sufficient evidence remains to show that in organization, teaching and the stubborn retention of fundamentals, the movement continued widespread through the country. The English rulers found themselves absorbed in issues first of foreign war with France and then of civil, dynastic disorder at home, but yet the steady notice of Lollard activities from different parts of England indicates fairly enough that the belief persisted, together with the writings of its faith – the Scriptures in English, some of Wycliffe's vernacular works, notably *The Wicket*, and tracts based on them by his followers. In London, a Lollard was burned in 1438, and two years later Richard Wyche, the veteran from earlier days, was executed as a relapsed heretic. Notices of recantations by five Lollards in Surrey came in 1441, whilst in the 1450's other members were active in Bristol, Somerset and East Anglia as well as around London. They were known by their scorn for priests, denial of transubstantiation and their iconoclasm, but above all for their claim to possess and read the Scriptures in the vernacular. Among the errors admitted and abjured by William and Richard Sparke of Somersham in Huntingdon in 1457 was the assertion about the Eucharist that "a priest has no more power to make the body of Christ than the wheat stalk has. After the words of consecration the bread remains only bread as before; and in fact is debased by having had such spell-words pronounced over it". These ideas were common in Lollard teaching, but where no educated leader was at hand in control, all kinds of extreme beliefs could sometimes be added. The teaching of a Lollard martyr William Smith at Bristol was spread

[1] Aston, op. cit., p. 30, does not regard such silence as conclusive and considers that Lollardy in 1450 could still have political overtones.

among groups in the Chilterns by James Willis, who was himself eventually executed in 1462 following a trial before the Bishop of Lincoln. Willis could read and possessed the New Testament in English, as did his followers such as Geoffrey Symeon and Henry Smith, though their ideas at times appeared crude or extreme on their own confessions. But clear evidence of the continuing vigour and appeal of Lollard work and ideas is found in the fact that Bishop Pecock wrote at length to point out their errors, and in so doing was himself condemned for heresy.

Of all the English bishops of the fifteenth century, Reginald Pecock revealed one of the most attractive personalities as well as a boldness in thought, where his learning was influenced by Humanistic enquiry even if it did not always match his arguments. Ordained in 1422, Pecock was first appointed Master of Whittington College in London, then Bishop of St. Asaph, and finally in 1450 he was advanced to the see of Chichester. Through the years he was closely interested in Lollardy, and tried by argument and in writing to convince individual Lollards of their mistakes. He wanted to convert, not condemn, and wrote in English for easy reading by the clergy and the Lollards; in this, he went further than Wycliffe, whose extended theological treatises had all been in Latin, and whose sermons and short pamphlets alone had appeared in the vernacular. Pecock's most substantial work was *The Repressor of Over Much Blaming of the Clergy*, in which he analysed Lollard arguments to answer them point by point, and at the same time attempted to defend the existing ecclesiastical structure and life. Understandably enough, his arguments in favour of the English Church lacked force but the positive attack on the Lollards' ideas and practices was more impressive. He took as fundamental their belief in the authority and infallibility of the Bible, and set out three "trowings" or beliefs which the Lollards deduced from this, and which he claimed to refute. These "trowings" were first, that no law of the Church was binding on Christians without Biblical warrant; secondly, that any Christian man or woman, willing to understand the Scriptures, would infallibly perceive their true meaning, even in books like Revelation; and thirdly, that anyone with this insight should thereafter listen to no argument to the contrary raised even by a cleric.[1]

To answer such opinions of the "Bible men", as he called them, Pecock invoked the "doom" or judgment of reason for assessing Scripture, authority and the like:

[1] Gairdner, op. cit., pp. 202 f., summarizes Pecock's career and life; V. H. H. Green, *Bishop Reginald Pecock* (Cambridge, 1945), and E. F. Jacob, "Reynold Pecock, Bishop of Chichester", in *Proceedings of the British Academy* XXXVII (1951), pp. 121–153, give more rigorous analyses.

> Whenever and wherever in Holy Scripture or out of Holy Scripture be written any point or any governance of the said law of kind (i.e. Nature), it is more verily written in the book of man's soul than in the outward book of parchment or of vellum; and if any seeming discord be betwixt the words written in the outward book of Holy Scripture, and the doom of reason written in man's soul and heart, the words so written without ought to be expounded and be interpreted and brought forth for the according with the doom of reason in the same matter.

Although he clearly accepted that God had ordained the written Scriptures for articles of faith, Pecock's underlying appeal was to the "inward Scripture of the law of kind, written by God Himself in man's soul when He made man's soul in His image and likeness". The Bible served in matters of faith but could not suffice for everything in the "moral law of kind" where both reasoning and explanations of learned men were necessary. The "Bible men", Pecock argued, relied on "humility" and not reason for interpreting Scripture aright, and were therefore split by their views into many sects and groups. By appealing to experience and reason, he tried to deal with Lollard arguments, and claimed that the movement which had grown so widely through loving God's Word in English had foundered in lacking the guidance of trained leaders.

Pecock's work was broad in sympathy and unusually perceptive in considering many of the genuine weaknesses of Lollardy, but the basis of his argument displeased the orthodox English hierarchy as much as that of the Lollards. In one way, indeed, Pecock himself built on Wycliffite scholasticism by giving such prominence to "reason", and in another he was undoubtedly influenced by critical attitudes in Humanism. Like Valla and Piccolomini, he was able to reject the Donation of Constantine as a forgery in papal claims, but he went too far for orthodoxy in placing reason as the final authority above Scripture and God's revelation. Moreover, in the 1450's, he unwisely belittled the Christian Fathers and even more dangerously claimed that the Apostles' Creed had never been written by the apostles, and that since originally it had not contained the clause about Christ's descent into hell, this phrase was not an article of faith. Such views were startling and not easily forgotten, and in the seesaw of English politics after 1450, Pecock's enemies had their chance as the Yorkists took control from the Lancastrian party. He was cited to appear at Lambeth in May, 1457, and there had to abjure his ideas, after which he publicly burned his own books and was imprisoned first at Canterbury, finally in Thorney Abbey in Cambridgeshire, where he died in 1460. His condemnation fairly illustrated what control the government and hierarchy had over the English Church, for

Pecock secured the Pope's support and two bulls demanding in vain that he be restored to his see. In the event, he died in disgrace, his works condemned as worse than those of Wycliffe. Edward IV in 1475 wrote somewhat alarmingly of the spread of Pecock's ideas, but the bishop's reputation and record were so thoroughly expunged from contemporary comment that a century later he was given an honourable place as a Lollard martyr in Foxe's work.

Edward IV's concern about heresy was stirred by Lollard activity as much as by Pecock's speculations, and it seems that the movement continued to thrive in the latter part of the century in London, Lincoln and the West Country. The account of the burning of John Goose, one of Willis's disciples, in London in 1474 showed sympathy with the courage and teaching of a man who asked for a meal before his execution and commented, "I eat now a good and sufficient dinner as I have a sharp but short shower to pass through after supper". In 1489, Stephen Swallow abjured Lollard doctrines which he admitted to having taught for over thirty years, and five years after, Joan Boughton, of good social standing and aged eighty, was condemned and burned at the stake. She was defiant in claiming to be a disciple of Wycliffe "whom she accounted a saint", and proclaimed that "she was so beloved of God and His holy angels, that she passed not for the fire; and in the midst thereof she cried to God to take her soul into His holy hands".[1] Meanwhile, Lincoln diocese became so troubled with Lollards that in 1491 the bishop personally copied out passages from the older anti-Lollard tract of Netter, "against the Wycliffites, whose most insane doctrines have infected many of the common people of our English religion", and had these extracts arranged for use in dealing with suspects. Henry VII generally showed himself more zealous in championing orthodoxy than his Yorkist predecessors, and in the 1490's and after the numbers of Lollards prosecuted greatly multiplied. The king himself figured in one episode at Canterbury as having converted a Lollard from error before his execution, and Henry publicly declared his intention of dealing harshly with heretics. It seems clear that Lollard teaching was then spreading more widely than before not only in the small communities around London and in the cloth-working areas of the Chilterns, Bristol and Yorkshire, but also through a deeply-rooted network or organization stretching across the whole countryside. There were far more Lollards in England than ever came into contact with the authorities, where followers avoided official enquiries that might reveal their heresies, and the numbers dealt with at times pointed to the strength of this "secret multitude". There were forty-five indictments in the Chiltern

[1] Foxe, op. cit., IV, pp. 7 f.

region in 1506 and 1507, as many in Kent around Tenterden in 1511, a hundred prosecutions between 1510 and 1518 in London, and more than this in the Newbury area of Amersham.[1] These examinations and trials reflected the changes in Lollardy and how it was viewed by the authorities, for the accused were almost all lay people, and their trials were summary, conducted for the purpose of conviction – or recantation – on the legal grounds of heresy. No longer was there concern as even in 1450 to argue, convince or convert the erring priest or layman. Rather, the civil magistrates were anxious to stamp out heresy which appeared to be growing stronger despite official action. Lollardy no longer had its early overt revolutionary flavour, nor did Henry VII or Henry VIII image that it did, for all their anxieties about their throne. But in terms of orthodox faith and in the wider context of religious discontent in Europe, the movement appeared menacing to the Church in a way which Sir Thomas More noted some time before the Reformation came in England.

In these affairs, Humanistic studies and scholarly demand for reform in England also had their place, if crossing only incidentally with Lollardy and a wider anti-clerical sentiment. Renaissance interests in England found early echo in the confused ideas of Pecock, but more systematically they were introduced by individual Englishmen who travelled to Italy and encouraged classical studies in their own country. Duke Humphrey of Gloucester, Henry V's brother, aided men like Adam Moleyns or Andrew Holes in their pursuit of Italian ideas, friendships with Humanists and interest in the classics. Holes served Eugenius IV for a number of years before returning to England to hold a succession of ecclesiastical appointments until his death in 1470. William Grey, who was provided to the Bishopric of Ely by Nicholas V and later became Treasurer under Edward IV, travelled all Europe, was friend to Poggio and Bessarion, and lavish in his own patronage of scholars. So, too, was John Tiptoft, Earl of Worcester, who was notoriously cruel in the Wars of the Roses and was executed in 1470, but nevertheless aided immensely in spreading knowledge and books in the new studies. Others like John Free and John Gunthorpe enjoyed noble support and were more truly scholars in their learning, whilst stimulus to all studies came with the introduction of printing to England by William Caxton in 1476. Caxton himself was far more than just a printer, for he translated works from other languages and directed what were the best books to study. His publications ranged widely over all Humanistic interests, but he nevertheless gave special attention to religious or devotional works, and this tradition was encouraged further by Margaret of Beaufort, the

[1] Details are summarized in Deanesly, *Lollard Bible*, pp. 363 f.

Duchess of Richmond. She helped men like Theodoric Root, who printed one of Rolle's treatises in 1483, and Wynkyn de Worde, who issued a whole series of devotional books at the turn of the century. Conspicuous by their absence were publications of the Bible in English because of the law against vernacular versions.

Academic interests more specifically were nurtured in England by William Grocyn (1446–1519), who provided an all-important link between the old and new learning and taught at Oxford where his students included Thomas Linacre (1460–1524) and John Colet (1466–1519), as well as others like William Latimer and William Lily. In 1489, Grocyn visited Italy at a time when Linacre was already in Florence under the patronage of Lorenzo de' Medici. In the following years, Latimer and Colet also journeyed to the city, and it was not unimportant that these English Humanists knew not only the work of Ficino's Academy but also Florence at the height of Savonarola's influence. They returned to England deeply concerned with religion in their Humanism. To their circle in 1493 was introduced young Thomas More, precocious and brilliant in study, but it was John Colet above all who took the lead in advocating new ideas, austere and zealous as he was in his convictions.

Colet's personality was commanding, and in his studies he gave primary attention to religious and spiritual problems. His learning in the Bible and the Fathers was deep, but at the same time his classical scholarship embraced Neoplatonism and the reading of heretical books. His sincerity, it seems, impressed and won men. From 1497 onward, he lectured with striking appeal at Oxford on St. Paul's Epistles, and in this he abandoned the well-known methods of exposition for more challenging discussion. Instead of analysing each text in turn in different senses – literal, allegorical, moral and anagogic – he took and expounded a letter as an historical document and pointedly drew out contrasts between the primitive Church and the Church of his own day. He made the Bible living and relevant to illustrate the corruption in the England of 1500. From Oxford, Colet went on to St. Paul's in London, where he was installed as dean in 1505. This move greatly enlarged his audience to include ordinary people as well as scholars, and where he spoke on the Gospels rather than the Pauline epistles, it was recorded that crowds flocked to hear him. Amongst his congregations were Lollards who enthusiastically approved of what Colet said and his simple exposition of the Bible in sharp criticism of contemporary faults in the Church. He called men to a revival of spiritual life, to repentance and renewal of what they were supposed to profess, and for all his Humanism and Neoplatonic outlook, he placed faith in some sense over against reason, the foolishness of the Cross against philosophy. Such a ministry plainly endangered the hierarchy in its abuses and through the rest of his life and work at St. Paul's, Colet found himself at loggerheads with Bishop Fitzjames of London, who was an able and learned ecclesiastic but opposed to the new ideas in Humanism. He was deeply suspicious of Colet, and the two men clashed over preaching and also over education. Colet aimed to have children properly instructed in Christian affairs and founded St. Paul's School with the declared purpose "to increase knowledge and worshipping of God and Our Lord Jesus Christ, and good Christian life and manners in the children".

In his preaching and scholarship, Colet sounded a clarion call for a return to spiritual life and his influence was profound upon other Humanists in England and Christendom, notably upon More and Erasmus, who each became involved in the Reformation crisis. But whereas Erasmus stood more broadly upon the foundation of Christendom in his life and attitudes, and merits separate consideration, More in his Christian Humanism remained closely confined to English boundaries and problems and eventually lost his life in such entanglements. Born in 1478, his enthusiasm in classical study drew him particularly to revere Pico della Mirandola for his wide accomplishments, and More himself came to display a variety of skills and a breadth of knowledge that astonished contemporaries. In his early manhood, he was attracted briefly to the ideal of monasticism and always retained a rigorous discipline in his own life, but he went into law, was called to the bar in 1501 and three years later entered Parliament. His close friendship with Colet and Erasmus meant that his home became the centre for Humanistic gatherings and studies, and these seemed to be on the brink of great success at Henry VIII's accession in 1509. The young king's patronage went well with More's own progress in public service; he became Under-Sheriff of London in 1510, a Privy Councillor in 1518, Speaker of the House of Commons five years later, and finally in 1529 Lord Chancellor in succession to Wolsey. From this post he resigned in the growing difficulties of Henry VIII's divorce, and it was therefore as a private citizen that he was executed in 1536 for continuing to uphold papal supremacy.

More was the Humanistic reformer in much wider terms than Colet, and his concern was never directed so sharply to the matter of religious corruption. He held firmly to orthodox faith, and it was this fact that made him both antagonistic to Lollards and Lutherans and also courageous in refusing to deny the authority of the Pope. But he wanted reform, and in contrast to the contemporary evils in England, he sketched out an ideal State in *Utopia* which was published in 1516. More condemned the lack of justice, the social inequalities, poverty and hardships of his day, and he blamed the clergy insofar as they were concerned in creating these evils. In Utopia, he argued, there was common possession of all wealth, free justice and a freedom in religion which allowed none to impose their beliefs on others; such was the ideal for peace, within society and between States. But Utopia as More intended it was an ideal in which Man achieved his highest end without the knowledge of God's revelation in Christ; and in the practical world of Christendom he held as strongly as any conservative to the truth of Roman orthodoxy. His later arguments against Tyndale and reaction to Lutheranism revealed the dilemmas that faced him in a Christendom divided, however full of promise his Humanistic schemes had been.[1] Earlier, however, both his activities and those of Colet had crossed with Lollard affairs in the case of Richard Hunne.

Hunne was a merchant taylor and freeman of London and known for dabbling with Lollards in his anti-clericalism, though he was not regarded as a heretic. His baby died in 1514 and at its burial the priest claimed the bearing cloth as a mortuary fee. This Hunne refused to give on the ground that the infant had no property in the cloth, and on being sued and convicted in the consistory court, he had the priest cited for "praemunire" in the court of King's Bench. Fitzjames then examined Hunne for heresy, had his house searched where a number of banned books were found, and committed him to prison in the Lollards' Tower at St. Paul's. There a few days later Hunne was discovered hanged in his cell. The ecclesiastical authorities claimed this was suicide, the people believed it to have been murder, and the coroner's jury returned this finding, charging the diocesan chancellor Horsey and two of his servants with the crime. The bishop's answer was to set out what he alleged had been the heresies of Hunne, whose body he then had burned by the city's civil officers. When one of Horsey's servants admitted to the murder, stating that he had acted on his master's instructions, Fitzjames repudiated the confession and rashly claimed that the laity had no power over ecclesiastics, certainly not in an issue of heresy. Charges and counter-charges were debated at Blackfriars, where a friar named Standish vigorously put the civil case against the bishop and argued that no ecclesiastical law could have force in England until received there, let alone one alleged against the trial of clerics in the royal courts. Such anti-clerical ideas were very popular in London and the House of Commons, and when Fitzjames tried to have Standish answer for his views before Convocation, the friar sought the king's protection. In a second debate at

[1] Cf. T. M. Parker, *The English Reformation to 1558* (Oxford, 1950), pp. 31–2.

Blackfriars, the judge declared that the bishop had earlier been guilty of "praemunire" in dealing with Standish, and the controversy was resolved with Cardinal Wolsey's public submission to Henry VIII to excuse all the clergy and disavow any thought of harming royal authority. This apology the king accepted, and a compromise followed whereby Convocation withdrew its case against Standish, Horsey was tried and acquitted in the King's Bench and mortuaries were abolished. Henry's agreement displayed his control over the Church, but in part it was meant to divert the stormy anti-clerical feeling voiced in the Commons, which had been excited over Hunne and been dismissed in consequence before granting the king his badly needed financial supplies.

Behind the whole episode, and even Hunne himself (who was probably murdered),[1] there was evidence of Lollard activity and organization in London in close connection with more general anti-clerical sentiment. But these developments did not provoke reformation in England in 1515 or after until Henry VIII decisively rejected the traditional ties to papal authority over the question of his marriage with Katharine of Aragon; and with all the upsets of the 1530's, Protestant doctrinal changes were not more completely introduced until Edward VI's reign. In the 1520's feeling against the Pope and the clergy was deepened in England by Wolsey's unwise flaunting of power as Lord Chancellor, papal legate and Archbishop of York, but Lollardy remained non-revolutionary and played a rôle which did not fit easily into the public course of events in England or Scotland. Lollards kept their few basic tenets of belief and after 1520 gave place intellectually and academically to Lutheran teaching from the Continent, and to the new translation of the New Testament and parts of the Old by William Tyndale. In personal terms there were significant contacts between Lollard evangelists and those who secretly began to spread Luther's ideas and to study the Bible in English,[2] and Bishop Tunstal of London in 1524 judged that Lutheranism only added details to the older movement. In Scotland, too, Lollardy persisted, with individuals suffering martyrdom for their faith, the arrest of thirty adherents after a raid in Kyle in 1494, and the work of Murdoch Nisbet and the Gordons of Earlstown in the early sixteenth century, who made their own translations into Scots from the Wycliffite New Testament. These people and communities had their ties with the Lutherans and Calvinists who later evangelized in Scotland.

[1] Cf. A. Ogle, *The Tragedy of the Lollards' Tower* (Oxford, 1949), for a full analysis of the evidence about Hunne's death.

[2] Cf. E. G. Rupp, *Studies in the Making of the English Protestant Tradition* (corrected edition, Cambridge, 1949), Chapter I.

But Lollardy in England and Scotland was not identical with Lutheranism or Calvinism, nor was its legacy either so direct or shortlived to the new movements. Doctrinally the Lollards valued St. James in his practical advice more than Luther did and gave no special place to St. Paul and justification by faith; whilst their ideas of the Church and the sacraments by no means coincided with those of Luther or Calvin. Lollardy persisted as the faith of artisan groups who neither sought publicity nor to make that decisive challenge to traditional authorities and beliefs which required the more thorough doctrinal restatements of Luther, Zwingli or Calvin, and in England the action of king and Parliament. But its influence lasted on beyond the 1520's and cut across the turbulent developments of the Reformation in England and, more faintly, across those in Scotland as well. Professor Dickens has shown[1] that the dramatic changes in doctrinal and ecclesiastical structures in the sixteenth century for long concerned the majority of Englishmen far less than their deeper accustomed faith and attitudes. Politically, the break was made from papal control by Henry VIII in 1533, and in doctrine the Continental ideas were brought into England under Edward VI; these changes were consolidated more moderately by Elizabeth after 1558, following the interlude of Mary's Catholic reaction. But until about 1580, that is to say, halfway through the reign of Elizabeth, ordinary Englishmen remained Lollard rather than Anglican, Lutheran or Presbyterian, and handed their outlook on to those of independent or sectarian belief. In Scotland, too, it seems that decisive changes came not in 1560 but only about twenty years later, and that for decades, popular attitudes remained a mixture of traditional Catholic and Lollard views as much as Calvinist.[2]

These Lollards of the sixteenth century continued to be the heirs of Wycliffe in challenging Church authority and order by appeal to Scripture and the Christian's right and ability to understand it for daily life. They were essentially nonconformist and sought to draw a barrier between Church and State whereby the individual could be free to believe as he would and preserve his conscience against the commands of others. Though there were Lollard martyrs, these principles did not necessarily issue in heroic action. Nevertheless, they deeply impugned Catholic fundamentals in England as on the Continent; and they conflicted hardly less with those arguments of the sixteenth-century Reformers in favour of authority, doctrinal uniformity and obedience for the fight against Rome.

[1] In *Lollards and Protestants*.

[2] Cf. G. Donaldson, *The Scottish Reformation* (Edinburgh, 1962).

CHAPTER XII

THE FRENCH CHURCH (1438–1516)

GERMANY IN THE FIFTEENTH CENTURY PRE-EMINENTLY KNEW THE evils of a powerless central authority and local corruption that stoked the fires of political, social and religious rebellion. By contrast, France, like England, showed how a strong monarchy could control and direct ecclesiastical affairs, especially in recovery from the exhaustion of conflict in the Hundred Years' War, which proved far more destructive for the French than the English. The later stages of that struggle fitfully crossed the Conciliar developments, where Henry V's brilliant victories were impossible to consolidate and his death in 1422 took most of the energy from the campaign to unite the crowns of France and England. His rival Charles VI died in the same year, but it was not until 1429 that the Dauphin could be crowned as Charles VII, and longer still before he was strong enough to recover his dominions and be acknowledged by other subjects against both the English and the Burgundians. The first stages of his struggle were dominated by Joan of Arc, whose national and religious enthusiasms brought her to trial for heresy in 1431 after her capture by the English. She recanted after judgment, but relapsed and was burned as a heretic, where Charles did nothing to save her when he could. Significantly his emergence later into undisputed control over the strongest State in Latin Christendom was marked by the rehabilitation of Joan in 1456 and repudiation of the process and judgment against her. Generally the Hundred Years' War is taken as having ended with the battle of Castillon in 1453, though no formal peace treaty was then signed and raiding continued for some years. There were no further widespread campaigns, nor serious thought by the English of conquering France. Both Edward IV and Henry VII sent expeditions into French territory on later occasions, but solely to have handsome indemnities paid to call off the attacks.

In these political and military developments there was considerable misery brought upon the people and clergy of France, but for their part the French kings came into control of ecclesiastical affairs at the expense of both the Pope and the national hierarchy. The great centre for conciliar argument and thought before and during the Council of Constance was the University of Paris, and French diplomacy for long was directed to ending the Schism. In these movements, there lay deeply embedded the tradition of Gallicanism, that is to say, the conception of the French Church as ultimately under the Pope's authority but nationally and independently organized with the king at its head as a sacral, anointed ruler, the "first ecclesiastical personage of the realm". These ideas had been trumpeted at the start of the fourteenth century in the struggle between Philip IV and Boniface VIII, and they were cited repeatedly in the conciliar discussions. But after Constance and Martin V's concordat with the French king in 1418, older papal abuses in appointments and taxation continued whilst Charles VII struggled against the English. The situation altered considerably after 1431, for Eugenius IV became entangled with the Council of Basel and Charles VII in 1436 recaptured Paris with all its prestige and power as a capital. From these developments there followed two years later the Pragmatic Sanction of Bourges. Charles VII summoned at Bourges an assembly composed of leading French ecclesiastics, including twenty-five bishops, under the leadership of Gerard Machet, the Bishop of Castres and the royal confessor. At times the king himself presided over the discussions, and it was in his name that a series of decrees was issued; these were ominously given the title of a "pragmatic" to describe a solemn settlement of the affairs of the French Church by the king and his bishops without reference to Pope or Council. The Pragmatic Sanction of Bourges was in many ways similar to the concordat being negotiated by the Germans and later confirmed at Vienna, but there were notable differences. The German and French settlements alike aided Eugenius IV in his conflict with Basel, but beyond this the Pope gained far less at Bourges than in his dealings with the Emperor and the princes of Germany.

Some of the members at Bourges appealed to a "pragmatic" supposedly issued by Louis IX in the thirteenth century, but documentary proof adduced to verify this appeal was forged, most probably by Machet himself. What in fact was done in 1438 was new. The Pragmatic began by affirming that the French king had to defend Holy Church, and the work at Basel was cited as justification for summoning a French assembly. It was made quite clear that the king and his ministers would deal with abuses and corruption, and the Pragmatic repeated twenty-four decrees of the Council of Basel, including *Sacrosancta* and *Frequens* which unequivocally stated the superiority of the General Council over the Pope. Thereafter, however, only French issues were dealt with in detail. Papal provisions and reservations were declared invalid, annates were prohibited, and all appeals to Rome disallowed unless adequate justice could not be provided by French ecclesiastical tribunals. In addition there were broad condemnations of abuses in excommunications, interdicts and clerical behaviour, and the king was given the right to intervene in matters of ecclesiastical discipline. The Pragmatic Sanction appeared to consolidate the earlier Gallican demands of Gerson and the University of Paris, but in the vital matter of appointments this was not so. Conciliar regulations restoring canonical elections in benefices were repeated at Bourges, but with the proviso that the synod "does not consider it as reprehensible if the King (of France) and the princes of his kingdom sometimes use benign and benevolent recommendations in favour of persons (to be elected to these benefices)". The French had long sought to have free elections of their own clergy, but what the Pragmatic gave in restricting papal interference was much less than this, for royal control was sanctioned. Some papal abuses were cut out, but the settlement was by no means satisfactory where so much was dependent on royal initiative. The Popes were never willing to recognize the Pragmatic, but the French kings vacillated about implementing it, according as they wanted to threaten or make alliances with particular pontiffs. In these circumstances the disorder and corruption in the French Church, so far from being checked, grew steadily worse with the years.

Until his death in 1461, Charles VII maintained the Pragmatic in force, though to threaten the Popes rather than as a means for bringing about genuine reforms in appointments, clerical life or renewed spirituality. His constant refusal to accept Eugenius IV's deposition by the Council of Basel earned the Pope's gratitude, and later with the aid of Calixtus III he obtained Joan of Arc's rehabilitation, an event of profound public importance for the king. Assemblies in 1450 and 1452 confirmed the Bourges settlement, and in answer to Pius II's condemnation in *Execrabilis* of any appeal to a General Council, the French Procurator General invoked the authority of such a body against the bull. But nothing came of this defiance which was conveniently treated by the Pope and Charles VII as only a threat, not an irrevocable action. Charles's concern remained to exploit the situation so that he should retain control over the French Church, but Louis XI, who succeeded him in 1461, immediately withdrew the Pragmatic as part of a policy for conciliating the Pope. Three years later he partially re-imposed it, once again forbidding papal reservations and the despatch of money from France to the Curia. Eventually in 1472, Louis negotiated a fresh settlement with Sixtus IV to resolve the financial issue, but he continued to apply the Pragmatic intermittently with considerable harmful effects on the French Church in its leadership and work and on the general standards of spiritual and moral life. Both king and nobles practised abuses in their controls of appointments and the older programme of reforms was left a dead letter. Partly as a result of the interruption of early Humanistic studies in the civil conflicts, the University of Paris lost much of its former zeal and any great figures to formulate positive measures for eradicating evils, and it was divided for some years over support for the Pragmatic. Paris also suffered from the defeat of Conciliarism, and it was only late in Louis XI's reign that any progress came in new studies which the king himself promoted.

For the most part the religious houses showed little desire for reform and in their allegiances to the Pope were often largely withdrawn from French ecclesiastical life. In the war with England and the civil strife, the great monasteries of northern France fell into considerable decay, bringing disorder in what they did or failed to do. On occasion their abbots could argue that corrupt practices should not be disturbed, for if evil priests did not harm, say, the consecration of the elements in the Mass, then even the worst monastery or abbey still helped to divert God's wrath from the rest of his creatures. Yet before Louis's death in 1483 there were numerous signs of concern for dealing with ecclesiastical failings among seculars and religious alike. In 1476, the Abbey of Cîteaux revolted against misgovernment and the long-standing system of papal provision, and elected its own abbot, John of Cirey, who was a reformer. In his work, Cirey was supported increasingly by the French kings and at last in 1487 he obtained authorization from Innocent VIII to reform the whole Cistercian Order in France. Meanwhile Louis XI retained some sense of religious needs despite his unpleasing personality, and after a stroke in 1482 he summoned the Italian hermit Francis of Paolo to France. Francis was renowned for his own austerity and holiness in the Franciscan Order, and he not only advised Louis in his last days, but stayed as royal confessor to his son, Charles VIII, and died in France in 1507.

At his accession in 1483, Charles VIII was only thirteen, and his character and life aroused more comment than his father's, where his physical deformity and delusions in ambition appeared unnatural to contemporaries. But with him there was positive concern about the state of the French Church and genuine attempts on more than one occasion to implement reforms. In the Estates General at Tours in 1484, growing disillusion among the secular clergy was voiced in demands for reconstruction of the orders, the proper application of the Pragmatic and changes in the general methods of appointments to ecclesiastical offices. As a result the king began negotiations with the Popes which dragged on through the following years, but papal opposition to radical action about appointments prevented any success. Attempts by the Archbishop at Sens in 1485 to introduce measures for raising standards of nominations and clerical behaviour were ignored or flouted through the country where neither king nor Pope was prepared to give effective support. More vigorous response came through the actions of individuals who were themselves not leaders in the hierarchy, and developments in the closing years of the century pointed to a reviving spirituality and earnestness for tackling the grave problems of the French Church. One such person was Olivier Maillard, a Franciscan Observant who became Vicar-General of the Order in 1487, and was given a respected place at Charles VIII's court as well as a commission from the Pope to secure the abrogation of the Pragmatic Sanction.[1] Maillard's real concern was with reform, where he was outspoken in preaching and criticism of spiritual faults in clergy and laity and cared nothing for the unpopularity which he evoked. In a similar way, John Raulin, the Principal of the College of Navarre, castigated the vices of the Church and poured scorn on the scandals of appointments. "Of old," he claimed, "one became a bishop by the grace of God; nowadays the man had better call himself bishop by the king's favour .... Ecclesiastical functions are given to children; we commit men's souls to a boy whom we would not trust with an apple." Raulin refused to have anything to do with the preaching of indulgences, and rejected alike the sterile idea of religion as merely intellectual or that it was to be found in the popular appeals of the friars. He was not concerned with restating doctrine but in restoring spiritual life particularly in study of the Bible and personal faith in Christ. By his denunciations, Raulin gained increasing favour from Charles VIII but spurned his successes in his preaching and pursuit of reforming ideals. Following a visit to Cluny in 1497, he joined with another reformer, John Quentin, who had been impressed by Francis of Paolo and proclaimed a return to asceticism to meet Christian laxity and the materialism of the day.

Both Raulin and Quentin, however, came into contact with a more remarkable figure, John Standonck, whose programme they enthusiastically endorsed. Born about 1450 at Mechlin in Brabant, Standonck was trained by the Brethren of the Common Life at Gouda, from which he went on to Louvain in 1469 and thereafter to Paris, where like Quentin he came eventually under the influence of Francis of Paolo. In 1483 he was appointed Principal of the College of Montaigu, and this he hoped to use educationally for bringing in reform of the whole body of the clergy, much as Groote and Radewyns

[1] The work of Maillard and others is outlined by G. G. Coulton, *Five Centuries of Religion*, Vol. IV (Cambridge, 1950), Chapter XXXVI; and in A. Renaudet, *Préréforme et Humanisme*, 2nd edition (Paris, 1953).

had planned in the Netherlands a century earlier.[1] Standonck extended the college's premises by 1490 so that students could live communally and in strict discipline, and three years later, he founded a new school with a further eighty students under his care. This project was warmly supported by influential authorities, including the Chapter of Notre-Dame, the Vicar-General of the Dutch Dominicans, Bishop d'Amboise of Albi, and the Admiral of France who gave financial help. Standonck, however, did not devote himself solely to plans in education, and in 1493 he also presented his more general ideas before Charles VIII at Tours. In common with others in the assembly – such as the Abbots of Cîteaux and Marmoutier – Standonck criticized prevailing laxity in life and discipline which, he claimed, affected all society and sprang to a large extent from royal and papal exploitation. He outlined his scheme for life and teaching on the pattern of the New Devotion and was able to join with Raulin and other reformers in having his ideas debated and accepted. Whilst Charles VIII lived, the work at Montaigu was actively encouraged, but the accession of Louis XII in 1498 brought a setback. Standonck incurred the new king's dislike by condemning his marriage to Anne of Brittany, who had formerly been betrothed to Charles VIII. In 1499, he was expelled from France, but support for him was so strong that he was allowed to return to Paris only a year later. He completed his work at Montaigu and secured official approval of its constitution in 1503, together with an annual royal grant for the maintenance of the college.

In the ten years following 1493, three hundred missionaries were trained and sent out from Montaigu to other colleges and to reform religious houses, and at Standonck's death in 1504 there were over two hundred students in his school. Montaigu stood out as the lively centre from which reforming work could be carried far and wide through France, and though the general pattern of work was such as had been laid down by Groote, Standonck gave it an austere, even reactionary, flavour which did not win support from everyone in his age. His own upbringing at Gouda seems to have been conclusive for his outlook, for Gouda was poor and strict in comparison with the Brethren's communities at Deventer or Zwolle. Standonck in consequence held to an educational programme that estranged him from those more Humanistic and liberal in attitude. In addition, he owed something to Francis of Paolo and therefore made the sort of protest to be found with Savonarola in Italy or in Luther's reaction against materialism and corruption in the Renaissance Church. What most clearly illustrated the temper of his reforms was that Erasmus

[1] For Standonck, cf. Hyma, op. cit., pp. 236 f.

studied for a year at Montaigu and later always spoke adversely of its harsh and narrow-minded discipline.

Nobody could doubt the truth of Standonck's criticisms, and in other ways, too, hopes for far-reaching action were stimulated when missionaries from Windesheim were invited to reform the great Abbey of St. Victor in 1497. Standonck arranged for the request, following the earlier reform of the smaller monastery of Château-Landon by a party from the Netherlands, led by John Mombaer. The attempt to deal with problems at St. Victor, however, failed for the time being as Charles VIII's death in 1498 ended active royal support for the work. When Mombaer himself died in 1501, only four additional houses had been reformed and in 1505 these were constituted on the model of Windesheim as a new chapter, like a number of Benedictine houses which were also organized in a separate congregation. Ten years later the formal adherence of St. Victor to these reformed bodies was ordered by the Bishop of Paris. But the first enthusiasms in monastic reconstruction soon waned, and Mombaer's influence was longer-lasting in his writings which echoed many of the older mystical themes in the New Devotion. His *Rosary of Spiritual Exercises* owed much to à Kempis and Gansfort, both of whom Mombaer probably knew, but it drew upon earlier manuals as well and became widely popular in clerical and lay circles, not least of all amongst the French Humanists.

The spread of Humanism in France came late but rapidly, in the wake of Charles VIII's invasion of Italy in 1494 and with the continuing involvement of his successors, Louis XII and Francis I, in Italian wars against the Habsburgs. Louis XII and his leading minister d'Amboise became enthusiastic patrons of things Italian after 1500, welcoming scholars at their court and encouraging Frenchmen to visit Italy, and Francis I later posed as the perfect Renaissance prince in rivalry to Henry VIII. In these developments, two men stood out pre-eminently as Humanists and reformers – Badius Ascensius and Lefèvre d'Étaples. Both of them knew much of the ideals of the New Devotion and shared in the hopes for reconstruction of religious life around 1500. Badius was born in 1462, and after schooling at Windesheim and Louvain, travelled to Italy before returning to France to devote himself primarily to printing. In 1494 he published Occam's works, but thereafter turned to the writings of the Brethren of the Common Life and other fifteenth-century reformers; under Louis XII he became the leading figure for promoting Latin studies in France. In close association with him, Lefèvre d'Étaples, who was born in 1455, developed interests that led more completely into reforming aims. Lefèvre was greatly influenced by Cusa's works, and had

Badius print them as well as Mombaer's *Rosary*, and he achieved early renown as a teacher in mathematics and physics before his first visit to Italy in 1492. Under the inspiration of Ficino and the Florentine group he turned his attention to editing and translating into French various works of Aristotle, and in lecturing upon Greek philosophy in Paris he developed a method of exposition similar to that used by Colet with regard to Scripture. But Lefèvre moved on further. Following a conversion experience in 1507, he thought first of becoming a monk but on deeper reflection decided to employ his abilities in studying and expounding the Bible. In 1509 he published a Quintuplex edition of the Psalms, setting five versions side by side in columns to show the most correct text, and three years later he issued the Pauline Epistles, again in parallel columns with the Vulgate and his own Latin translation from the Greek, together with comments. These works followed directly in the tradition of critical scholarship and questioning of the Vulgate begun by Valla, and had their counterparts in the contemporary activity of Ximenes and Erasmus.[1] Lefèvre similarly published the Gospels in 1522, and then produced his own French translations of the New and Old Testaments. His scholarship was not so commanding or careful as that of others, as his commentaries on the texts revealed, but his work and ideas were both invaluable at that juncture. Luther employed Lefèvre's edition of St. Paul's Epistles until the more skilled works of Erasmus appeared, whilst Lefèvre instructed Farel – the older companion of Calvin – and stood close to the Reformers in his ideas and conclusions.

Lefèvre gave Scripture a high place in his theology and saw the Old as well as the New Testament speaking throughout of Christ, where Scripture was to interpret Scripture. Although allowing an important place for Man's freewill, his ability to choose or reject God's grace, he outlined what amounted in effect to the doctrine of justification by faith. To believe in justification by works, he argued, was to deny God's grace and any meaning in Christ's death, where faith could only be the free gift of God. But in Pauline terms, and like Gansfort before him, Lefèvre took the thought further in urging the individual to confide "neither in faith nor in works, but in God, who alone justifies". He also stressed that the Mass was a memorial of Christ's sacrifice rather than the sacrifice itself, though he did not reject traditional Eucharistic doctrine or other ideas on the structure and functioning of the Church. His concern in reformation was to restore a purer life and leadership, and after 1512 he became closely

[1] Cf. *Cambridge History of the Bible – The West from the Reformation to the Present Day*, edited by S. L. Greenslade (Cambridge, 1963), pp. 80 f. (dating of the Psalter and Epistles wrongly printed).

connected with Bishop Briçonnet of Meaux, who gathered around him a group of reformers that included Lefèvre and pupils like Farel and Roussel. The Meaux circle enjoyed the patronage of Margaret of Angoulême and through her the favourable interest of Francis I for some years after 1516. Lefèvre's work and that of his associates continued through the crisis of Luther's struggle with Rome, and he himself was condemned at the Sorbonne for heresy in 1521. As arguments about Lutheran ideas and influences arose, it became possible to question some of Lefèvre's own views, though his hope remained for reform within the existing structure. Lefèvre fled to Strasbourg in 1525, and some of his followers were executed in the developments, but even before 1520 it was plain that reform faced strong opposition from king and Pope alike.

Despite the movements around 1500, the general control and structure of the French Church remained in disorder, largely because of the rivalries of the kings and Popes, which involved political ambitions in Italy. Charles VIII's appearance in the peninsula to sweep corruption from the Renaissance Papacy had been lamentable, Louis XII's attempt in 1501 to use authority with d'Amboise to undertake the wholesale reconstruction of the French Church faded away where the Pragmatic remained to allow abuse by monarch and minister, and later the conflict with Julius II led to the abortive French attempt to maintain a Council at Pisa against that summoned at Rome. Great play was made with conciliar ideas in France, but to little avail, and Louis had to abandon opposition to the Pope. His successor, Francis I, had to agree to a compromise in 1515 with Leo X, before the French victory at Marignano in Italy gave the advantage back to the King. The result was the Concordat of Bologna signed in 1516. By its terms, all great appointments in the French Church thereafter were to be made by the king, without any pretence of election in chapter or ecclesiastical control as in the Pragmatic. The Pope retained the right of institution to benefices but this was only symbolic and royal power over appointments was left supreme. Nevertheless Leo X did not go unrewarded. Though no explicit reference was made to the fact, he regained the payment of annates which had been treated throughout the preceding century in very cavalier fashion by the French kings. The new understanding pleased both Francis I and the Pope in practical terms far more than the earlier Pragmatic, not least of all by cutting out any irritating claims for clerical independence. It regularized what the kings had tried to practise, and though clergy, lawyers and Parliament alike protested at the settlement as attacking the French Church's government of itself, they were compelled to accept the terms. Still Gallican in sentiment, the Church's leaders became royal agents first and foremost, and clerical wealth the wealth of the kings. Unlike Henry VIII therefore, Francis I and his successors remained content with existing papal ties and had no interest in promoting reform that would upset this situation. The concordat of 1516 did not stifle demands for dealing with corruption, but it did not itself in any way bring remedies – beyond curtailing papal influence over appointments – and those planning reform found little genuine official support.

Montaigu continued to influence its students, among them Calvin, and Lefèvre inspired followers who later challenged the ideas and ties of Rome. At the same time, there came from much of this teaching those leaders who later resisted Protestantism and brought the Counter-Reformation in France. But developments in any direction were delayed in a situation in which the king himself kept tight control over the hierarchy and was happy with his relations with Rome, whilst conspicuous by their absence were the complicating issues to be found in other countries. France did not know the national social unrest which troubled Germany, nor the militant movement of Hussitism, or even the more pietistical and stubborn tradition of Lollardy in England. The dissatisfactions in French spiritual and ecclesiastical life remained largely unresolved through the fifteenth and early sixteenth centuries. But the storm nonetheless came in the end, for the attempt by the Huguenots to introduce reformation after 1550 brought violence in civil war. In that conflict, political, dynastic and religious aims became hopelessly entangled and together destroyed the vision of those reformers who had tried to renew purity of life and spirit in a united French Church in earlier years.

CHAPTER XIII

SPAIN AND REFORM

IN THE HISTORY OF LATIN CHRISTENDOM THE SPANISH PEOPLE POSSESSED a unique and long tradition. Over the centuries their national development was forged in the fire of religious war, and the common aim to recover the peninsula from the Moors gave them similar ideals and hopes that also had repercussions more widely through the Christian world. Yet Spain was divided into three Christian realms – Portugal, Castile and Aragon – which knew further internal divisions, and as a more united kingdom it only came to participate in European affairs in the latter half of the fifteenth century. At the same time, however, it was the one country to introduce overall ecclesiastical reforms before the crises of the following age.

The Great Schism split the allegiances of the various Iberian kingdoms but in the councils afterward they all counted as one of the "nations", and a similar unity of outlook religiously made them stronger in the cause of papal authority than for the Pope's enemies. Such support helped to determine the final issue between Eugenius IV and the Council of Basel. But politically the history of the Iberian peninsula continued to be that of shifting competition, alliances and wars between the three realms – apart from Moorish Granada – until the 1470's made it clearer how these States might be fused in any greater structure. Their involvements in missionary and commercial exploration formed part of the external history of Christendom,[1] but in domestic affairs each realm had the problem of Christian conquest and consolidation, Castile notably with Granada, whilst the Aragonese looking out to the Mediterranean sought in addition to extend their power eastward. Alfonso V, who became King of Aragon in 1416, made himself master of Naples by 1433 and at his death in 1458 left an inheritance divided between his brother John II, who reigned over Aragon and Sicily for a further twenty years, and his illegitimate son Ferrante, who managed to hold Naples and south Italy during his lifetime. But by 1494 when Ferrante died, the pattern of union and development had been resolved in Spain. Varying hopes for possible alliances between Castile and Portugal or even France were frustrated in 1469 by the secret marriage of John II's son Ferdinand to Isabella, heiress to the Castilian crown. Five years later Isabella

[1] See Chapter VIII, pp. 132 f. above.

became Queen of Castile and in 1479 Ferdinand succeeded his father as King of Aragon, though both rulers had to confirm their governments and the union of the crowns. In land, population and wealth, Castile far outweighed Aragon and in many respects the two monarchs continued to enjoy separate authorities over their respective kingdoms, but Ferdinand and Isabella sought to build up the organization of a more united State and it was in this context that their religious work had its place.

The fundamental task was to make the monarchy strong against all rivals, whether the nobles, the local Cortes or assemblies, the towns, or not least of all the Spanish Church, which was well-entrenched under episcopal control and possessing a tradition of missionary zeal reaching back through the centuries. Heresy as well as Moorish beliefs had recognized ties with different peoples in the peninsula, and even Wycliffe's influence was to be found where some of his ideas had been brought into Castile by Lancaster's daughter Catherine, who was the wife of Henry III and the grandmother of Isabella. Wycliffite doctrines about predestination and damnation were welcomed by groups retaining older Albigensian principles, but by contrast the ecclesiastical and political leaders in Spain were among the most loyal and active in defending and restating papal claims. The champion who emerged to argue anew for the Pope's supremacy against the Council was the Spaniard John Torquemada, and he was no less active in papal diplomatic service until his death in 1468. Nevertheless, it was quite clear that as the Spanish monarchs in the closing part of the century unfolded a policy for unifying their possessions, they intended to bring the Church closely under royal control, reorganized and reformed but carefully protected from excessive papal interference. Precedents existed for such policies where in earlier years rulers and assemblies alike were vigilant in checking clerical abuses and curbing the claims of the Popes; as early as 1348 the King of Castile had been granted the right to approve or refuse any papal bull before it could be promulgated in his realm. Royal patronage and control over ecclesiastical appointments were sought at a council in Seville in 1478, and four years later a concordat with Sixtus IV gave the Spanish rulers the right of nomination to benefices, together with that of visitation which was assumed to include the power to depose individual clerics from their offices. Such claims were made effective in Granada after 1486 and in the Spanish American possessions by 1508, even though it was not until Charles V's reign that they were extended through all the territories of the Crown.[1]

[1] Cf. J. H. Elliott, *Imperial Spain*, 1469–1715 (London, 1963), pp. 89–90, and more generally for the account of the union of the crowns and royal policy.

But this position was only what all the national kings schemed to achieve at the Pope's expense by 1500, and more positively a general policy of reform was attempted in the Spanish Church. Of prime importance in this work was the creation of the Spanish Inquisition to enforce religious unity, whilst the reform programme as a whole was summed up in the lives and achievements of two men – Thomas Torquemada and Francis Ximenes of Cisneros.

As a general instrument of papal policy, the Inquisition dated back to the 1230's and its organization by Gregory IX in the hands of the Dominicans as an international order. Its work was technical, the examination and determining of heresy so that individual men and women could be made to recant and be punished temporally by secular Christian authorities. The machinery was international in scope and ultimately under papal control, and in the thirteenth century its effectiveness was harshly demonstrated in many lands of Christendom.[1] But such power and respect as the Inquisition commanded greatly declined with the scandals of Avignon and the Great Schism, together with the rise of national rulers who did not always want its services. When Ferdinand and Isabella therefore asked to have the Inquisition set up in Spain, they were restoring something which had largely become moribund, but in significantly different terms – the new organization was to be national in scope and work, not universal. Behind the monarchs' desire for such an authority stretched a history of the treatment of religious groups in Spain and the enforcing of orthodoxy that went back to the preceding century. Spanish society contained two groups – the Jews and the Moors – which stood out from the rest in faith and race and in the wealth which they were able to amass. Through the centuries a policy of assimilation brought profit to the nascent Spanish kingdoms where both groups provided converts to Christianity and economic prosperity. The kings generally had been more tolerant than the Church in allowing Jews and Moors to retain their beliefs and customs at the same time as they contributed actively to banking, commerce and industry. Where some accepted Christianity they were often given privileges and protection above that accorded to ordinary Christian subjects in the realms. But under the influence of ecclesiastical leaders who wished to stamp out heresy, the spirit of tolerance steadily dwindled, whilst at the same time the practice used by Spanish princes of giving specific quarters in towns to Jews and Moors tended to prevent their fuller integration into Iberian society.

In the fourteenth century, growing intolerance was marked in the councils of Zamora (1313) and Valladolid (1322) which restricted the

[1] Cf. H. C. Lea, *The Inquisition of the Middle Ages – Its Organization and Operation* London, 1963).

social intercourse of Christians with either Jews or Moors. Thereafter popular resentment among the Christians was deepened in the hardships of the Black Death and inflamed by preaching that led to riots and massacres of Jews in particular in Castile, Aragon and Navarre. The most significant of these disturbances came in 1391 when a whole series of massacres occurred in the towns of Seville and many of the wealthy and learned Jews, until then secure in royal protection, accepted Christian baptism as the only means of saving their lives. Such conversions were spurred on in 1391 and through the following twenty years by the missionary work and fanatical preaching of Vincent Ferrer. Persecutions culminated in 1412 with a Castilian decree requiring Jews and Moors to wear distinctive clothing and barring them from many careers or professions in society. The Jews in particular suffered from official and popular attacks but many became Christians under the force of circumstances, and the events of 1391 and after brought the consolidation of a new class of Conversos or Marranos in Spanish society. These people were hardly ever genuine converts to Christianity, but they retained their wealth and influence and were even more resented and feared in Spain in the fifteenth century than the Jews who were known and persecuted.

Concern for religious uniformity steadily developed through the Conciliar period, ill-judged though the policy was in creating communities of discontented subjects who reluctantly adopted Christianity and who, as occasion arose, tried to return to the faith of their forebears. The danger that such groups would keep their traditional practices behind the mask of orthodox Christian ceremonial was noted at Basel, and in 1451 John II obtained from Nicholas V an official with inquisitorial powers in Spain. Little, however, was accomplished in the following years, partly because John was politically weak, but criticism of Jewish practices continued and, it is suggested, rumours about plans by Jews and Conversos to hold a secret festival on the night of Good Friday in 1478 impelled Ferdinand and Isabella to make their request to the Pope for establishing the Inquisition in Castile, where Isabella was already queen. Sixtus IV complied, empowering the rulers to appoint three suitably qualified bishops to have jurisdiction over heresy in Castile. Two years later, two Dominican friars were made inquisitors in Seville and provided with assistants for their work, which was soon evidenced in public recantations, burnings and the tribunal's enquiries around the region. The inquisitors' activities led to an attempted conspiracy among the Conversos which only encouraged support for the new court from other members of the people and brought additional tribunals in Castile. But Ferdinand's attempts next to introduce the Inquisition into his own realm of Aragon were met with opposition from more than one quarter – the people preferred the less efficient Papal Inquisition which still functioned intermittently and without too much harm in Aragon, and Sixtus IV was anxious to prevent any extension to a Spanish Holy Office which was under royal rather than papal control. He eventually gave way to Ferdinand in allowing Torquemada, already Inquisitor in Castile, to have this office as well in Aragon. Local opposition persisted and the Conversos in Saragossa at last took desperate action in murdering an inquisitor named Arbues. Popular reaction in favour of the Inquisition led to a purge of noble families throughout Aragon, in which scarcely one household was untouched and heretical ideas of all kinds were rooted out. For years the Aragonese remained jealous of their privileges, and their Cortes sought to circumscribe the powers and work of the Inquisition, but its jurisdiction was inexorably developed and it became an integral part of Spanish religious life.

The climax in the policy to secure religious uniformity in Aragon as well as Castile, at the expense of Jews and Moors, came in association with the final campaign from 1483 to 1492 to conquer Granada. In terms of religious feeling, there was strong emotional reaction among the people and in the government at completing the Reconquista of centuries with the destruction of the last Islamic power in the peninsula, and this was cruelly reflected in action taken against the non-Christian bodies. The Jews were the first to be dealt with as it was felt that they were no longer so necessary with their financial support as before the fall of Granada. In March, 1492, they were given four months in which to choose between leaving the country and changing their religion. It was said that two of the wealthiest of the Spanish Jews tried to avert this order by offering three hundred thousand ducats to Ferdinand, who was himself of Jewish blood and disposed to accept the money, but that he was prevented by Torquemada's appearance and taunt, "Behold the Crucified whom the wicked Judas sold for thirty pieces of silver! If you approve this deed, sell Him for a greater sum". The decree was enforced, and amid popular outrages against the Jews, it is possible that as many as one hundred thousand went into exile and another fifty thousand were baptized. According to one authority, the work of the Inquisition was done so well that no Jews remained for baptism in Granada. The Moors on the other hand were treated well at first in the fall of the city and given guarantees by the Spanish rulers that their property and religion would be respected. The first Archbishop of Granada, de Talavera, who was Queen Isabella's confessor, did not seek forcible conversions of the Moors but instead he evangelized among them and won their confidence. This attitude was speedily replaced when Ximenes as Archbishop of Toledo undertook their enforced acceptance of Christianity in Granada. In 1501 he forbade them to go to other parts of Spain where Moslems were still tolerated, and a year later, all Moors were ordered to leave Castile and Leon, a command amounting to one of conversion since no neighbouring doors were open through which refugees could pass into other lands. Similar measures were extended to Aragon by Charles V in 1525 and persecution of the Moors continued through the sixteenth century.

Even where allowance is made for the religious motives in the monarchs' actions, their policy it seems was intentionally directed towards achieving national uniformity for a strong State, and the Inquisition fully fitted into this scheme. The moving spirit in shaping the Spanish Office was Torquemada, who was a nephew of the cardinal, and after training as a Dominican at Valladolid, had become Prior of Segovia and then confessor to the Spanish monarchs. Though he was not the first Grand Inquisitor, he became intimately associated with the development of the Court and made it notorious. In the new Spain where government was exercised by a number of great councils under the monarchs, the Inquisition itself was constituted as one of these bodies and acted with well-nigh independent authority through the country. It framed its own rules, appointed its own officials under the Inquisitor-General, had use of all the State's resources for conducting enquiries and enforcing decisions, and allowed an inquisitor in making his investigations to supersede all local civil or religious powers. In the actual proceedings in Spain, an inquisitor set up his tribunal in a district and asked for information from anybody concerning suspicions of heresy. Individuals were defamed and then examined without adequate means of making a defence or with loop-holes for recantations; they could be punished as heretics by burning, with the confiscation of their property and ruin of their families. Torture and imprisonment were normal parts of questioning to determine the truth about the accused; and those convicted of heresy and refusing to recant, or persistently denying that they were guilty, or any who were relapsed heretics, were handed over to the secular power for burning on the ground that such people should not be suffered to live. Whilst Torquemada was Grand Inquisitor from 1483 to his death in 1498, possibly as many as one hundred and fourteen thousand people were brought before the Inquisition, and of these ninety thousand were found guilty or recanted and no less than two thousand were burned.

The attitudes and actions were shameful but widespread in the age and it is to be noted that the numbers of those martyred were far fewer than popularly believed afterward, whilst individual inquisitors tried to act with clemency and justice within the limits of their harsh principles. Both Torquemada and Ximenes – who became Inquisitor-General in 1507 – were over-zealous rather than lacking all humanity in their attention to orthodoxy, though it is no easier to justify their use of the Inquisition than the fifteenth-century legislation and action concerning heresy in England. Ximenes carried out a general review of the personnel and machinery of the Inquisition after a scandal over one inquisitor Lucero who illustrated the lengths to which obsession and zeal could go. Convinced apparently that there was a great conspiracy to supplant Christianity with Judaism in Spain, Lucero accused and condemned many orthodox believers in his examinations, suggesting finally that Archbishop de Talavera was a Jew in his sympathetic behaviour to the inhabitants of Granada. Public complaint led to Lucero's trial and dismissal from his post, and thereafter Ximenes tried to prevent recurrence of unsatisfactory behaviour by inquisitors.

Apart from the Jews and Moors, the Inquisition dealt with any who appeared to deviate from Catholic faith, and after 1500 these could include certain Franciscans who recruited support from suspected Marranos in the movement of Illuminism. In this development individuals sought mystical experiences and claimed that the human soul could be lost in God. At times their ideas moved out of Christian categories to embrace millennial hopes of a New Jerusalem, as in one friar's visions in 1512. Ximenes was not intolerant of Illuminism in its simpler forms and concern for communion with God, but it could not always be distinguished from more extreme hopes, and later inquisitors eventually condemned it as heretical. Spanish mystics there were of great power and insight, and among them was Ignatius Loyola in the 1520's, but their hopes had to be bound inside the traditional acceptance of the Church's order and authority in Spain. At Ferdinand's death in 1516, the Holy Office was already an essential and commanding instrument for preventing the spread of other than traditionally orthodox ideas through the country, and its future was even more important as it came to be the weapon for countering Protestantism and the model for a renewed Papal Inquisition.

But there were other developments under Ferdinand and Isabella in religious and ecclesiastical affairs that set Spain on a different path from the rest of Christendom in the sixteenth century. The introduction of the Inquisition was but one aspect – certainly the darkest – of a general reform of the Spanish Church planned by the monarchs and coupled throughout with Ximenes, one of the most remarkable men of his age. His interests and work straddled asceticism and Humanist principles in reform, religion and politics, and he gave Spain its particular character for the shock of Protestant struggle. In his early life, Ximenes studied law and theology at Salamanca University before going to Rome to work for some years in the Curia in his training. He returned to Spain in 1465 with promise of provision to an important benefice, but the appointment was locally resented in Toledo and the archbishop went to the length of imprisoning Ximenes in disputing the title. When he was released, however, he became chaplain to Cardinal Mendoza, and used the opportunities of study and travel to learn oriental languages until in 1484 he abandoned his career to join the Franciscan Observants in the search for ascetic purity of life. As he developed, Ximenes withdrew even further into the solitary pursuit of a hermit, gaining thereby an increasing reputation for holiness and rigorous principles, and it was from such a life that he was recalled through Mendoza's intercession to become confessor to Queen Isabella in 1492. This post he was reluctant to take, despite Isabella's enthusiasm for Christian affairs, and he was loath to accept the rapid promotions which followed in offices of Church and State. He was made Provincial of the Franciscan Order in 1494, and succeeded Mendoza a year later as Archbishop of Toledo, a post recognized as the highest and most influential in the realm after that of the sovereigns, and one of the most important in the Latin Church below the Pope. When Isabella died in 1504, Ximenes remained to advise her son-in-law Philip of Burgundy whose succession to the Castilian throne Ferdinand did not dispute. When Philip in turn died two years later, the archbishop ruled the kingdom until Ferdinand returned from Naples in 1507 to assume control for his infant grandson Charles. For his services at the time Ximenes was made a cardinal, and he continued to govern Spain under Ferdinand until the king's death in 1516, when once again he held the reins of power before Charles arrived from the Netherlands a year later.

In this career Ximenes moved into the centre of work for reform and reorganization of the Spanish Church, and he built on the foundations laid in earlier days. Apart from royal control over the Church in appointments and the right of visitation, episcopal courts were limited by the sanction of appeals to civil tribunals, and the king directly ruled the three Spanish military and ecclesiastical orders as their Grand Master. Ximenes exploited to the full such royal powers in reforming the Church, himself setting an example of true clerical life in Franciscan self-denial, personal devotion and asceticism. He began by trying to impose Observant ideals upon all the orders in Spain in place of those of Conventuals, and made personal visitations of monasteries to insist upon strict return to the disciplines envisaged by their founders. It was said, probably with exaggeration, that more than a thousand friars left Spain and fled to Africa, preferring the liberty of self-indulgence under infidel protection to submission to Ximenes in their native country. In his lifetime, Ximenes's efforts met with success among the Franciscans at the expense of earning the Conventuals' enmity, and jealous rivalry from the Dominicans who were concerned with their own reforms. Beyond the orders he dealt with the houses of regular canons attached to cathedrals, compelling them to give up lives of wealth and leisure and to return to simpler devotion and rigour in Christian service. More generally, he endeavoured to eradicate immorality, corruption and disorder among the ordinary secular clergy throughout Spain. In his work, he was able to use the civil machinery of the State and, with Isabella's support, to overcome what direct opposition he met, even that of Alexander VI who protested initially at the high-handed behaviour of the archbishop in dealing with the clergy. As a result, a renewed spirit of devotion and standard of life were undoubtedly bred in the Spanish clergy from the start of the sixteenth century which were not to be found in other Latin hierarchies at the time.

But Ximenes went further in his schemes for reconstruction, and showed how much he himself owed to quickened interests in Humanistic culture. He planned to remove ignorance, illiteracy and incompetence in the clergy and to have an episcopate learned and spiritual in its leadership of the Church. Individual prelates he dismissed from their offices where their failings were obvious, whilst he laid down that in every chapter in Castile and Aragon two prebends were to be set aside for scholars, one to be a student in canon law, the other an expert theologian. More widely he encouraged university studies, not only in the older schools of Salamanca and Valladolid but also in new foundations at Avila, Palma, Seville, Santiago and Alcala. The University of Alcala, opened in 1508, was founded largely upon Ximenes's own private income and given lavish additional endowments with the purpose of training leaders in the Spanish Church. It was staffed with eminent scholars from Italy and France, and Ximenes even tried – unsuccessfully – to persuade Erasmus to come to teach there. Composed of a number of small colleges in which the students gained intensive instruction in theology, law and languages, Alcala retained older courses, with stress on the teaching of Augustine and Aquinas at the expense of extreme Nominalism, but Ximenes added fresh studies on Biblical exegesis and Greek, Hebrew and Latin. In aiding reform, his attention to education and scholarship bore abundant fruit, for the Spanish clergy that emerged was able to meet the later Protestant challenge far better than most in western Christendom.

Ximenes, however, contributed in another way that revealed most clearly how Humanistic ideas could be used for Christian purposes. From 1502 onward, scholars worked under his patronage and guidance to prepare a comprehensive edition of the Bible in different languages. The work was started to commemorate the birth of Charles, grandson of the Spanish monarchs, and before Alcala University was founded, but it was finished at that centre and later given the title *Complutensian Polyglot* from "Complutum", the classical Latin name for Alcala. The edition was a "polyglot" with the Old Testament arranged in parallel columns of Hebrew, Greek and Latin, and the New in similar columns of Greek and Latin; in addition, there was included an Aramaic version of the Pentateuch with its own Latin translation. The whole product was designed to give a critical study of the Bible. The New Testament was printed in 1514 and therefore had the distinction of being the earliest Greek text to be printed in western Europe, but publication was delayed until the rest of the Bible was ready, and as a result Erasmus's edition of the Greek New Testament was the first to be issued publicly in 1516. Even after Ximenes's death in 1517 the Polyglot remained in private hands until Leo X gave permission for its publication, and in the end it appeared in full only in 1522. Memorable both for contributing Humanistic scholarship to aid Biblical study and in the printing itself (which was of the highest quality in the day), the work showed convincingly what standard of reform Ximenes sought in Spain.

His achievement was considerable in that at the start of the sixteenth century he faced and overcame in Spain the kinds of abuse, disorder and materialism which were generally so rampant in Christendom, not least in the Papacy itself. Typically enough, he denounced in scathing terms the ineffectual work of the Fifth Lateran Council after 1512 and opposed the great indulgence campaign of Leo X for building St. Peter's. But not all corruption was stamped out even in Spain, some ecclesiastics remained too rich and what was gained was at a cost, where authoritarianism, rigid control and orthodoxy were enforced in the Inquisition as a permanent part of Spanish government. In the New World there were protests and visionary ideas about the Spanish treatment of natives and Christian responsibility for their conversion voiced from 1511 onward by the Dominicans Montesinos and Las Casas; to these men, missionary endeavour through following years owed no little debt. But in Old Spain, Ximenes was Inquisitor-General and had taken a fanatical if not completely ruthless part in treating the Moors and Jews. To that extent, therefore, it can be argued that the Spanish reformation moved backward in allowing no room for speculation or exploring of ideas beyond certain limits.

It demonstrated plainly what could be found in renewed spirituality and order within accepted assumptions, but this meant suppressing much that had been sought after or stated through preceding centuries, not least of all in the fruitful enquiries and exchanges of ideas between different peoples and cultures. Spanish religious developments – no less than those political – that led into the age of the Reformation were moulded too sharply by the particular conditions and stresses of the long struggles against the Moors, and too easily they permitted the use of force to impose orthodoxy and uniformity. The key position of the Inquisition in the new State demonstrated most of all the reactionary direction of Spanish ecclesiastical reform, with the continuing vigilance against any sign of heresy.

The idea of toleration or free enquiry was generally not very acceptable in western Christendom in the sixteenth century – possibly less so than in the previous hundred years – and nearly all the protagonists in religious struggle believed it right to equate heresy and nonconformity with civil disobedience or even treason. But for many this attitude was progressively to be tempered by a growing tolerance, the thought that the individual should be allowed to believe and worship as he wished without persecution. The Spanish leaders, however, took and kept the principle of authoritarian control and repression as fundamental for purifying and unifying their Church. In all Ximenes's attention to scholarship and the textual study of the Bible there was lacking that thought of the Scriptures for ordinary reading by the laity or of the freedom urged so passionately by Erasmus. Mystical interests and spirituality which drew in no small measure from the New Devotion were taken up eagerly by Ximenes's own nephew, Garcia of Cisneros, but were so modified in the experience of Ignatius Loyola that he founded an order in the Jesuits perfectly suited to the whole temper of the Spanish Church and the Inquisition in the sixteenth century. When the crisis came, the Church leaders in Spain were able at first to welcome much in Luther's criticisms, but this reaction was transient, and the man who supremely hoped to carry out Spanish ideas in papal reconstruction – Adrian VI – not only roused the united opposition and protests of all in the Roman hierarchy, but also stood out as adamantly against Luther as had Leo X before him. In Spain, reformed in its fashion, Protestantism later took only shallow root and was quickly swept away; and from the Spanish Church came those conservative and uncompromising forces that led the Counter-Reformation and stated its principles at Trent.

CHAPTER XIV

SAVONAROLA AND THE CRISIS IN ITALY

AT PRECISELY THE TIME WHEN XIMENES COMMENCED HIS WORK OF ecclesiastical reform in Spain, the general decadence of the Latin Church, particularly of the Papacy, was highlighted in events that convulsed Italy and gave sudden hope of action to deal with prevailing evils. Alexander VI's pontificate (1492–1503) coincided with political developments that ended Italy's isolation with the irruption of the French and Spanish into the peninsula, but it also ran parallel to the turbulent career of Savonarola in Florence. From this age sprang directly the situation which cradled Luther's revolt. More than religion was entangled in the issues at stake but they nonetheless revealed what was at fault in papal attitudes, organization and life in 1500, and why some of the reforms envisaged by Ximenes within Spanish limits could not more widely be adopted.

Although the figures of the second Borgia Pope and the Florentine Dominican stood in vivid contrast to each other, Alexander VI was not so markedly worse than some other pontiffs of the Renaissance – Sixtus IV, for example – nor particularly original in his reprehensible activities. At the same time, Savonarola was by no means unique in the fifteenth century where popular preachers as well as ecclesiastical scholars and conciliarists had denounced the Papacy and general abuses in violent terms. Nevertheless, the clash between these two personalities was seen at the time and in later years as symbolic of something greater than either of the men concerned. The Borgia Pope came to be taken as epitomizing all that was most evil and corrupt in the Renaissance Papacy, and Savonarola as the archetype of Luther's defiance against Rome. Both images have some value for providing an insight into the situation which framed the crisis after 1517, but neither is correct where they can only properly be measured against the context of events twenty years earlier. Savonarola was born at Ferrara in 1452 of good middle-class family known for its service to the noble d'Este family in the city, and in his early years Girolamo was trained for a medical career.[1] But after the regular courses of study in scholastic philosophy and Aquinas as preliminaries for his profession, he abandoned the plan and in 1475 entered a Dominican

[1] R. Ridolfi, *The Life of Girolamo Savonarola* (London, 1959), is the most balanced and scholarly recent study of Savonarola.

house at Bologna, renowned for its strict life on the Observant pattern. Six years of further theological training at Bologna and then again at Ferrara prepared Savonarola for higher scholastic work, but also seemed to provide him with opportunity for reaching more certain conclusions about the evils of his day and the need for returning to Biblical principles for reforms of life. He went out on his first preaching tour in 1484 but met with no success, nor did he fare better on moving a year later to the Dominican Convent of St. Mark in Florence. Under the patronage of Cosimo de' Medici, St. Mark's had become famous for its learning and studies, but Savonarola's career there continued undistinguished for several years. His preaching was theologically learned, but rough and uncultured in comparison with that of a popular Florentine friar like Mariano of Gennazzano. Only after tours in neighbouring towns in 1484 and subsequent years did Savonarola find his vocation more surely in the prophetic condemnation of contemporary evils, with visions and fastings, and in 1489 he was eventually recalled to Florence by his superiors. From his first sermons at St. Mark's in August of that year he quickly gained a reputation for fiery and apocalyptic attacks on life, morals and government in Florence, and through the last eight years of his life his following took him far beyond the confines of a friar's usual activities into the maelstrom of Italian and papal politics.

In fifteenth-century Italy, there were many such men and women in the orders who preached austere reform, and apart from Bernardino, Capistrano and Francis of Paolo, Catherine of Genoa was closely contemporary to Savonarola himself in the Observant tradition. Even in a city like Florence there was nothing new in an indictment of society such as Savonarola made; indeed, the very culture of the day made possible his return and criticisms, even though he so vehemently repudiated its standards and materialism. Under Lorenzo de' Medici Florence knew the full flowering of Renaissance studies in art, literature and scholarly work, and this not least of all in the pursuits of Ficino and the Platonic Academy. In all his captivating brilliance, Pico della Mirandola knew and appreciated Savonarola in the early 1480's and it was he who persuaded Lorenzo to have the friar recalled in 1489, whilst more generally he influenced him in his Greek and Hebrew studies, and was in turn so impressed that he had Savonarola clothe him in the Dominican habit on his deathbed.

Like Ximenes with the Franciscans in Spain, Savonarola demanded reform within his own order and set about achieving this once he had become Prior of St. Mark's in 1491. At the time the Dominicans in north Italy were so organized that Florence was associated with the Lombard communities more widely, but two years later Savonarola had his convent freed from any intermediate control and placed directly under papal authority, with Cardinal Caraffa as its protector at Rome. This rearrangement enabled him to carry out a rigorous reformation of life among the Dominicans at Florence, where wealth was abandoned, a strict return to simple study and devotion enforced, and members were trained to evangelize in and around the city. But Savonarola also condemned society more generally, laity and secular clergy as well as the regulars, and he went back to the Old Testament for his denunciations. He did not flinch from criticizing Lorenzo himself at whose feet he placed the responsibility for all the corruption and wrongs to be found in Florence. For his part the Medici ruler tried to keep on good terms with Savonarola, even when his gifts to St. Mark's were received with the demand that he should repent for his sins, and his threat that the Dominican would be exiled was met with the prophecy of his own imminent death. In such an attitude about reform, Savonarola became embroiled in politics and was unable to withdraw from this position when Lorenzo died early in 1492. The event enhanced his reputation as a prophet but it also left him prominent in opposition to the continuing rule of Lorenzo's son, Peter de' Medici.

These political events involved all Italy, for Lorenzo alone had been able to preserve the balance between Naples and the Sforza of Milan and to keep Charles VIII of France at bay. His death ended any further hope of stability, since Lodovico Sforza, the Regent of Milan, speedily invited the French into Italy and Peter de' Medici was wholly incapable of meeting the crisis. In 1494, with the connivance of the Sforza and Alexander VI's enemies, Charles VIII crossed into Italy, ostensibly to launch a crusade against the Turks from southern Italy, but in fact to seize Naples for himself and possibly initiate papal reform by summoning a General Council. Savonarola looked to Charles as the "new Cyrus" and his coming as God's way to sweep away corruption, much as Dante in 1311 had hailed the Emperor Henry VII's expedition into Italy. In Florence the Medici government was overthrown and a republic proclaimed by the people shortly before the arrival of the French. Given the promise of a subsidy and an alliance, Charles accepted the new government and dealt with Florentine affairs without trying to bring back the Medici. This meant that the life of the new republic depended in no small measure upon a French alliance and that similarly Savonarola's fortunes were bound to those of France. The hopes placed on Charles VIII, however, were signally disappointed, for he was outmanoeuvred by the Pope at Rome and failed to summon a General Council. His overthrow and occupation of the Neapolitan kingdom in 1495 were short-lived and the French army had to retire precipitately from Italy in the face of a new alliance of enemies, narrowly escaping disaster at Fornova. Florence therefore was left without immediate support, though French resources were not too distant and Charles hoped to return.

In these events Savonarola emerged into a dominating if unofficial position in Florence where he helped to frame a new government. He was reluctant to be drawn further into politics, but complied with requests by recommending the adoption of a mixed constitution that left the commercial middle classes holding the reins of power. In addition he used his influence to have introduced measures for fair justice and taxation. But his abiding preoccupation and his goal in reconstructing the State were reforms in moral and religious terms, and generally he tried to stand above politics or party. His own support came from more than one group – the merchant-industrialists, the enemies of the Medici, the Dominicans, the people swayed by his sermons – and not all wanted the same ends or even the moral reconstructions which he desired. Such support was fickle in many strands and what was remarkable was that Savonarola kept his controlling position for nearly four years when his demands were morally severe and spiritually high. His ideal was nothing less than the Kingdom of God on earth, Christ as the Ruler of Florence, and the reforms to bring in the Millennium he expounded in his Lenten sermons of 1495. The secular carnivals which had earlier become so riotous that even Lorenzo had tried to check them were turned by Savonarola into great religious festivals, with children organized to impose good behaviour. Gambling and prostitution were rooted out, extravagant or costly dress prohibited, and finally in 1497 great bonfires – the "Burning of Vanities" – were held at which Florentines committed to the flames their luxuries, indecent books or paintings. Botticelli was one who burned some of his works in this ceremony and who thereafter gave himself more completely to religious art. Positively, Savonarola encouraged alms-giving for the poor and organized social work for the sick and the churches. His criticisms were not unlike those of Bernardino fifty years earlier, but their impact was dramatic at this later stage in Renaissance history, for they represented a sweeping revulsion from much that had been achieved in Florence, the cradle of Humanistic culture under the Medici. Savonarola's protest was basically conservative in asserting that true Christian religion lay in the austerity of earlier days rather than in the lax morals and concern for Man in Humanistic studies. But even during his lifetime there was scarcely lasting renewal of moral life in Florence, for on occasions when Savonarola was unwell or forbidden to preach, it was noted that the traditional ways quickly reappeared.

Savonarola's criticisms indeed soon made him enemies whose opposition grew as hopes of further French action receded, but it was only when developments were well advanced that the Pope joined the other groups against him. Alexander VI was not necessarily antagonistic at the outset nor even bothered at Savonarola's activities in Florence so long as they did not touch the Papacy or Rome. The Pope was a diplomat by training and could consider that it would be unwise to offend a Florentine government allied to France by objecting to Savonarola; for his part, the Dominican did not immediately look outside Florence in his denunciations. But in 1495 he spoke so vigorously of what Charles VIII might accomplish in reforming the Church that Alexander cited him to appear at Rome to explain his prophecies. Savonarola refused to go on the grounds of ill-health, and then declined the cardinal's hat which the Pope offered, it seems, in the hope of making him leave Florence. For the time being, however, Savonarola complied with the papal order to stop preaching, and he only resumed this early in 1496, at the Signory's request. In his Lenten sermons, he directly attacked the Pope who, he claimed,

> cannot command me to do anything which is in contradiction to Christian charity or the Gospel. I am convinced that he never will; but were he to do so, I should reply: "At this moment you are in error and no longer the chief pastor or the voice of the Church."

He condemned Rome for its immorality and likened it to Babylon in confusing all tongues. The Pope took no specific notice of these criticisms in 1496, since he hoped that Savonarola could be removed from Florence in a reorganization of the Dominican congregations, but following the sermons of Lent, 1497, Alexander at last excommunicated him, supposedly for his defiance and views. Savonarola tried to avoid publication of the bull and wrote humbly to the Pope who seemed mollified, but the decree was nonetheless announced. It was rejected as invalid, based on false evidence, and castigated by Savonarola as a command "opposed to charity and the Law of God", and others agreed with him in judging the sentence as irregular and void. Yet he respected the sentence and the Signory's wish to the extent of refraining from any priestly action until Christmas Day, 1497, when he celebrated Mass once again.

In the meantime, he became inextricably involved in party politics and increasingly hated by certain groups in Florence. An abortive attempt by the Medici to recover the city in April, 1497, was followed by the trial and condemnation of five of Peter's adherents, and Savonarola did not intervene to save the men. Much of his support was therefore waning when early in 1498 he began preaching once more and claimed that the Pope had shown himself to be no longer an instrument of God but a "broken tool", and that the scandals at Rome were worse than those of the Turks and Moors. More ominously, in March he appealed to a General Council against Alexander and supported his attack by addressing letters to the leading rulers of Christendom. The Pope answered by threatening to place Florence under interdict unless Savonarola were stopped from preaching, and the Signory, sensitive to the disastrous economic consequences that could follow in the city if such a threat were realized, ordered him to be silent. There came then the notorious episode of the proposed ordeal by fire, and this sealed Savonarola's fate. The incident arose out of a rash boast to defend his views in such a test, and though he quickly discounted the idea as neither practical nor sensible, some of his Dominican followers insisted on pursuing it in rivalry to their Franciscan enemies in Florence. A public ordeal was arranged, chiefly because Savonarola's opponents saw that whatever happened it could only harm him. This fact the Signory underlined by stating that in the test a Dominican and Franciscan were each to enter the fire, and that if his champion perished Savonarola was to be banished from the city; but nothing was said about the Franciscans. The spectacle, arranged for April 7th, 1498, proved in the event to be a fiasco, for delays and disputes about conditions for entering the fire were capped by a torrential storm, and the Signory finally abandoned the proceedings. In disappointed rage the mob swung against Savonarola and his supporters, sacked the Convent of St. Mark on the following evening of Palm Sunday and seized Savonarola, who was then brought to trial with two other friars. After lengthy examination and torture, all three were found guilty of heresy, schism, deceiving the people and inciting them to rebellion, and on May 23rd they were hanged in the city square, their bodies were burned and the ashes scattered in the river Arno. The Pope, it seems, genuinely wanted to have Savonarola dealt with otherwise, but the friar's execution undeniably aided papal interests in Italian politics, and came when temporarily no French help was at hand; Charles VIII died on the same day as the planned ordeal by fire. In the straightforward clash between the two men, it can with fairness be claimed that Savonarola provoked the Pope beyond reasonable limits, even though much of his criticism was just. Yet such was the opinion of the Papacy that barely a decade after his death the friar could be portrayed as a saint in painting, whilst Alexander VI's reputation was taken to typify all that was worst in a corrupt Renaissance Church.[1]

[1] Julius II in 1505 said he would gladly have canonized the friar, though the remark was to help blacken Alexander VI's character. (Cf. Ridolfi, op. cit., p. 295.)

Savonarola was largely the victim of Italian communal politics, not least in his dream of the New Jerusalem in social as well as religious revolution, but his criticisms ranged far over all ecclesiastical abuses, he was officially condemned as a heretic and the Papacy was intimately concerned in his death with its own material interests. Quite where he stood in relation to other critics of the age remained difficult at times to assess, particularly in any dispute about his contribution to Protestant ideas. It seems, however, clear that Savonarola saw himself as fully orthodox in doctrine, engaged above all in restoring purity of life and authority in a degenerate Florence where Renaissance practices had brought corruption. Until his final days he moved no further than many contemporaries and did not even attack the papal office. There was no central doctrine of justification by faith such as could be glimpsed in Gansfort or Lefèvre or as propounded later by Luther, and Savonarola not only insisted on his readiness always to submit to the Church's judgment but also emphasized that it was heresy to separate from accepted Roman teaching. But under the pressure of circumstances, particularly as Alexander VI endeavoured to discipline him with increasingly severe measures, Savonarola stepped beyond orthodox bounds, and dangerously so, in defining obedience and the place of individual judgment to show whether or not any authority in the Church should be accepted. His appeal in 1498 to a future General Council to sit in judgment on the Pope and bring reform was a formal and recognized challenge to papal orthodoxy, and Alexander VI was acutely sensitive to the threat, but Savonarola had already gone further in claims for the individual. He was repeating earlier thoughts in his final sermon in March, 1498, when he stated that "in the Church, the believer must first apply to his priest or confessor; failing these to his bishop or the Pope; and finally, if all the ecclesiastical hierarchy be corrupt, he must turn to Christ, who is the primary cause, and say – Thou art my confessor, my bishop and my Pope; provide Thou against the ruin of the Church; let Thy vengeance begin". Every individual had the right to resist a corrupt order, to appeal in the last resort to Christ Himself, and in claiming this, Savonarola was no less radical than Wycliffe or Hus before him, or Luther afterward. He was antinomian in setting private judgment against authority, though beyond this he did not go, certainly not in rejecting monasticism or a righteous Pope. It can well be argued that he never resolved the contradictions into which events drove him, and that the radical ideas upon which he touched were well known to others who had already challenged the Papacy without any more fully worked out evaluation of Christian faith and salvation. But his actions and preaching pinpointed the glaring faults in Italian religious affairs, and even if valued wrongly in the developments of the early sixteenth century they helped to prepare the path for Luther.

Florentine ambitions were not realized in Savonarola's death, and his dire prophecies for the future came true with the struggles of the Spanish and French in Italy in the years afterward. Charles VIII's ill-planned expedition only heralded further French designs, and though he himself never returned, Louis XII wasted little time in declaring his intentions by adopting the title of Duke of Milan and imprisoning Lodovico Sforza in France for the rest of his life. Further French efforts to seize the Kingdom of Naples had to be carried out in alliance with Ferdinand of Aragon, who willingly agreed to partition the realm with Louis XII in 1500 before gathering his forces for more positive action in Italy. The allies soon came to blows where the French nearly succeeded in driving the Spanish garrisons out of south Italy. Under Gonzalo of Cordova, however, and with additional reinforcements from Ferdinand, the Spanish eventually took the initiative, recovered all their possessions and central Italy by 1504, and restricted French power to the northern plains and the Alps. In the following decades, this balance was repeatedly upset as the French and Spanish-Habsburg forces fought in Italy, but it was against this background that the Popes as Italian princes and leaders of the Church found their ambitions swallowed up in the interests of outside powers. This situation ensured that much-needed ecclesiastical reform in the Curia and in papal government was all but completely ignored and that even where it was thought of, the undertaking was found to be impossible.

More than once through the latter part of the fifteenth century reconstruction in papal affairs had been considered by Popes and demanded in the college of cardinals as well as threatened from outside with thoughts of appeal to a General Council. Neither the Popes nor the cardinals were wholly unaware of what was wrong and whilst Pius II in 1460 or Sixtus IV later could have bulls drafted, though not published, for reforming the papal court, the college itself numbered among its members not only the politically ambitious but also some of the ablest and single-minded ecclesiastical leaders of the day. Yet in the event reforms were not brought in before the Lutheran revolt, and nothing more vividly illustrates the situation than the attempt briefly made to face the problems and to legislate for them during Alexander VI's pontificate. Savonarola's criticisms, like those of the French or Spanish kings, came from outside the Curia and Rome, and could be discounted in part for their bias; those advanced seriously and soberly within the Vatican itself could not be so regarded, and in consequence carried all the more weight. This was what happened under Alexander VI. In full pursuit of his political, dynastic ends, he was cut short in the summer of 1497 by the murder of his second son, Duke John of Gandia. Shocked, it seems sincerely, for a time into contemplating his proper functions and claims as the Vicar of Christ, Alexander appointed a Reform Commission to examine abuses in the Curia and papal organization and to recommend measures for overcoming corruption. The commission was more than a sham and clearly intended to make an honest and searching report, for it was composed of the most eminent, respected and able men of the college – Cardinals Caraffa, Costa and Piccolomini – and with ecclesiastical jurists of distinction to assist in the work. To everyone's surprise at Rome, the commission worked thoroughly for some months, and with the Pope drafted out a reform bull of such comprehension and honesty that undoubtedly its authors knew what was wrong in the practices of the Renaissance Papacy. Reforms were proposed for cutting down curial staff, for ending corrupt financial and judicial practices, and for a return to a more austere, responsible and Christian life by the Pope and cardinals. All these issues involved general complaint about the Papacy and genuine action at this stage would have been welcome on every side, but the bull remained a draft and was never publicly promulgated.[1] The Pope possibly had difficulties with outside threats from Spain and France but it seems more likely that he recovered from remorse over his son's death and was thus able to wind up the commission's work before the end of 1497. He made a scapegoat of one of his private secretaries whom he had accused, condemned and imprisoned for life for malpractices and forgeries which had offended the Spanish monarchs, but otherwise he resumed the familiar path of Renaissance papal ambition. No other attempt was made to contemplate such reforms before the time of Luther and conceivably they would have been too difficult to implement then even by a man of sincerity and spirituality. When Adrian VI attempted to sweep away curial materialism, bureaucracy and corruption in 1522, he met with blank opposition and brought on his own speedy collapse and death. More genuinely and widely supported efforts at dealing with the evils had to wait until the Council of Trent.

In the first twenty years of the sixteenth century, the Popes continued to show themselves too completely immersed in politics and Italian ambitions to give proper attention to the wider religious or spiritual issues of Christendom. In material terms and for a stable resolution

[1] L. Pastor, *The History of the Popes*, Vol. V, edit. by F. I. Antrobus (London, 1908), pp. 512–8.

of the Italian turmoil, Alexander VI's hopes were centred upon a principality for his son Cesare, with continuing Borgia control of the Papacy. Machiavelli saw in Cesare political ability, ruthlessness and trickery for uniting Italy, but also great failure, for Borgia ambitions ended in 1503 with Alexander VI's death. Reaction against the Spanish family amongst the Roman people, in the college and throughout Italy illustrated unhappily how Italian and isolated the Papacy was from Christian needs and opinion at large, and after Pius III's reign of a month, Julius II ascended the throne. He completed the destruction of Borgia power, but also built upon and completed his enemy's work by consolidating papal authority over the Church's lands in central Italy. In this task he was demonstrably successful, notable for his lack of interest in family fortune and for ability and steadfastness in devotion in making his own conquests, within the limits allowed by Franco-Spanish rivalries. Julius was the warrior Pope who, it is said, had thrown the keys of St. Peter into the River Tiber but had kept the sword of St. Paul and led his own armies into battle. By 1506 he had subdued cities like Perugia and Bologna which had long treated papal overlordship lightly, and thereafter he exploited the balance between French and Spanish forces in Italy to humiliate Venice in 1508. Finally, though unsuccessfully, he tried to capture the small Duchy of Ferrara, and narrowly escaped defeat himself at the hands of the French in 1510. In this naked pursuit of power, the Pope made numerous enemies, and in 1511 the Emperor Maximilian and Louis XII gave their support to a number of dissident cardinals who summoned a General Council at Pisa and cited Julius to appear before it.

This appeal was dangerous for the Pope at such a juncture, but when the Pisan assembly met, the cardinals were not united, Maximilian changed his mind to join Ferdinand in support of Julius, and Louis XII alone remained to recognize the council for what it claimed to be. Effectively it achieved nothing in condemning the Pope, who completely countered any threat by summoning his own assembly – the Fifth Lateran Council – which met in May, 1512. Some delegates came to the opening sessions enthusiastic for genuine reforms in the Church, but Julius II had not the slightest intention of engaging seriously in such work. His primary concern was to nullify any danger from the cardinals' council, which had to move from Pisa to Milan and was duly condemned at Rome. Apart from this, only a decree against simony was passed before the Pope died in 1513. Julius II's achievements outside Italian politics embraced administrative reform but only for increasing efficiency in taxation and for beautifying Rome, in which he was notable for starting the construction of the new St. Peter's in 1506 and for patronage of Michelangelo and

Raphael. He was understandably popular with the Romans, but this reputation bore no relation at all to the urgent needs of reform in the Church.

Julius's successor, Giovanni de' Medici, who took the title of Leo X, was chosen for his mildness, but he inherited papal political aims and if crafty rather than bellicose was scarcely less materialistic in his pursuits. He is credited with having remarked that he intended to enjoy the Papacy, and in his extravagance he was as good as his word. Yet papal independence became less of a reality than ever before, where it consisted in the precarious balance between France and the dynastic power of the Habsburgs in their control of the Empire, Spain and the Netherlands. This balance was destroyed first by the French victory at Marignano in 1515, and then a decade later by their defeat at Pavia which led to the imperial sack of Rome in 1527. At the start of his reign, Leo X inherited the Lateran Council and he was presented by two Venetian monks with a radical programme for dealing with corruption. But he was no more concerned than Julius with such schemes. In 1513 he reached an understanding with Louis XII for French abandonment of the rival council, and for a draft agreement to replace the Pragmatic Sanction. The new Concordat of Bologna finally signed in 1516 followed Francis I's victory at Marignano and conceded much more to the French king than Leo earlier had hoped. As the Council's most notable achievement, it was significantly a move backward from genuine ecclesiastical reform, whilst the assembly itself was dissolved in March, 1517, with emphatic reaffirmations of papal supremacy over the Church. But these claims were hardly related to reality where the Renaissance Papacy had lost contact with feeling throughout Christendom about the need to remedy evils. It was illuminating that the Curia was most efficient and most keenly praised or execrated in its financial work, in which a massive campaign for selling indulgences was deemed essential to continue building St. Peter's and to launch other papal projects. Leo X's notorious authorization of such sales was bitterly criticized in Spain; and when the wider challenge came in Luther's protests, the Papacy could not command authority to contain a threat far greater than that in the local defiance of Savonarola in Florence. Instead, it was Charles V who as Emperor after 1519 determined and checked Luther's path, and showed that hopes of reform could still be entertained.

In becoming embroiled in the pursuit of political and material ambitions, the Popes failed to live up to their exalted claims as the Vicars of Christ. The depth of that failure is to be measured by the fact that the storm did not burst until 1517, that reverence for the

Papacy could endure for so long even though individual pontiffs were patently unspiritual and corrupt. Ideas for reform abounded through the fourteenth and fifteenth centuries but they only came to fruition insofar as the Papal organization was ignored. Where the Popes entered affairs, it was as a rule to oppose any change that would inevitably harm their coveted privileges. Such opposition, repeatedly registered and coupled to the abuses patent in the Curia, contributed weightily to the searing nature of the Lutheran revolt when it came. But it also destroyed what hope there was for a new world in Christian Humanism, a hope exemplified above all in the life and work of Erasmus.

CHAPTER XV

ERASMUS AND THE HOPE OF CHRISTIAN HUMANISM

THE RENAISSANCE IN ITALY GAVE RISE DIRECTLY TO NON-CHRISTIAN, even anti-Christian, ideals and attitudes, though there were the enquiring textual studies which led some scholars into the paths of Biblical exegesis and criticism. Savonarola repudiated the Renaissance in its pagan materialism but at the same time was himself the friend of Florentine Humanists and kindred in spirit to those who gave their minds to study of the Bible. But north of the Alps, the spread of Humanism and classical studies was tempered far more positively by other intermingling influences, including the tradition of the New Devotion, and the result was that ideas for the reform of Christian life were nurtured within the framework of Humanistic principles as much as outside them. The new learning was praised and pursued for its service in aiding the reconstruction of Christendom, and the "Christian Humanists" (as they were called) who were won by this ideal worked in every country and kind of condition for religious and ecclesiastical change. Among such leaders were Ximenes with his Spanish programme, Lefèvre d'Étaples in France, Reuchlin in Germany and the Englishmen Colet and More; they all shared many similar aims, but their achievements were clearly governed by the varying situations with which they were faced. The outstanding figure of the movement, however, was Erasmus who was associated with scholars and learning throughout Christendom, and whose career straddled the crisis that led to Luther's break from Rome. More than any other person, Erasmus expressed what was the vision in Christian Humanism, and showed not only how earnestly reform was sought at the start of the sixteenth century but also why any step short of that taken by Luther was almost inevitably bound to fail.

Erasmus "of Rotterdam", as he called himself, was born in Gouda about 1469 of illegitimate parentage insofar as his father was a priest and never known to him.[1] Though such a situation was not uncommon nor regarded as a bar to advancement in the age, Erasmus's outlook was deeply moulded by the fact of his early dependence upon a

[1] For general studies of Erasmus and his work, see P. Smith, *Erasmus* (New York, 1923), and M. M. Phillips, *Erasmus and the Northern Renaissance* (London, 1949).

mother rather than a father whom he thought of as disgraced. He went to school at Deventer where the stricter principles still applied before Hegius's advent in 1485, and though he later condemned the teaching as "barbarous" in its treatment of the classics, he undeniably learned much from the Brethren of the Common Life. His first enthusiasm for Biblical study and his mystical concern derived probably from the early years of training at Deventer. In 1486, he entered the monastery of Steyn, at first on probation and then more definitely committed to the life, with, it seems, some conviction despite his subsequent criticisms of monasticism. During his training he cultivated a strong love for classical literature and thought, and as early as 1490 wrote a defence of Valla and his critical work. It was partly in pursuit of these same interests that in 1492 or 1493 he abandoned Steyn to become secretary to the Bishop of Cambrai, who ordained him a priest. In his new post, Erasmus enjoyed valuable opportunities for travel and study where the Netherlands stood at the centre of political and cultural life in the dynastic structure binding the country to the Empire and to Spain. He went to Paris in 1495 to study for his doctorate in theology and stayed the year at the College of Montaigu where Standonck was in control. Erasmus's later recollections were of the grim and unhelpful nature of Standonck's methods, but though the régime was certainly severe, such reaction was illuminating chiefly for showing what the Dutchman came to consider was – and was not – necessary in reform. After a brief final visit to Steyn in 1496, he returned to Paris, confirmed in the decision to leave the monastic life, though for years he remained worried about repudiating his vows and finally secured a papal dispensation to set his mind at rest. At Paris, he showed his particular interests in studying in the new liberal courses rather than in scholastic theology for his degree, and he met like-minded teachers and fellow-students at the very moment when French excitement over Italian ideas and culture was at its height after Charles VIII's expedition across the Alps.

Through the introduction of one of his pupils, Lord Mountjoy, Erasmus travelled to England in 1499 and spent some months in Oxford before returning to the Continent. It was at Oxford that he met Colet, More and other Englishmen in the Humanistic movement, and this association proved to be of signal importance for his career and ideas. The friendship started with More was life-long, but at the time Erasmus's discussions with Colet counted most, though to what extent his theological outlook was changed remains debatable. He was basically a Humanist in his absorption in the classics, whilst Colet stood out as the Christian evangelist and scholar concerned with Humanism only insofar as it aided Christian and Biblical studies.

Erasmus was influenced profoundly by Colet and increasingly sought Christian objectives rather than those primarily Humanistic, but his views were never cast precisely in the same mould as those of the Englishman. He was not won over to Colet's fierce passion for Christ so much as spurred on to greater zeal in classical studies, together with a renewed appreciation of those principles of belief and life known from childhood in the teaching of the Brethren of the Common Life.[1] All that he later attempted to do and wrote suggests the blending of Christian and classical principles in a reasoned explanation for daily living rather than an uncompromising conviction of truth in God's Word alone and the experience of conversion found in Colet and a little later in Luther. Erasmus's outlook was and remained more closely in tune with that of More through their long years of friendship. In 1499, Colet suggested that he should stay on in England and lecture on some part of the Old Testament in the style already used for St. Paul's Epistles. Erasmus refused, on the ground that he could not teach what he himself had never learned, and suggested instead that he should spend his time in mastering Greek for wider Biblical studies.

The following five years he therefore spent on the Continent in such linguistic study, and during that time published his first works of renown. The *Adages* showed his classical knowledge, for it was a collection of proverbs and pithy sayings from ancient authors, with explanations and notes by Erasmus; originally slight in form, it was steadily extended in size and depth so that by 1508 it ranked as a study of consequence, not least of all in being a commentary on contemporary Christendom and problems. The work enhanced Erasmus's reputation but also pointed clearly to his development in scholarship as a critic of the evils of his own day. His whole attitude to Christian affairs, however, was already made plain in another work published in 1503, the *Handbook of the Christian Knight*. As a manual intended to be the "sword" of the Christian soldier, it was addressed supposedly to a nobleman to recall him to the true practice of his faith and life. It set out the bases and weapons for the struggle and contained all that was essential in Erasmus's thought, even though later he discussed some subjects more fully in other treatises. His starting-point was the need for the Christian to be watchful and to take care not to rely too excessively on God's grace at the expense of human reason in fighting against Satan. "We will conquer through Christ," he asserted, "if we fight according to His example. Wherefore we ought to steer a middle course between Scylla and Charybdis, so that we neither act too securely because we rely on divine grace, nor cast

[1] Cf. A. Hyma, *Renaissance to Reformation* (Grand Rapids, 1951), Chapter IX.

away our mind with our arms because we are dispirited by the difficulties of war." For this conflict, the weapons were prayer and the study of the divinely-inspired Scriptures; as introductions to such study, Erasmus argued that attention could be given to the Greek philosophers, particularly the Platonists, and then more completely to those Christian Fathers who followed St. Paul and "departed as much as possible from the literal sense" in laying bare the supernatural meaning in the text of Scripture. For Erasmus, these authorities were Origen, Ambrose, Jerome and Augustine who did not fight bitterly over the letter of the word like the contentious scholastics of later centuries.

In more detailed discussion he considered how the Christian should practise the art of "knowing himself" and what weapons were necessary for eradicating special sins. It was characteristic of his approach that he should speak of the principle of Reason as uniquely manifest in the Johannine Logos but to be found generally in the prophets and in all men. On this basis, he was able to appeal to Plato and Socrates as well as to the Hebrew prophets and the Christian Fathers for witness of the Divine Reason that had its complete, visible expression in Christ. Erasmus's argument was similar to that of the early Christian Apologists and the Alexandrian Fathers – Clement and Origen – who likewise could regard Socrates as preparing the way for the Gospel. In his Christian understanding, there was room for philosophy, above all for Greek thought, and this was in marked contrast to the views of Christians like Tertullian, Colet in his Biblical concern, or Luther who set the foolishness of the Cross and faith over against reason and the wisdom of philosophy. Furthermore, in applying his ideas to the problems of Christian living and reform, Erasmus laid considerable weight on Man's reason and ability to know and gain the mastery over himself. This was essentially the kernel of individual inner reform familiar as the theme of the New Devotion and implying rejection of institutional or sacerdotal religion. To a large extent in Erasmus's argument, ignorance was sin and the way to salvation in Christ lay in knowledge and the study of the Scriptures. The accompanying stress on self-reliance at the expense of God's grace – if admittedly in an allegorical discussion – was indicative of Erasmus's differences from Colet and of what was to divide him theologically from Luther.

In the years after 1503, Erasmus anchored his positive hopes for action upon a monumental work of scholarship and study to recover the true framework of primitive Christianity. Once this had been achieved, his expectation was that the leaders of Christendom would accept and use such knowledge in reforming the Church. After a second stay in England in 1505, Erasmus visited Italy where he remained for three years in literary study; he seemed to have been entirely unaware of Renaissance cultural splendour in what he saw, but his eyes were opened to much that was wrong in the Papacy. When Henry VIII came to the throne in 1509, Erasmus returned once more to England, and on the journey conceived the plan of his most brilliant satire, *The Praise of Folly*. The work he completed soon afterward and dedicated to More whose name he punned in its Latin title (*Moriae Encomium*). Though writing the satire at white-hot pace, Erasmus delayed publication until 1511 and then arranged that it should appear anonymously so that, if need be, he could deny authorship or any dangerous accusations for what he had said. The work was supposed to be a set speech by the goddess Folly in her own defence, and it followed a literary tradition of "fool" writing well known in the age. The most striking and successful earlier example was *The Ship of Fools* of Sebastian Brandt published in 1494, which lampooned society by recounting in poetry the habits and idiosyncrasies of all kinds of fools in a boat. Brandt's satire inspired many imitators in the early sixteenth century, and what Erasmus wrote therefore appeared in a situation where his discussion could be appreciated for its humour and criticism. Light and witty it certainly was, where Folly presented herself as the deity who made life bearable for men in all their mistakes, but much of the peroration was in fact deadly serious criticism of Christian life and supremely a condemnation of ecclesiastical malpractices, monasticism and the papal hierarchy. Erasmus perhaps said more than he intended, and for ever after he declared his innocence of any thought of radical criticism of the Church but his remarks plainly showed what were general attitudes in Christendom and there could be little doubt as to his purposes. Folly as a figure provided him with ample scope for making sharp attacks on all religious practices under the cloak of good humour, and more positively to state, with a similar disarming lightness of touch, what he himself believed to be the heart of Christianity. In his dedication to More he claimed to have praised folly "in a way not altogether foolish", and this serious intent ran through the whole discourse.

In the opening sections, Folly appeared as little more than abundant good humour to make Man's existence possible, where too serious a concern with affairs in the world was ridiculed. The half-wits, Folly claimed, "after a life of jollity and with no fear of death or sense of it, go straight to the Elysian fields, where they entertain the pious and leisurely shades". Erasmus appeared to deride Christian ideals and attitudes in praising enjoyment of days as they came, but his purpose was more subtle, namely, to show the barrenness or futility of much that was regarded as all-important and to suggest that people should be more tolerant and willing to let anxieties of ordinary life concern them less. And from this opening, Erasmus turned to criticize as folly the practices of ecclesiastics, theologians and monks and the whole formal religious system in terms that could hardly be mistaken, even under cover of humorous satire. Indeed, he seemed to forget about Folly as the speaker in his tirade. He pilloried scholasticism in its meaningless concern with details and ignorance of true religion. "Paul could exhibit faith," Folly exclaimed, "but when he said, 'Faith is the substance of things hoped for, the evidence of things not seen', he did not define it scholastically. Although he exemplified charity supremely well, he analysed and defined it with little logical subtlety in his first Epistle to the Corinthians, chapter thirteen." For their materialism and self-seeking, their pride and illiteracy, the monks and friars were mercilessly condemned, whilst for all ecclesiastics the ideal of a return to primitive apostolic poverty was held out. "Finally," Folly summed up,

> ... if the Supreme Pontiffs, who are the Vicars of Christ, tried to imitate His life, His poverty, labours, teaching, His cross and contempt for life; if they stopped to consider the meaning of the title of Pope, a Father, or the epithet Most Holy, who on earth would be more overwhelmed? Who would purchase that office at the cost of every effort? Who would retain it by the sword, by poison, and by every other way?

Such criticism was a thinly-veiled attack on Julius II and was common enough, though others did not always voice complaints so bitterly and so skilfully in their writings. Erasmus's charges were all the more weighty and ominous because of their polished presentation.

But Folly's speech did not end at this point, and in a shorter concluding section Erasmus once again struck a different note, deeper and more personal, and resuming some of the opening thoughts of the speech. Christianity itself was drawn under inspection as Folly posed the idea that "the Christian religion on the whole seems to have some kinship with folly, while it has not at all with wisdom", and went on to instance the attitudes and behaviour of those "possessed with true Christian piety", who appeared to despise material interests and hardships and disdained life "as if their souls lived elsewhere and not in their bodies". There were two kinds of people, two kinds of living, and Erasmus clearly commended the one that was spiritual and pious in terms revealing his own continuing attachment to the principles of the New Devotion. The foolishness of Christian behaviour and ecstatic, mystical experience was seen as the essence of true faith, where men counted ordinary mundane affairs as nothing against the joy of communion with God, and could know on earth a foretaste of heavenly pleasures to come. In these thoughts, Erasmus probed most deeply where his stress, as in the *Handbook*, was upon a simple Christian piety with its roots in an inner spiritual experience at the expense of the priesthood or formal religion, and entirely separate from abuses and corruption which were the product of ecclesiasticism. For all its frivolity, the *Praise of Folly* was of wide consequence and influence in popularizing discussion of the failings in the organized Church and religious life at the time.

In the enthusiasm accompanying the start of young King Henry VIII's reign in 1509, Erasmus had visions of a great Christian and Humanistic enterprise, but though he and others like More were welcomed at court and their ideals respected, all too little came of their high hopes. Erasmus was honoured by being appointed to the newly-created Lady Margaret Chairs of Divinity and Greek at Cambridge, but he found the years there frustrating rather than rewarding. Nevertheless, he continued to work steadily on those projects which academically and in Christian terms constituted his most enduring and positive achievement, more substantial and momentous than the popular *Praise of Folly*. His ideal for reform remained the primitive Church and the teachings of the Christian Fathers, in contrast to the accretions and corruption of later scholastics, theologians and philosophers. Through the years Erasmus used his energies and knowledge in editing and having printed the complete texts of the works of Jerome, Hilary, Epiphanius, Ambrose, Irenaeus, Augustine, Chrysostom and Origen. This achievement alone was sufficient to mark him out as a giant among Christian scholars, but massive though it was, it belonged almost entirely to the years when Luther was already engaged in conflict with Rome. Erasmus's most important contribution in Biblical scholarship came before that date, namely, his publication in 1516 of a complete text of the New Testament in Greek. More than any other single work, it has been claimed, this represented what Christian Humanism specifically could contribute to the cause of reform. From the time when he first met Colet, Erasmus was concerned with such a project for he was acutely aware that the existing versions of the Latin Vulgate were far removed from the text of Jerome, and even more distantly from the Greek that had been Jerome's source. In common with others like Ximenes and Lefèvre, Erasmus wished to return to this source as closely as possible, so that the title deeds of true Christianity could be clearly seen. Over the years therefore he sought to collect and collate Greek manuscripts for printing a New Testament in the original tongue, working contemporaneously with those scholars whom Ximenes encouraged in Spain. But though in fact Ximenes greatly admired Erasmus and invited him more than once to go to Alcala, and Erasmus for his part praised many of the reforms undertaken in Spain, it seems that until late in the day there was little knowledge that both men were working on a similar project. Then information that the Spanish had printed their edition and were delaying its publication spurred a Dutch printer in 1515 into persuading Erasmus to complete his work at speed; a year later the New Testament was published, six years before the appearance of the Complutensian Polyglot.[1]

The edition presented by Erasmus contained the New Testament in Greek, his own translation into Latin alongside it to illustrate corruptions in the accepted Vulgate text, and detailed annotations to explain textual points and the spiritual meanings of passages. As it emerged in 1516, the work was by no means perfect, for it was full of typographical mistakes and was based by Erasmus for the most part on only four manuscripts to which he had easy access in his haste. None of these texts possessed the last six verses of Revelation, and so Erasmus obligingly supplied his own rendering back into Greek from the Vulgate! His Latin translation was more careful, and so too were the annotations which had been prepared over a number of years, although they did not always correspond to the readings given in the printed work. The mistakes gave room for criticism, which fed also upon the resentment of the older schools to Humanism and to any tampering with the Vulgate text as it stood. That Erasmus dared to omit I John 5:7[2] because the verse was not in his Greek manuscripts aroused a furore and led him to promise, somewhat rashly, to include it if it could be found in any Greek text. This he did in his revision of 1522, on the authority of one late and wholly unreliable manuscript unearthed by his enemies at Dublin.[3] Many of the mistakes were remedied in the second edition of 1519, in which Erasmus introduced better readings, and at his death in 1536 a fifth edition was being issued. The work overwhelmingly captured the imagination and interst of Christendom, symbolizing the widespread concern for Biblical truth and the sources lying behind the corruptions of the institutionalized Church. It embodied the hope for reform through the study of the Bible itself, and far more completely than any other textual or critical study of the Christian Humanists it summed up the deepest ideals of the movement. Part of the quality of Erasmus's New Testament was to be found in his annotations which plainly set

[1] Cf. *Cambridge History of the Bible*, pp. 58–60, 81–2. See p. 205 above.

[2] In the Authorized Version – "There are three that bear record in heaven, the Father, the Word and the Holy Ghost: and these three are one".

[3] *Cambridge History of the Bible*, p. 60.

out the interpretation of Scripture, placing side by side the literal and spiritual expositions, and acknowledging that Christ always stood authoritatively to make clear by His Spirit the inner meaning of the written Word.[1] But it also owed much to the tone of the preface – the *Paraclesis* – which Erasmus provided for the first edition of his work.

This preface was brief and written at speed, but it was forceful and a succinct, challenging statement of Erasmus's deepest aspirations.[2] His theme was the "philosophy of Christ", which he placed in contrast to other philosophies whose students read and mastered the writings of their founders. Christians, he claimed, scorned and neglected the study of Christ and His teachings, which was shameful,

> For Christ is the only doctor to come to us from Heaven, He is the only one to teach certain truth, since He Himself is eternal wisdom; as the unique author of human salvation He alone has taught the things necessary for salvation, and He alone perfectly realized in practice what He taught and was able to show forth in reality what He had promised.

Christian truth, Erasmus argued, was not so complicated that it had to be hidden amongst a handful of men. Unlike other philosophies, Christianity suited itself to every need and person and was "within the reach of the lowest, just as it is the admiration of the greatest". The knowledge of Christ was the way of truth for all and Erasmus utterly condemned any restriction of the Scriptures to Latin. His plea that all should read them in the vernacular was eloquent:

> I wish that even the most humble women should read the Gospel and the Epistles of St. Paul. And these should also be translated into every tongue, so that they might be read and known not only by the Scots and Irish, but also by the Turks and Saracens . . . . Would that the ploughboy recited something from them at his plough, that the weaver sang from them at his loom, and the traveller whiled away the tedium of his journey with their tales, indeed, that the speech of Christian men were drawn from them.

No argument for the open Scriptures could be put more strongly by a Wycliffe or a Luther, and Erasmus's own fundamental work of scholarship logically demanded translations into the vernacular such as followed in Reformation developments. Moreover, there could be no plainer description of the nature of true Christian life than what he added in deriding the claims of monks and other clerics to be theologians. "He is truly a theologian," he claimed, "who teaches not with syllogisms and contorted arguments, but with compassion in his eyes and his whole countenance, who teaches indeed by the

[1] Ibid., p. 82.
[2] Cf. M. M. Phillips, op. cit., pp. 77 f. for a masterly evaluation of the *Paraclesis*.

example of his own life that riches are to be despised, that the Christian man must not put his faith in the defences of this world but depend entirely upon heaven." Anyone "inspired by the spirit of Christ" and who taught such things was "a true theologian and a great doctor, even if he should be a ditch-digger or a weaver". Such ideals were simple, too simple indeed in scholastic terms, but for Erasmus they were the essence of Christ's teaching. If they were followed, so he believed, peace and reform could be brought in Christendom.

The *Paraclesis* revealed how great was the contribution that Christian Humanism could make to the cause of reform; but it also betrayed no less clearly the movement's weaknesses for securing positive action to sweep corruption away. In his enthusiastic proclamation of the central theme of Christianity – the knowledge of Christ taught and learned with the Scriptures for all to read – and his rejection of much that was inessential or debased, Erasmus went to the root of many of the religious problems of his day. During the last twenty years of his life, when he served briefly as a councillor for Charles in Brussels before retiring first to Basel and then to Freiburg in Switzerland in the effort to continue his studies in peace, he was classed by many traditionalists with Luther and other Protestant leaders. Such judgments Erasmus always rejected, and he was too much of a Humanist in outlook ever to stand completely with Luther or to approve the practical means which he adopted to deal with the Roman Church. Erasmus valued Man's reason in learning, but also in his response to Truth, and he could never accept that the human will was wholly depraved and unable of itself to contribute in some way to salvation. The dispute over freewill and predestination in 1525 divided Erasmus theologically from Luther, but already much earlier in the *Handbook* he had voiced the hope that Man would do good though fallen; and in his own Latin translation of the opening verses of St. John's Gospel, he deliberately changed Jerome's *Verbum* for "Word" into *Sermo*, which denoted "Reason" or "Mind" in a much wider sense. Erasmus's rationalism indeed was always limited where he drew so strongly upon the principles of the New Devotion and praised the Holy Spirit's teaching in Scripture against the claims of the schoolmen. But alongside the plea for simplicity in religion and a faith based only upon the Scriptures and the Apostles' Creed, he put too much trust in Man's reason.

Erasmus looked optimistically upon the world, and though his optimism faded before his death in the bitterness of events, he retained his trust in men's reason and a respect for the individual in defending tolerance for their beliefs and actions. Toleration was part of the wider attitide of the Christian Humanists and marked what was great in Erasmus and others of similar mind, but in his age his plea was given as little attention as that of all groups or sects – the Waldensians, the Lollards, the independents of the new generations – who claimed their individual rights to live as they wished, to know the Scriptures and to worship God in their own ways. Repeatedly Erasmus insisted on the supreme importance of practical Christian living and scorned theological dogma, just as more generally he repudiated force and war. The attitude was courageous, but Erasmus found it impossible to maintain with any consistency. He praised Ximenes's work as the model for Christian Reformation, but only by ignoring the fact that scant respect was given to the ideal of toleration in Spain. His Dutch friend who became Adrian VI and of whom there were great hopes for a few brief months was moulded by that same harsh Spanish training in the Inquisition. And when events compelled him to make a choice, Erasmus was unwilling to challenge the final authority claimed by the Pope and the Roman Church for order and understanding. Although he championed the right of every Christian to demonstrate his belief in life rather than in the niceties of assent to dogma, he could not envisage having the organized unity of western Christendon rent, he could not welcome defiance or rebellion if such seemed necessary to attempt reformation. There was a limit to his defence of individual freedom to read and understand the Scriptures, and this was implicit in his sanguine belief that such reading would directly bring agreement, peace and greater unity in Christendom. When such consequences did not follow, Erasmus could not happily face the crisis of defiance by peoples who no longer would tolerate corruption. With other Christian leaders like Lefèvre and More, he assumed that for reformation there had to be a united, visibly ordered Christian world, and his hope was that this would embrace the Orthodox Churches as well as other bodies in some continuing allegiance to the Pope. Reform that shattered such unity he could not regard as reform, and in consequence would have nothing to do with it. In the years after 1517, Erasmus increasingly strove for an end where a "third" Church would emerge, different from the corrupt Roman body and from the new Protestant groups, and restored to an ancient apostolic form that left a pre-eminence still for the Bishop of Rome. But these efforts only underlined the dilemma and tragedy in Erasmus's whole outlook; in his last years, the contradictions in his position made him the outcast of Rome and the Protestants alike, just as they had left him unable to meet the crisis before it came.

In 1516, he dedicated his Greek New Testament to Leo X and praised the Pope for what he had already done, in encouraging letters, in dealing with disorders at Rome and in giving the lead for restoring true Christian piety. These views can be explained to some extent on the ground of relief felt by Erasmus at the death of Leo's predecessor, Julius II, but they were nonetheless surprising, and more generally the Dutchman was full of enthusiasm for the future at that time. Early in 1517 he wrote to a friend to hail the dawn of a new age in Christendom, with the promise of reform and cultural splendour. His hopes for renewed morality, Christian faith and learning he centred upon what he believed the Pope and the Emperor, Francis I, Henry VIII and other rulers were doing and were willing to do; he himself stood close to the Habsburg heir, Charles of Spain, for whom he wrote a manual on the conduct of a prince. Erasmus was a citizen of Christendom, not of Holland or any particular country or empire, and with his scholarship and devotion to Christian Humanism, he was welcomed in the highest circles in all lands. But his universal outlook and the allegiance which he proclaimed were in many respects antiquated by 1517, for the rivalries of national rulers had long been familiar in European affairs, and the Christian leadership of the Pope had for most become farcical, certainly in any spiritual sense. To that extent, therefore, Erasmus was deluding himself in his hopes where those leaders whom he thought he knew and could trust were plotting their next strokes in political ambition and cared little for united Christendom, whilst not the barest glimmer of spiritual responsibility or authority was to be discerned in Leo X.

In the same year that Erasmus wrote so optimistically the storm broke with Luther's challenge for debate about indulgences and papal authority. How Erasmus fared in the following crisis is part of the history of Luther and Protestantism, but though he lived on for another two decades he did not see reform as he wanted it realized. Rather, his dream was shattered, despite the fact that his ideas and achievement largely opened the way for Luther. He refused to break from allegiance to the Pope, preferring, as he put it, "to submit when Pope and Emperor command what is wrong". Lefèvre in France decided similarly, and did not follow some of his own disciples who joined the Protestant movement and were martyred for their stand; whilst in England, Sir Thomas More and Cardinal John Fisher were executed for refusing to abandon papal obedience and the ideal of a united Christian Church. Through the confusion of Continental developments, Erasmus could only seek shelter in towns where Protestantism did not disrupt his continuing, urgent work of Christian scholarship. Even so, his last years were not peaceful and he was increasingly harried by events around him before his death in 1536. The image of reform that he held out in Christian Humanism was in some ways the noblest in the age, and Erasmus himself brought together many earlier hopes, whether expressed in Wycliffism or the Hussite movement, in the schemes of the conciliarists or in mysticism. But at the same time his plan demonstrated that it remained humanly impossible to secure remedies for so much that was wrong in the Roman Church by any action short of rebellion against existing authority. And though the developments that came were far from Erasmus's hopes, they owed to him some of their most profound principles and objectives. This was true not least of all where Erasmus and Luther both defended the worth and standing, the responsibility and judgment, of the individual before God and in his possession of the Scriptures. But in this defence, too – regardless of differences in doctrine or order – Wycliffe and Hus supremely shared; and thereby they heralded that mighty movement of God's Spirit in the sixteenth century which is called the Reformation.

CHRONOLOGICAL TABLES

POPES (1305–1534)

Anti-popes of the Great Schism and Conciliar age are starred (*).

1305–1314	Clement V
1316–1334	John XXII
1334–1342	Benedict XII
1342–1352	Clement VI
1352–1362	Innocent VI
1362–1370	Urban V
1370–1378	Gregory XI
1378–1389	Urban VI
1378–1394	*Clement VII
1389–1404	Boniface IX
1394–1424	*Benedict XIII
1404–1406	Innocent VII
1406–1416	Gregory XII
1409–1410	Alexander V
1410–1415	John XXIII
1417–1431	Martin V
1424–1429	*Clement VIII
1431–1447	Eugenius IV
1439–1449	*Felix V
1447–1455	Nicholas V
1455–1458	Calixtus III
1458–1464	Pius II
1464–1471	Paul II
1471–1484	Sixtus IV
1484–1492	Innocent VIII
1492–1503	Alexander VI
1503	Pius III
1503–1513	Julius II
1513–1521	Leo X
1522–1523	Adrian VI
1523–1534	Clement VII

HOLY ROMAN EMPERORS (1346–1556)

1346–1378	Charles IV
1378–1400	Wenzel
1400–1410	Rupert
1411–1437	Sigismund
1438–1439	Albert II
1440–1493	Frederick III
1493–1519	Maximilian I
1519–1556	Charles V

KINGS OF ENGLAND		KINGS OF FRANCE	
1327–1377	Edward III		
1377–1399	Richard II	1364–1380	Charles V
1399–1413	Henry IV	1380–1422	Charles VI
1413–1422	Henry V		
1422–1461	Henry VI	1422–1461	Charles VII
1461–1483	Edward IV	1461–1483	Louis XI
1483	Edward V		
1483–1485	Richard III	1483–1498	Charles VIII
1485–1509	Henry VII	1498–1515	Louis XII
1509–1547	Henry VIII	1515–1547	Francis I

KINGS OF BOHEMIA

1346–1378	Charles I
1378–1419	Wenzel IV
1419–1437	Sigismund
1438–1439	Albert
1440–1457	Ladislas Postumus
1458–1471	George
1471–1516	Ladislas II
1516–1526	Louis II

RULERS OF HUNGARY

1382–1395	Maria of Anjou
1385–1386	Charles of Durazzo
1387–1437	Sigismund
1437–1439	Albert
1440–1444	Ladislas I
1444–1457	Ladislas Postumus
1458–1490	Matthias Corvinus
1490–1516	Ladislas II
1516–1526	Louis II

BIBLIOGRAPHY

I. Works of Reference

General surveys, with full bibliographies, of developments in late medieval Christendom are to be found in the *Cambridge Medieval History*, Vols. VII and VIII, and *Histoire de l'Église*, edited by A. Fliche and V. Martin, Vols. XIII–XV; the *New Cambridge Modern History*, Vol. I, deals with the early sixteenth century, but provides no bibliography. Helpful for information on western Europe is *The Oxford Dictionary of the Christian Church*, edited by F. L. Cross (1958), but it must be supplemented on Bohemian and Orthodox affairs in general encyclopaedias and studies included in section III below.

II. Texts

No comprehensive set of sources exists but for English works there are the publications in the Rolls Series, the Camden Society and the Early English Text Society. Selections of the most important public documents translated into English are provided in H. Gee and W. J. Hardy (editors), *Documents Illustrative of English Church History* (London, 1896), H. Bettenson (editor), *Documents of the Christian Church*, second edition (Oxford, 1960), and S. Z. Ehler and J. B. Morrall (editors), *Church and State through the Centuries* (London, 1954).

The Cloud of Unknowing, translated by C. Wolters (Penguin, 1961).

Cusa, *Unity and Reform: Selected Writings of Nicholas de Cusa*, edited by J. P. Dolan (Notre Dame, 1962).

Erasmus, D., *The Praise of Folly*.

Fasciculi Zizaniorum, edited by W. W. Shirley (London, 1858).

Forshall, J. and Madden, Sir F., *The Holy Bible in the earliest English versions made by J. Wycliffe and his followers*, four vols. (Oxford, 1850).

Hus, J., *Positiones, Recommendationes, Sermones*, edited by A. Schmidtová (Prague, 1958).

Hus, J., *Tractatus de Ecclesia*, edited by S. H. Thomson (Cambridge, 1956).

Julian of Norwich, *Revelations of Divine Love*.

Kempe, Margery, *The Book of Margery Kempe* (Oxford).

The Lay Folks' Catechism, edited by T. F. Simmons and H. E. Nolloth (London, 1901).
The Lay Folks' Mass Book, edited by T. F. Simmons (London, 1879).
Loomis, L. R. (translator), *The Council of Constance*, edited and annotated by J. H. Mundy and K. M. Woody (New York, 1961).
Pecock, R., *The Repressor of Over-Much Blaming of the Clergy*, two vols., edited by C. Babington (London, 1860).
Petry, R. C. (editor), *Late Medieval Mysticism* (London, 1957).
Spinka, M. (editor), *Advocates of Reform from Wyclif to Erasmus* (London, 1953).
Wyclif, J., *Latin Works*, Wyclif Society, 1883 onward.
Wyclif, J., *Trialogus*, edited by G. V. Lechler (Oxford, 1869).
Wyclif, J., *English Works* hitherto unprinted, edited by F. D. Matthew (London, 1880).
Wyclif, J., *Select English Works*, three vols., edited by T. Arnold (Oxford, 1869–71).
Wyclif, J., *Select English Writings*, edited by H. E. Winn (Oxford, 1929).

III. General Works

Aston, M. E., "Lollardy and Sedition", in *Past and Present* 17 (1960).
Atiyah, A. S., *The Crusade in the Later Middle Ages* (London, 1938).
Baynes, N. H. and Moss, H. St. L. B. (editors), *Byzantium* (Oxford, 1949).
Bernard, P. P., "Jerome of Prague, Austria and the Hussites", in *Church History* XXVII (1958).
Bett, H., *Nicholas of Cusa* (London, 1932).
Betts, R. R., "English and Czech Influences on Hus", in *Transactions of the Royal Historical Society*, fourth series, XXI (1939).
Betts, R. R., "The Influence of Realist Philosophy on Jan Hus and His Predecessors in Bohemia", in *Slavonic and East European Review* XXIX (1950–1).
Betts, R. R., "Jan Hus", in *History* XXIV, new series (1939–40).
Betts, R. R., "Jerome of Prague", in *University of Birmingham Historical Journal* I (1947).
Brandt, M., "Wyclifism in Dalmatia in 1383", in *Slavonic and East European Review* XXXVI (1957–8).
Bruce, F. F., *The English Bible* (London, 1961).
Cassirer, E., *The Individual and the Cosmos in Renaissance Philosophy*, translated by M. Domandi (New York, 1963).
Cohn, N., *The Pursuit of the Millennium* (London, 1957).

Coulton, G. G., *Five Centuries of Religion*, Vol. IV (Cambridge, 1950).
Creighton, M., *A History of the Papacy from the Great Schism to the Sack of Rome*, six vols. (London, 1897).
Deanesly, M., *The Lollard Bible* (Cambridge, 1920).
Deanesly, M., *The Significance of the Lollard Bible* (London, 1951).
Dickens, A. G., *Lollards and Protestants in the Diocese of York*, 1509–1558 (Oxford, 1959).
Dugmore, C. W., *The Mass and the English Reformers* (London, 1958).
Elliott, J. H., *Imperial Spain*, 1469–1716 (London, 1963).
Elton, G. R., *England under the Tudors* (London, 1955).
Figgis, J. N., *Studies of Political Thought from Gerson to Grotius*, 1414–1625, second edition (Cambridge, 1923).
Foxe, J., *Acts and Monuments*, edited by S. R. Cattley (London, 1837), Vols. III and IV.
Gairdner, J., *Lollardy and the Reformation in England* (London, 1908), Vol. I.
Gill, J., *The Council of Florence* (Cambridge, 1959).
Gilmore, M. P., *The World of Humanism*, 1453–1517 (New York, 1952).
Green, V. H. H., *Bishop Reginald Pecock* (Cambridge, 1945).
Green, V. H. H., *The Later Plantagenets* (London, 1955).
Greenslade, S. L. (editor), *Cambridge History of the Bible – The West from the Reformation to the Present Day* (Cambridge, 1963).
Gwynn, A., *The English Austin Friars in the Time of Wyclif* (Oxford, 1940).
Haller, W., *Foxe's Book of Martyrs and the Elect Nation* (London, 1963).
Hay, D., *Europe, The Emergence of an Idea* (Edinburgh, 1957).
Heymann, F. G., "John Rokycana – Church Reformer between Hus and Luther", in *Church History* XXVIII (1959).
Heymann, F. G., *John Žižka and the Hussite Revolution* (Princeton, 1955).
Holmes, G., *The Later Middle Ages*, 1272–1485 (London, 1962).
Hunt, E. W., *Dean Colet and His Theology* (London, 1956).
Hyma, A., *The Brethren of the Common Life* (Grand Rapids, 1950).
Hyma, A., *The Christian Renaissance* (Grand Rapids, 1924).
Hyma, A., *Renaissance to Reformation* (Grand Rapids, 1951).
Jacob, E. F., *The Fifteenth Century*, 1399–1485 (Oxford, 1961).
Jacob, E. F., *Essays in the Conciliar Epoch*, second edition (Manchester, 1952).
Jacob, E. F., "Gerard Groote and the Beginnings of the 'New Devotion' in the Low Countries", in *Journal of Ecclesiastical History*, III (1952).
Jacob, E. F. (editor), *Italian Renaissance Studies* (London, 1960).

Jacob, E. F., "Reynold Pecock, Bishop of Chichester", in *Proceedings of the British Academy* XXXVII (1951).

Jedin, H., *A History of the Council of Trent*, translated by E. Graf, Vol. I (London, 1957).

Kaminsky, H., "Chiliasm and the Hussite Revolution", in *Church History* XXVI (1957).

Kaminsky, H., "The Free Spirit in the Hussite Revolution", in *Millennial Dreams in Action*, edited by S. L. Thrupp (Hague, 1962).

Kaminsky, H., "Hussite Radicalism and the Origins of Tabor (1415–1418)", in *Mediaevalia et Humanistica* (1956).

Kaminsky, H., "Wyclifism as Ideology of Revolution", in *Church History* XXXII (1963).

Kenyon, F., *Our Bible and the Ancient Manuscripts*, fifth edition, revised by A. W. Adams (London, 1958).

Knowles, D., *The English Mystical Tradition* (London, 1961).

Knowles, D., *The Religious Orders in England*, Vols. II and III (Cambridge, 1955, 1959).

Latourette, K. S., *A History of the Expansion of Christianity*, Vol. II (London, 1939).

Lea, H. C., *A History of the Inquisition of Spain*, Vol. I (New York, 1922).

Lea, H. C., *The Inquisition of the Middle Ages, Its Organization and Operation* (London, 1963).

Leff, G. *Bradwardine and the Pelagians* (Cambridge, 1957).

Loserth, J., *Wiclif and Hus*, translated by M. J. Evans (London, 1884).

McFarlane, K. B., *John Wycliffe and the Beginnings of English Nonconformity* (London, 1952).

Mackinnon, J., *The Origins of the Reformation* (London, 1939).

McKisack, M., *The Fourteenth Century*, 1307–1399 (Oxford, 1959).

Manning, B. L., *The People's Faith in the Time of Wyclif* (Cambridge, 1919).

Mollat, G., *The Popes at Avignon*, 1305–1378, translated from ninth French edition (London, 1963).

Moorman, J. R. H., *A History of the Church in England* (London, 1953).

Morrall, J. B., *Gerson and the Great Schism* (Manchester, 1960).

Myers, A. R., *England in the Later Middle Ages* (Penguin, 1952).

Odložilik, I., "Wycliffe's Influence upon Central and Eastern Europe", in *Slavonic Review* VII (1928–9).

Ogle, A., *The Tragedy of the Lollards' Tower* (Oxford, 1949).

Origo, I., *The World of San Bernardino* (London, 1963).

Owst, G. R., *Literature and Pulpit in Medieval England*, second edition (Oxford, 1961).

Owst, G. R., *Preaching in Medieval England* (Cambridge, 1926).
Pantin, W. A., *The English Church in the Fourteenth Century* (Cambridge, 1955).
Parker, T. M., *The English Reformation to 1558* (London, 1950).
Parry, J. H., *The Age of Reconnaissance* (London, 1963).
Partner, P., *The Papal State under Martin V* (London, 1958).
Pastor, L., *History of the Popes*, Vols. I–VIII, translated by F. I. Antrobus and R. Kerr (London, 1891–1908).
Pepler, C., *The English Religious Heritage* (London, 1958).
Petry, R. C., "Emphasis on the Gospel and Christian Reform in Late Mediaeval Preaching", in *Church History* XVI (1947).
Phillips, M. M., *Erasmus and the Northern Renaissance* (London, 1949).
Poole, R. L., *Illustrations of the History of Medieval Thought and Learning*, second edition (London, 1920).
Poole, R. L., *Wycliffe and Movements for Reform* (London, 1911).
Prestage, E., *The Portuguese Pioneers* (London, 1933).
Rashdall, H., *Universities of Europe in the Middle Ages*, three vols., revised by Powicke and Emden (London, 1936).
Renaudet, A., *Préréforme et Humanisme à Paris pendant les premières guerres d'Italie* (1494–1517), second edition (Paris, 1953).
Richardson, H. G., "Heresy and the Lay Power under Richard II", in *English Historical Review* LI (1936).
Ridolfi, R., *The Life of Girolamo Savonarola*, translated by C. Grayson (London, 1959).
Robson, J. A., *Wyclif and the Oxford Schools* (Cambridge, 1961).
Rupp, E. G., *Studies in the Making of the English Protestant Tradition*, corrected edition (Cambridge, 1949).
Seebohm, F., *The Oxford Reformers* (Everyman, London, 1929).
Seton-Watson, R. W. (editor), *Prague Essays* (Oxford, 1949).
Smalley, B., *The Study of the Bible in the Middle Ages*, second edition (Blackwell, Oxford, 1952).
Smith, H. M., *Pre-Reformation England* (London, 1938).
Smith, P., *Erasmus* (New York, 1923).
Spinka, M., *John Hus and the Czech Reform* (Chicago, 1941).
Spinka, M., "Peter Chelčický, The Spiritual Father of the Unitas Fratrum", in *Church History* XII (1943).
Spitz, L. W., *The Religious Renaissance of the German Humanists* (Harvard, 1963).
Stacey, J., *Wyclif and Reform* (London, 1964).
Summers, W. H., *Our Lollard Ancestors* (London, 1904).
Thompson, A. H., *The English Clergy and Their Organization in the Later Middle Ages* (Oxford, 1947).
Thomson, S. H., *Europe in Renaissance and Reformation* (London, 1963).

Thomson, S. H., "Learning at the Court of Charles IV", in *Speculum* XXV (1950).

Thomson, S. H., "Luther and Bohemia", in *Archiv für Reformationsgeschichte* XLIV (1953).

Thomson, S. H., "The Philosophical Basis of Wyclif's Theology", in *Journal of Religion* XI (1931).

Thomson, S. H., "Pre-Hussite Heresy in Bohemia", in *English Historical Review* XLVIII (1933).

Tierney, B., *Foundations of the Conciliar Theory* (Cambridge, 1955).

Trevelyan, G. M., *England in the Age of Wycliffe* (London, 1909).

Turberville, A. S., *The Spanish Inquisition* (Oxford, 1932).

Ullmann, W., *The Origins of the Great Schism* (London, 1948).

Ullmann, W., *Principles of Politics and Government in the Middle Ages* (London, 1962).

Vernadsky, G., *The Mongols and Russia* (New Haven, 1953).

Villari, P., *Life and Times of Savonarola*, second edition, translated by L. Villari (London, 1889).

Waugh, W. T. "The Great Statute of Praemunire", in *English Historical Review* XXXVII (1922).

Williams, G. H., *The Radical Reformation* (London, 1962).

Wood-Legh, K. L., *Studies in Church Life in England under Edward III* (Cambridge, 1934).

Workman, H. B., *John Wyclif*, two vols. (Oxford, 1926).

Zernov, H., *Eastern Christendom* (London, 1961).

INDEX

www.ingramcontent.com/pod-product-compliance
Lightning Source LLC
LaVergne TN
LVHW050620100826
845148LV00011B/1670